Commonsense Darwinism

Commonsense Darwinism

Evolution, Morality, and the Human Condition

JOHN LEMOS

OPEN COURT
Chicago and La Salle, Illinois

To order books from Open Court, call toll-free 1-800-815-2280, or visit our website at www.opencourtbooks.com.

Open Court Publishing Company is a division of Carus Publishing Company.

Printed and bound in the United States of America.

Library of Congress Cataloging-in-Publication Data

Lemos, John, 1963-
    Commonsense darwinism : evolution, morality, and the human condition / John Lemos.
        p. cm.
    Includes bibliographical references (p.) and index.
    Summary: "Examines the philosophical implications of evolutionary biology" —Provided by publisher.
    ISBN 978-0-8126-9632-5 (trade paper : alk. paper)
    1. Ethics, Evolutionary. 2. Evolution (Biology)—Philosophy. I. Title.
BJ1335.L46 2008
171'.7—dc22

                                                                    2008032378

To my wife Laura and my three children,
Rosa, Billy, and Michael

Contents

Acknowledgments

The writing of this book would not have been possible without the support and encouragement of various entities and persons. First, I should thank the Philosophy Department at Duke University for the excellent education and financial support they provided for me during my graduate studies there. I am especially grateful to Michael Ferejohn who served as the thesis advisor for my Ph.D. thesis at Duke. While this book is not related to the subject of my dissertation, Professor Ferejohn did very patiently teach me how to read and think like a philosopher and for that I am forever in his debt. I also want to thank Coe College for providing me with a good teaching job, for granting me tenure, and for its continued support of my research through its summer faculty research stipends. I am especially grateful for the friendship and support of my two colleagues in philosophy at Coe, Jeff Hoover and Peter McCormick. I am also indebted to the head of the Honors Program at Coe College, Ed Burke. Many years ago he recruited me to teach a course called "Topics in Scientific Inquiry," and he paid me to engage in summer research to prepare for the course. It was in preparing to teach that course that I developed a keen interest in the philosophical implications of evolutionary biology.

My father, Ramon Lemos, read a complete draft of the manuscript and gave me extensive and very helpful editorial advice. I am grateful for this and the love and support that he offered me over the years. Thanks are also owed to my mom, Mamie Lou, and to my brothers—Noah, Bill, and Chris—all of whom have provided guidance and support for me over the years. Regrettably, my mom passed away quite a few years ago, and much more recently both my father and my brother, Bill, did so as well. It's a shame that they could not have been with us longer.

Perhaps the biggest debt of gratitude I have is to my wife, Laura, whose beauty and wit have lifted my spirits over the years. She has provided me with three fine children and her care of them has allowed me much of the time to write this book.

Finally, it should be noted that permission has been granted to use material from the following previously published articles: "Evolution and Ethical Skepticism: Reflections on Ruse's Metaethics," *The Journal of Social and Evolutionary Systems* 21:2 (1998), pp. 213–221; "Bridging the Is/Ought Gap With Evolutionary Biology: Is This a Bridge Too Far?," *Southern Journal of Philosophy* 37:4 (1999), pp. 559–577; "A Defense of Darwinian Accounts of Morality," *Philosophy of the Social Sciences* 31:2 (2001), pp. 361–385; "Evolution and Free Will: A Defense of Darwinian Non-Naturalism," *Metaphilosophy* 33:4 (2002), pp. 468–482; "Theism, Evolutionary Epistemology, and Two Theories of Truth," *Zygon* 37:4 (2002), pp. 789–801; "A Defense of Naturalistic Naturalized Epistemology," *Critica: Revista Hispanoamericana de Filosofia* 35 (2003), pp. 49–63; "Rachels on Darwinism and Theism," *The American Catholic Philosophical Quarterly* 77:3 (2003), pp. 399–415; and "Psychological Hedonism, Evolutionary Biology, and the Experience Machine," *Philosophy of the Social Sciences* 34:4 (2004), pp. 506–526.

Introduction

In this book I raise questions like: Does evolutionary biology require us to give up the notion of objective moral truth? Does evolutionary biology require us to reject a libertarian conception of freedom? Does it require us to give up a correspondence theory of truth? My answers to these questions are: No, No, and No. This book is intended to support such answers, as well as answers to other questions, and in doing so it supports what I would call a "commonsense Darwinism." Darwinism, I maintain, is no threat to free will, reason, morality, belief in God, or—for that matter— the moral rectitude of eating meat.

The study of the philosophical implications of evolutionary biology is nothing new. One of Darwin's nineteenth-century contemporaries, Herbert Spencer, was a widely studied advocate of evolutionary ethics, and his views were influential until G.E. Moore's famous critique of ethical naturalism became widely accepted in the early twentieth century. Following Moore's critique, interest in the philosophical implications of evolutionary biology ceased, for the most part, for quite some time. During much of the twentieth century philosophy was dominated by logical and conceptual analysis. However, in the last twenty years there has been a renewed fascination with the philosophical implications of evolutionary biology. Besides the resurgent interest in evolutionary ethics, there has also been a growing attention to evolution's religious implications, its epistemic implications, and its implications for traditional philosophical problems about the nature of human motivation and freedom of the will.

This book is a critical study of some of the literature that reflects this renewed interest in the philosophical implications of evolutionary biology. Like many of the authors who are discussed in this book, I am fascinated by the study of what evolutionary biology might mean for the traditional problems of philosophy. Over the years I have engaged in extensive research in this field. Through my studies my own position on the philosophical implications of evolutionary biology has emerged. This book might reasonably be viewed as a defense of this position. In this introduction I will briefly explain my positions on some of the issues that will be discussed in this book and also briefly explain how I will address these points in the book.

I believe that the Darwinian theory of evolution by natural selection gives us a correct account of the origin of species. This is to say that I think the great diversity of species we see in the biological world today originated from some one or a relatively few original life forms and that natural selection is the primary mechanism through which speciation occurs. The theory of natural selection tells us that there is competition for survival and mates within the populations of species. Those organisms with traits that favor their survival or reproductive success in their environments are the ones that tend to fare well in the competition to survive and reproduce. Thus, their genes tend to get passed on at a greater rate into future generations, meaning that the traits associated with those genes are passed on to future generations, thus shaping the nature of the species over time. Various factors, such as the development of random favorable mutations or significant environmental changes, play an important role in guiding the course of evolution.

There is abundant evidence in support of the Darwinian theory of evolution. A great place to start in understanding the nature of the theory of natural selection and the evidence for it is Darwin's own book, *On the Origin of Species* (1859). Also, see the Norton Critical Edition, *Darwin*, edited by Philip Appleman (2001). This Norton Edition contains extensive excerpts from *On the Origin of Species* as well as *The Descent of Man*. It also contains various articles summarizing twentieth-century developments and research supporting the Darwinian theory of evolution. See especially the piece entitled "Scientific Method in Evolution" issued by the National Academy of Sciences (pp. 289–300 of the Norton Critical Edition). This contains an excellent summary of the relevant empirical evidence supporting the Darwinian theory. This piece originally appeared in *Science and Creationism: A View from the National Academy of Sciences* (Washington, D.C., 1999). Michael Ruse's *Taking Darwin Seriously* (1998) also provides a very clear and readable account of the evidence for the Darwinian theory.

Given that I accept the truth of the Darwinian theory of evolution by natural selection, I also believe that both the physical and behavioral characteristics of human beings have been shaped in significant ways by evolution. Thus, I take seriously the suggestion of sociobiologists that there is a plausible Darwinian explanation for the existence of a natural altruistic impulse in human beings. I believe that we have innate desires to help others even at some risk to ourselves and that these desires can be explained with reference to the stock-in-trade of sociobiological explanation, the theories of kin selection and reciprocal altruism. In the first chapter, I explain Michael Ruse's sociobiological account of the origins of the moral sentiments and defend it against a variety of criticisms published in the literature.

While I accept the Darwinian theory of evolution by natural selection and the view that our moral sentiments have been shaped by such evolution, I also believe that there are objective moral truths that we can discover through reason and argumentation. I have long felt that an Aristotelian approach to ethics is our best hope of providing a defensible objectivist ethic, and over time I have come to the conclusion that the Darwinian theory of evolution can play an important supporting role in the defense of such an objectivist ethical theory.

In defending an objectivist approach to ethics, I part company with Michael Ruse. Chapter 2 presents an exposition and critique of his nonobjectivist evolutionary ethics. In Chapter 3, I explain and critically engage with a variety of recent objectivist approaches to evolutionary ethics. In Chapter 4 I go on to present a sketch of my own Aristotelian approach to evolutionary ethics, arguing that it escapes the various problems of the other objectivist approaches while not falling prey to other kinds of problems.

The first four chapters, then, deal with issues in ethical theory. While many contemporary thinkers are interested in these theoretical questions, there are also philosophers interested in the implications evolutionary biology has for specific issues in applied

ethics. One of the most noteworthy applications of evolutionary
biology to issues in applied ethics has been its application to questions about the moral status of nonhuman animals. In Chapter 5,
I examine the work of one of the most rigorous defenders of the
view that evolutionary biology has very significant implications for
this issue. James Rachels argues that evolutionary biology tells us
things about humans and animals and the relationship between
them which make it clear that eating meat is wrong, as well as a
number of other practices relating to animals which are typically
regarded by most people as perfectly acceptable.

Rachels argues that most people believe animals do not possess
the same moral status as humans because they either accept (1) the
image of God thesis or (2) the rationality thesis, or both. The
image of God thesis states that only human beings, not animals,
are made in the image of God, and because of this it is inferred that
human beings have a special moral status which animals lack. The
rationality thesis states that human beings have rational capacities
which are different in kind from the other animals, and from this
too it is inferred that we have a moral status which animals lack.
Rachels argues that Darwinism undermines both of these theses,
thereby undermining the case for treating animals as though they
have a lesser moral status.

In Chapter 5, I explain his argument in detail and argue that
neither of these theses are undermined by Darwinism. The discussion of these issues, especially the image of God thesis, takes us
into the realm of religion. Chapter 5 includes a discussion of
design arguments for God's existence and the possible implications
that evolutionary biology might have for such arguments. Rachels,
like some other notable contemporary thinkers, most notably
Richard Dawkins and Daniel Dennett, thinks Darwinism undermines the design argument, but I argue that such is not the case.

While Chapter 5 is primarily focused on the ethical treatment
of animals and as such continues on the general topic of ethics that
is introduced in the earlier chapters, it *is* a transitional chapter since
it raises questions about Darwinism and the rationality of faith. In
Chapter 6 I go on to explore further the possible religious implications of Darwinism by examining the recent work of Alvin
Plantinga and some of his critics. Plantinga has argued that were
human beings the products of evolution by natural selection alone,
God having no hand in our creation, we could not know anything,

not even that the Darwinian theory of evolution is correct. He believes that to avoid the absurdity of this conclusion it is more reasonable than not to think God has a hand in our creation. My discussion of Plantinga's argument raises questions about the nature of truth, justification, evidence, and the implications evolutionary biology has for these questions. As such, Chapter 6 takes us into the domain of evolutionary epistemology. I examine Michael Ruse's and Evan Fales's replies to Plantinga and argue that while Ruse's reply is inadequate in several respects, Fales's reply can be made to work.

Chapters 7 and 8 take us more into questions about the nature of the human condition. In doing so, I take up two perennial problems of human nature that have been addressed by philosophers—psychological egoism and freedom of the will. Psychological egoism is the view that humans are fundamentally selfish. Our ultimate motive in whatever we do is to promote our own interests. Psychological hedonism is a version of psychological egoism. Psychological hedonism is the view that avoiding our own pain and increasing our own pleasure are the only ultimate motives people have. According to this view, every act a person performs is motivated by one or both of these self-interested goals. Elliot Sober and David Sloan Wilson regard psychological hedonism as the version of egoism that is the most difficult to refute. Thus, they believe that in refuting psychological hedonism one would in effect refute psychological egoism. In their book, *Unto Others: The Evolution and Psychology of Unselfish Behavior,* Sober and Wilson write:

> By pitting altruism against hedonism, we are asking the altruism hypothesis to reply to the version of egoism that is most difficult to refute.
>
> Although hedonism is a special variety of egoism, we believe that our argument against hedonism has more general implications. We will maintain that no version of egoism is plausible for organisms such as ourselves. Hedonism exemplifies the kinds of evolutionary implausibility into which egoism inevitably must fall. (Sober and Wilson 1998, 297)

The "altruism hypothesis" which Sober and Wilson defend is the view that sometimes human beings are motivated to act on an irreducible concern for the welfare of others. This hypothesis is incompatible with any form of psychological egoism. Thus, in defending the altruism hypothesis Sober and Wilson take themselves to be refuting both psychological egoism and psychological hedonism.

Sober and Wilson maintain that traditional attempts to refute psychological hedonism, such as Bishop Butler's argument and Robert Nozick's experience machine argument, have failed. In light of this failure Sober and Wilson go on to provide a new evolutionary biological argument against psychological hedonism, which they think is sufficient to refute it. In Chapter 7 I explain their argument and critically address it, arguing that it is flawed in some significant respects. However, I go on to argue that this gives us no grounds to think that psychological hedonism or egoism are true, since, contra Sober and Wilson and other critics, Nozick's experience machine argument actually gives us good reason to think these views are false.

In Chapter 8, I turn to the issue of free will. Bruce Waller has recently argued that evolutionary biology gives us some good reasons to think that human beings possess a certain kind of freedom of the will which is distinct from the kinds advocated by soft determinists on the one hand and libertarians on the other. I explain Waller's views and go on to argue, contra Waller, that a libertarian view of freedom is both defensible and compatible with the theory of evolution by natural selection.

I conclude the book with a final chapter in which I address some recent developments in the field. This book brings together a lot of research and writing I have done over the years, but the philosophy of biology is a very active field. During the time some of these chapters were written and while bringing the manuscript to publication, more important work on the philosophical implications of evolutionary biology has been done. In Chapter 9 I draw the reader's attention to some of this work and I try to explain the relationship between my work and it. In some places I go into more detail than others, developing certain points and criticisms more fully than others. It is my hope that this discussion of recent work will serve as a useful resource for those wanting information about some of the more recent literature and that it will reveal the significance of my own work for some of the issues addressed in this literature.

Chapter 9 contains sections devoted to each of the preceding eight chapters of the book. After reading each chapter, readers might consider skipping ahead to read the relevant sections of Chapter 9 instead of waiting until they've completed reading all eight chapters.

The preceding synopsis suggests that I hold views that are fairly commonplace among educated people today. I think there are objective moral truths that we can discover through reason and reflection, that we have the kind of freedom that can make sense of the concept of moral responsibility, that not everything we do is done only to promote our own interests, and that eating meat is morally acceptable. I also believe that we can know things, that truth involves a correspondence between beliefs and the world, that God's existence is a real possibility, and that Darwinism does nothing to undermine this belief.

Insofar as these views are held by many educated people today, they are part of what I want to call "a commonsense view" of the world. These views are not common in the sense that they are held by all people nor even in the sense that all educated people hold them. Rather, they are simply commonplace beliefs among many educated adults. It is in this respect that I take myself to be defending common sense, and this book can be viewed as one philosopher's attempt at defending such commonsense views through examining their fit with the facts of evolutionary biology.

1

Defending a Sociobiological Account of Morality

In the recent philosophical literature a number of articles have been published examining the metaethical implications of evolutionary biology. Michael Ruse has argued that evolutionary biology implies that there can be no objective justification for our normative ethical claims.[1] Other philosophers have argued that evolutionary biology provides the keys to an objectively justified system of ethics.[2] Both groups of thinkers—I will call them the nonobjectivists and the objectivists—appeal to the claims of sociobiology to support their theories. In particular they feel that sociobiological views on the origins and nature of morality have implications for their claims about the objectivity of moral discourse or, as in Ruse's case, the lack thereof.

Before one takes seriously the arguments these thinkers provide one should give serious consideration to the plausibility of the sociobiological theories on the origins and nature of morality that these theories use to make their cases. I will begin by outlining the central elements in Michael Ruse's sociobiological theory of the origins and nature of morality and then I will go on to look at various sorts of criticisms that have been made against such sociobiological theories.

I focus on Ruse's views in particular because I believe his sociobiological understanding of morality shows a philosophical sophistication that is not present in the work of many other sociobiologists.

---

[1] See Ruse 1986; 1990; 1993; 1998.
[2] See Arnhart 1997; Campbell 1996; Collier and Stingl 1993; Rottschaefer 1991; and Richards 1986a; 1986b; 1987.

I will show that the philosophical sophistication of his approach makes it immune to many of the traditional criticisms of the sociobiological theory of morality. After providing a defense of Ruse's sociobiological account of morality, I will go on in the next two chapters to explore the merits of the various nonobjectivist and objectivist approaches to evolutionary ethics.

Ruse's Version of the Sociobiological Account of Morality

According to Ruse, morality as we know it today with its complex system of moral rules, moral feelings, and conditions of responsibility is an outgrowth of the animal tendency to engage in altruistic behavior, behavior that involves one animal helping another at some risk to itself. Many examples of this sort of behavior have been discussed in the literature. Since sociobiology is infused with neo-Darwinian thinking, sociobiological explanations of such animal altruism must explain how these cooperative behaviors enhance the reproductive success of the individual animals that engage in them. The typically Darwinian explanations for these cooperative behaviors are given in terms of kin selection and reciprocal altruism. According to Ruse, we can expect to see animals, including human beings, helping other animals that are, or are at least likely to be, related to them as kin or family, because in doing so an animal increases the chances of having its genes reproduced in future generations through helping kin that carry copies of its genes. So, for instance, it makes sense for an animal to help its children or siblings survive at some risk to its own survival, since its children and siblings carry half of its genes. According to this theory of kin selection, the amount of risk an animal will take in helping others will reduce the more distantly related the kin. Thus, an animal, A, should not be expected to risk as much in helping distant cousins as it would its own children or its own siblings, since distant cousins do not share as many genes in common with A.

It is common to see both human and nonhuman animals helping their kin. However, much animal altruism is directed towards animals that do not stand in any kinship relations. Since, according to neo-Darwinian thinking, traits, including behavioral traits, are to be understood as adaptations favoring an organism's chances at reproductive success, some alternative to the kin selection theory must be proposed for explaining altruistic behavior that is not directed at kin. So the question arises as to how these sorts of cooperative behaviors arise. The traditional answer is given in terms of reciprocal altruism. According to the theory of reciprocal altruism, when an animal helps another animal at some risk to itself, it does so only with the expectation that the favor will be returned.

As noted, Ruse thinks morality as we know it today is an out-growth of animal altruism. And, as I have just noted, animal altru-ism is explained by sociobiologists in terms of kin selection and reciprocal altruism. But there is a lot more to human morality than altruistic, or cooperative behavior. Earlier I said that human moral-ity consists of complex systems of moral rules, and moral feelings, such as guilt, sympathy, and remorse, and conditions of responsi-bility. To give a Darwinian theory of the origins and nature of human morality some explanation must be given for the existence of these sorts of things. In *Taking Darwin Seriously* Ruse argues that morality exists as the naturally selected best way to get humans to act altruistically, sacrificing their own welfare for that of others. He argues that having such behavior hard wired into us as it is in social insects, like ants, would waste the brain power we have and the flexibility it gives us. Not all altruistic action is wise or just. If we were hard wired to help others whenever they were suffering or in danger, then we might help others whom we shouldn't be help-ing. Since we have the kinds of mental abilities that enable us to distinguish between justified assistance of others and unjustified assistance, and since much of the unjustified assistance would also be maladaptive, we would be wasting our brain power if we were hard wired to help others, instead of letting reason override such altruistic impulses on occasion.[3]

---

[3] To illustrate the point consider the following. Suppose that I have a brother who has no children and who is often drunk, getting into fights, and he is often endangering my wife and three children. Suppose that I am with him and he has unjustifiably harmed and angered some fellows in a bar. Since he is my brother, I am inclined to risk life and limb to protect him in a dangerous fight. Were altru-istic behavior hard wired into me, I would go ahead and risk my life for him. But, is this helping behavior wise or just? Probably not. Since my family depends upon me for support and love and since my brother has proven himself to be a threat to the health and well-being of my family, I should probably let him get a sound beating from these fellows rather than risk my own life to save him.

On the other hand, if altruistic behavior in humans resulted only from purely rational and self-conscious decision-making, this would demand too much of our brain power. According to Ruse, morality as a system of rules, sympathies, and so forth exists because our reproductive success is better served by allowing us the flexibility that comes with not being genetically hard wired to act altruistically and yet, since thinking painstakingly through every ethical decision we must make without guidance from moral rules or our sympathies would take too much thought and time, we have a system of moral rules and sympathies as a guiding mechanism. The system of morality is the naturally selected happy medium between genetically determined altruistic behavior in humans and purely autonomous decision making (Ruse 1998, 221).

So far I have spoken about Ruse's views on how altruistic behavior and the system of morality can be viewed as adaptive. But an *evolutionary* account of the origins and nature of morality must not only offer an explanation of how morality is adaptive, but must also explain the reasons that can be given for thinking that it is an outgrowth from earlier ancestral forms of life. Ruse deals with this problem in three steps. First, he talks about animal behavior in general noting that recent studies have shown how tight control is exercised on animal behavior by their genes (Ruse 1998, 223). He says there are various examples of kin selection and reciprocal altruism at work among animals, allowing for the persistence of altruistic behaviors in the animal kingdom. Ruse concludes his discussion of animal behavior in general by noting that since altruistic behavior in animals can be explained by kin selection and reciprocal altruism, and since humans are animals, the possibility and expectation of explaining human behavior in this way is obviously raised.

Second, Ruse examines the prevalence of altruistic behavior in the higher primates, the animals that share the closest genetic relationship to *Homo sapiens*. He believes that if we have innate predispositions to help other humans, as the Darwinian view of morality suggests, and if it is a product of selective forces, then we might reasonably expect to find something akin to our moral behavior in our closest animal relatives, the higher primates. Since we do see behavior akin to our moral behavior in the higher primates, he thinks we do have good reason to think our morality is a product of evolutionary forces. He cites the recent work of primatologists in supporting this argument, in particular the findings of Hrdy (1977), Goodall (1971), and de Waal (1982) are referenced. These primatologists have documented the prevalence of altruistic behavior in the higher primates.

Third, Ruse examines human morality with the hope of showing why it is reasonable to think that it is shaped by the forces of natural selection. At the beginning of this discussion he states:

> The claim is that human moral thought has constraints, as manifested through the epigenetic rules, and the application of these leads to moral codes, soaring from biology into culture. The question is not whether every last act of Western Man or woman is governed by kin selection or reciprocal altruism or some such thing. I am quite sure it is not. (Ruse 1998, 230)

It will be important to keep this passage in mind in understanding Ruse's sociobiological theory on the origins and nature of morality. He is not saying that every aspect of human behavior, nor every aspect of ethical behavior, is controlled by our genes. Rather the thesis is that our evolutionary and genetic heritage places constraints on our moral thinking. Ruse would be the first to admit that culture plays a huge role in shaping the particular set of moral rules that we live by. But at the same time there are genetically based constraints as to what humans can or cannot accept as a moral rule. An example that Ruse often uses to illustrate the existence of a genetically based constraint on morality is the prevalence of incest taboos across all cultures. There is a very good natural selective reason for this, since the progeny from the unions of close kin tend to be horrendously physically handicapped. Ruse also says that we have innate tendencies to help our kin with or without their reciprocation and to help non-kin when there is likely to be reciprocation. These tendencies get expressed in our moral thought as an intuited sense that we *should* help our family and we *should* help non-kin provided they (non-kin) are willing to reciprocate (Ruse 1998, 222). He also talks about how the fundamental principles of utilitarianism and Kantianism have intuitive appeal because respect for such principles serves adaptive ends (Ruse 1998, 251). I will discuss his views on the adaptiveness of utilitarian and Kantian principles in more detail later on.

Ruse goes on to state that:

The explicit goals sought by humans tend to be power and status and material riches and the like. Also actively pursued are peace and security, freedom from war and want, and from other humanly caused disasters and disturbances. Virtually all of these things translate readily into reproductive success, and their absence spells reproductive failure. (Ruse 1998, 231)

Ruse believes that insofar as the attainment of these various common human goals translates readily into reproductive success, this supports the hope of explaining the Darwinian factors at work in understanding human society. Also, since certain moral phenomena can be explained so well in terms of kin selection and reciprocal altruism, Ruse thinks this adds to the case for the existence of Darwinian factors at work in the shaping of morality. He talks about how Richard Alexander (1977; 1979) has shown that in those human societies where the adult responsible for the care of children is not the father but rather the mother's brother there is also considerable doubt as to paternity. From the Darwinian perspective it makes sense for mothers' brothers to provide for their children in these cultures. Since the men do not know if their own mates are carrying their young, they can at least see to it that they ensure their reproductive success by caring for their sisters' children, since they can be certain that their sisters' children carry twenty-five percent of their genes. This phenomenon is explained quite well in terms of kin selection. Ruse also notes that the common occurrence of the breakdown of cooperation among humans when there is not reciprocation suggests the plausibility of explaining many instances of altruistic behavior in humans in terms of reciprocal altruism.

Ruse also goes on to discuss the work of Marshall Sahlins, an anthropologist. Sahlins (1965) has shown that in pre-literate societies there are three levels of interaction between people. Among kin you see altruistic behavior with no expectation of benefit returned. Among non-relative acquaintances you see reciprocal altruism. And among strangers, especially threatening ones, you see "'negative reciprocity', where there is tension, suspicion, and the ever present possibility of violent conflict" (Ruse 1998, 233). According to Ruse this is the very kind of interaction you would expect to find among people whose modes of interaction with one another have been shaped in such a way as to promote their chances at reproductive success. Hence, we again have good reason to suspect that natural selection is at work in shaping the ways in which we interact with one another and that this shapes our conceptions of morality. Oddly enough, says Ruse, this discovery of Sahlins runs counter to his opposition to the Darwinian explanation of the origins and nature of morality.

In concluding his discussion of the evidence supporting the plausibility of the sociobiological account of the origins and nature of morality Ruse also notes that he has not made a complete case "for the evolution of the human moral capacity, even when it is agreed (as it must be) that we talk now only of the basic moral inclinations, leaving the full development to culture. . . . However, we do now have a strong hypothesis" (Ruse 1998, 235). Ruse wants to emphasize that a plausible sociobiological account of morality does not suggest that every aspect of morality is controlled by the genes or the drive for reproductive success. Rather, there is some genetic control over the basic moral intuitions that are used to construct a full blown morality that would contain a set of moral do's and don'ts. Ruse concedes that different cultures will be led to fill in the details of their moral systems differently due in many cases to non-biological factors.

A Supporting Point from Peter Singer

In *The Expanding Circle: Ethics and Sociobiology* (1981), Peter Singer provides some cross-cultural data that could be used in supporting Ruse's contention that there is a biological basis for the "basic moral inclinations" that are used to shape our various moralities. He writes:

> The idea of an impartial standard for ethics has been expressed by the leading thinkers of the major ethical and religious traditions. In Judaism the rule is to love your neighbor as yourself; a rule which Jesus elevated to the status of one of the two great commandments. . . . When Confucius was asked for a single word which could serve as a rule of practice for all one's life he replied: "Is not reciprocity such a word? What you do not want done to yourself, do not do to others." In Indian thought we find the Mahabharata saying: "Let no man do to another that which would be repugnant to himself; this is the sum of righteousness; the rest is according to inclination."

Among the Stoic philosophers of the Roman Empire, Marcus Aurelius argued that our common reason makes us all fellow citizens, and Seneca claimed that the wise man will esteem the community of all rational beings far above any particular community in which the accident of birth has placed him (Singer 1981).

Singer uses these points to argue that evolution has put in human beings a capacity for reason that allows them to extend the sphere of moral concern beyond kin and those with whom they stand in relations of reciprocity. Insofar as Singer believes that reason allows us to extend our moral concerns in this way he thinks that sociobiological theories of morality are problematic, since, according to Singer, such theories try to understand all altruism in terms of either kin selection or reciprocal altruism.

While I think that Singer makes a good point against, at least certain forms of sociobiological accounts of morality, I also think that his point helps to support Ruse's contention that the basic moral inclinations from which our moral systems are derived are a product of natural selection. Assuming for a moment that Singer is right that reason leads us to a more universal altruism than kin selection or reciprocity will allow, it is striking how you get the same fundamental ethical principles being pronounced and widely revered across diverse cultures. And this would suggest that rationality has been led to these principles from the same basic moral inclinations. But if it has been led from the same basic inclinations across diverse cultures, this just suggests that the basic moral inclinations are a product of our biology and not our culture. Thus, in Singer you get evidence that helps to support Ruse's vision of the biological element in the development of morality.

It might be objected that cross-cultural agreement on basic moral norms supports moral realism, not an evolutionary account of morality. Moral realism is the view that there are objective moral truths that we can discover through reason or reflection. We might equally well explain this cross-cultural agreement by saying that there are objective moral truths that people from diverse cultural backgrounds are equally capable of grasping. In this way cross-cultural agreement on basic moral norms could be said to support moral realism.

This objection is based on the assumption that moral realism is at odds with an evolutionary account of morality. The objection suggests that if cross-cultural agreement supports moral realism, then it cannot also support an evolutionary account of morality. However, I am an advocate of a certain kind of evolutionary account of morality and a moral realist, and I see no reason why the fact of cross-cultural agreement on basic moral norms could not play a role in supporting both theses. After all, if there are objective moral truths that people from diverse cultures are able to grasp, then it is likely that there are shared cognitive mechanisms placed in us by evolutionary forces enabling us to grasp these truths. Assuming that there are such objective moral truths, the task of an evolutionary account of morality would be to understand the nature of the mechanism that enables us to know such truths and the evolutionary forces which give rise to this mechanism. Human eyes and ears reveal objective truths about the nature of reality to us, and there is an evolutionary biological explanation for the development of human eyes and ears. Thus, the existence of an evolutionary account of the moral sense should not be viewed as incompatible with moral realism. For all of these reasons, I find the kind of objection considered in the preceding paragraph to be quite answerable.[4]

Critical Assessments of the Sociobiological Account of Morality

I turn now to consider a number of criticisms of human sociobiology and the extent to which, if at all, these criticisms suggest problems with Ruse's sociobiological account of morality. Rusean sociobiology was in many cases not the specific target of these objections. Indeed, several of the criticisms I will consider were published before Ruse had come to develop his own sociobiological account of the origins and nature of morality. However, even though Ruse was not always the specific target, the objections considered here have been presented as criticisms of sociobiological

---

[4] I defend moral realism in Chapters 2 and 4 of this book. In Chapter 2 I critically respond to Ruse's argument that an evolutionary account of the origins of the moral sentiments implies that there are no objective moral truths, and in Chapter 4 I try to sketch out the way in which an evolutionary account of morality might be combined with an Aristotelian approach to ethics. The approach I advocate in Chapter 4 is based on the assumption that there are some objective moral truths—as such it is a realist approach to ethics that I advocate. In Chapter 3 I discuss the views of a number of contemporary philosophers who, like myself, accept an evolutionary account of the origins of morality and who also embrace moral realism.

approaches to morality *in general*. These critics and many people familiar with these issues do think that any sociobiological approach to understanding morality, including Ruse's, is doomed to failure for some or all of the reasons that will be discussed. What I will show is that many of the criticisms do not present problems for the more philosophically sophisticated version of sociobiology that Ruse presents.

1. ARE WE ALL SELFISH? KITCHER'S CRITIQUE OF SOCIOBIOLOGICAL THEORIES OF ALTRUISTIC BEHAVIOR

Philip Kitcher's *Vaulting Ambition* (1985) provides an extended explanation and critique of the claims made by sociobiologists. I will focus my discussion of Kitcher's critique on what he says about sociobiological understandings of altruistic behavior. Kitcher is critical of sociobiologists' treatment of altruistic behavior, behavior that involves helping others at some risk to oneself, because it implies that humans are fundamentally selfish, having no real concern for the health and welfare of others. He cites various passages from sociobiologists wherein the fundamental selfishness of human behavior is asserted and goes on to provide two different interpretations of the sociobiological understanding of altruistic behavior. On one interpretation, "the sociobiological claim is that the apparent intention to promote the well-being of another person is a screen that hides some deeper motive. People really calculate the consequences of their actions in terms of their own inclusive fitness and act so that their inclusive fitness is maximized." And on the other interpretation, "human beings sometimes do intend the well-being of others and . . . such intentions sometimes move people to action; [the other interpretation] suggests, however, that the evolutionary explanation for the presence of such intentions and for efficacy in moving us to action lies in considerations of maximization of inclusive fitness. When we understand the evolutionary roots of the mechanisms that lead us to help others, then we may no longer be so impressed with the practice of evaluating people as altruistic or selfish (Kitcher 1985, 399–400)."

Concerning the first interpretation of the sociobiological thesis let me just say that if this is what the sociobiologists intend to say it is at worst false and at best an unjustifiable contention. Obviously, people seem to act out of a genuine concern for the health and well-being of others. So, if this thesis is going to work it will have to make reference to hidden self-interested motives, hidden to the agent himself, that are the real causes of altruistic behaviors. But this talk of hidden self-interested motives is simply not going to be empirically justifiable in many cases. Thus, if all sociobiological understandings of altruistic behavior were to be understood along the lines of the first interpretation, then there would certainly be a significant problem for these theories.

The second interpretation of the sociobiological thesis says that people may act out of a genuine concern for the health and well-being of others; however, since the possession of such a concern for others is placed in us through natural selection, it really exists for our own reproductive success. Thus, according to this second interpretation there is still no altruistic behavior that is really worthy of our moral praise (Kitcher 1985, 403). With good reason Kitcher finds this treatment to be problematic as well, but instead of discussing why he finds this problematic I will argue that Ruse's sociobiological account of morality does not understand altruistic behavior in the crude terms that these two interpretations do. Consequently, Ruse's version is immune to the sort of criticism raised by Kitcher in *Vaulting Ambition*.

Kitcher makes good points but it is important to realize that not all sociobiological accounts of altruistic behavior in humans suggest that humans are ultimately selfish. Ruse does not make this claim himself. He believes that we can act out of a genuine concern for the health and well being of others, even others who are not our kin, but he also believes that our tendency to act in this way is a product of natural selection. Ruse writes:

> . . . in the face of our general inclination to serve ourselves, because it is biologically advantageous to us to help and co-operate, morality . . . has evolved to guide and stiffen our will. We are moved by genuine, non-metaphorical altruism. To get 'altruism', we humans are altruistic. (Ruse 1998, 222)

'Altruism' is metaphorical. It refers to "co-operation which furthers the individual participant's reproductive interests" (Ruse 1998, 218). What Ruse is saying is that genuine altruism, that is, behavior motivated by a concern for the well-being of others, exists as a way of getting us to engage in 'altruism', co-operative behavior that improves our own chances at reproductive success. Thus, interpretation 1 above does not cohere with Ruse's position.

And since he never goes on to suggest that the fact that natural selection favors this tendency means that such altruistic behavior is not really altruistic or not worthy of our praise, there is no reason to think that interpretation 2 coheres with Ruse's views either.

For the reasons given here, I contend that Kitcher's critique of sociobiological accounts of altruism only works against certain versions of these accounts, but I do not think it works against the more philosophically sophisticated account that Ruse provides.

2. THE PROBLEM OF GENETIC DETERMINISM: FLEW'S CRITIQUE OF SOCIOBIOLOGICAL ACCOUNTS OF MORALITY

In a 1994 article Antony Flew argues that sociobiological accounts of morality cannot be correct because they imply that human behavior, including altruistic behavior, is genetically determined, meaning that it is causally necessitated. Since causal necessitation is incompatible with the fact of human choice, Flew concludes that any sociobiological account of morality must be mistaken. Flew gives an interesting argument for the fact of human choice that has been criticized by Peter Robinson (1995).

Rather than develop an explanation of Flew's argument for the fact of human choice and giving consideration to Robinson's reply, let me just note that Ruse's sociobiological account of morality is quite compatible with human choice. Thus, the charge of genetic determinism does not hold against the sort of sociobiological account that Ruse provides. Ruse believes that what the genes determine within us is an awareness of certain fundamental moral principles that are then developed into full-blown systems of morality through the influence of culture. Further, we are free to act or not act in accordance with these fundamental moral principles and their culturally developed correlatives. Ruse writes:

> I argue that precisely because Darwinian ethics does so strongly uphold the is/ought distinction, insisting that our sense of ethics is of a real demanding set of obligations, a dimension of human freedom is absolutely presupposed. If we had gone the route of the Hymenoptera, programmed to do blindly what we do, then there would be no true freedom. But we are conscious beings, aware of the dictates imposed by our epigenetic rules—aware of the prescriptions of morality. Far from Darwinism denying freedom, it demands it! And this demand is obviously met, for nothing has been said to negate our

phenomenological awareness of ourselves as free beings. Furthermore, we do break sometimes (often) with our sense of morality. Indeed, as we have seen, the Darwinian rather expects this to happen. (Ruse 1998, 259)

As noted earlier in my summary of Ruse's sociobiological account of morality, I said that according to Ruse it was adaptive for humans to have the kind of mental capacities that are incompatible with the kind of genetically hardwired altruistic behavior found in social insects like the Hymenoptera. And since it would also be nonadaptive for us always to think our way through adaptive behavior strategies on our own, morality came into existence as a means to lead us to the altruistic behaviors that it is generally adaptive for us to engage in. But if we are not genetically hardwired to act altruistically then we must be capable of choosing whether or not to act in accordance with the dictates of morality. Thus, Ruse's brand of sociobiology does not fall prey to the charge of genetic determinism.

3. THE PROBLEM OF UNDERSTANDING THE MORAL BELIEFS OF INDIVIDUALS: FLANAGAN'S DOUBTS

In an often cited article, "Is Morality Epiphenomenal?," Owen Flanagan (1981) argues that sociobiological accounts of morality are problematic, because you simply cannot understand all of the specifics of the moral beliefs of individuals by appeal to their tendency to promote reproductive success. Flanagan discusses at length a number of the particularities of the moral beliefs of Ludwig Wittgenstein and the Ayatollah Khomeini and shows quite convincingly that to understand the moral beliefs of these individuals you would have to look at social and historical factors that transcend biology.

As with the charges of Kitcher and Flew, I see this point as only carrying force against some versions of sociobiology, not Ruse's version. Ruse admits early on in his sociobiological explanation of morality that the idea is not to provide a biological explanation of every aspect of the moral beliefs and behaviors of human beings. Let me stress this point by quoting a passage I mentioned earlier:

> The claim is that human moral thought has constraints, as manifested through the epigenetic rules, and the application of these leads to

moral codes, soaring from biology into culture. The question is not
whether every last act of Western man or woman is governed by kin
selection or reciprocal altruism or some such thing. I am quite sure it
is not. Rather, the question is whether we have innate tendencies or
dispositions inclining us to social thoughts and actions, which latter
would improve our reproductive chances. (Ruse 1998, 230)

Clearly Ruse would not begin to think that biology could explain
all of the particularities of the beliefs of Wittgenstein or Khomeini
or anyone else. But he does think that natural selection plays a very
important role in shaping our conception of the most fundamental moral principles upon which culture builds more detailed systems of morality. Just as Kitcher's and Flew's critiques of
sociobiology are ineffective against Ruse's version, so too is
Flanagan's.

4. THE PROBLEM OF THE AUTONOMY OF ETHICS: NAGEL'S CRITIQUE CONSIDERED

Nagel (1980) argues that since ethics is, "a theoretical inquiry that
can be approached by rational methods, and that has internal standards of justification and criticism, the attempt to understand it
from outside by means of biology will be [of little value]." Most of
Nagel's article is a demonstration of the truth of the premise of this
short argument. Early on in the article he offers some reasons why
the conclusion follows from the premise. He writes:

> First, we have no general biological understanding of human thought.
> Second, ethics is not a fixed set of behavioral and intellectual habits
> but a process of development that advances by constant reexamina-
> tion of the total body of results to date. A being who is engaged in
> such an open-ended process of discovery cannot at the same time
> understand it fully from outside: otherwise he would have a decision
> procedure rather than a critical method. (Nagel 1980, 196)

Nagel concedes that the capacity to engage in ethical thinking
"presumably has some biological foundation." He continues:

> Biology may tell us about perceptual and motivational starting
> points, but in its present state it has little bearing on the thinking
> process by which these starting points are transcended. (Nagel
> 1980, 204)

In essence Nagel is arguing that since (1) we have no general biological understanding of human thought and (2) ethics is a subject matter that employs a critically reflective method as opposed to a pre-established decision procedure, it follows that biology will be able to tell us little if anything important about the nature of morality.

Ruse would agree that ethics is a theoretical inquiry having internal standards of justification and criticism, but he would have good reason to question whether Nagel's conclusion follows from this fact. Concerning Nagel's first point that we have no general biological understanding of human thought, Ruse might want to make reference to the increasing successes in the field of neuropsychology to argue that there is reason to think that this claim is at least debatable. But perhaps he would be better off simply arguing that insofar as human beings are part of the biological world and insofar as creatures in the biological world tend to get their characteristics including brain structure and functioning through the process of natural selection, there is good reason to think that our modes of thought can be understood in terms of their serving adaptive functions. Thus, we might understand human thought in biological terms by thinking about how certain modes of thinking serve to enhance inclusive fitness.

Concerning Nagel's second point that ethical inquiry is an open-ended process that involves critical thinking and is not simply a decision procedure, I think that Ruse would agree while also contending that the biological understanding of the nature of morality should focus on comprehending how the most fundamental principles of our ethical thinking exist as a matter of adaptive advantage. As I have noted several times already, Ruse believes that the fully developed moral systems that we operate with are a product of culture. Ruse would say that cultures develop their specific modes of ethical thought by critically reflecting on different developments of ethical thought from basic moral principles that are ingrained within our consciousness because of their adaptiveness.

For the reasons just given Ruse can argue quite plausibly that the conclusion of Nagel's argument does not follow from the premise. However, Nagel might want to reply that if this is all that the sociobiologists have to offer in the way of understanding morality, then they have relegated themselves to the realm of the trivial. The tone of Nagel's article suggests this as one of the responses he would make. However, I think that this sort of response calls for a much more detailed development because Ruse argues at length that, even given the limited role of biology in explaining morality that he supports, an understanding of the biological origins of morality does have significant meta-ethical and normative implications. He argues at length that a Darwinian theory of morality implies that our moral beliefs can have no objective justification (Ruse 1998, 250–56). And he argues that a utilitarian normative theory like that of Peter Singer is misguided because it defies our biologically enforced tendencies to act in ways that favor our reproductive success (Ruse 1998, 235–244). Before Nagel's triviality thesis is accepted Ruse's arguments need to be dealt with directly.

5. THE SINS OF "EVANGELICAL" SOCIOBIOLOGY: MILES'S CRITIQUE

James Miles (1998) argues that sociologists and anthropologists need not feel threatened by any plausible versions of sociobiology because its plausible versions do not suggest that all aspects of human social interaction, including morality, can be explained in biological terms. He lists Richard Dawkins, George Williams, and John Maynard Smith as proposing a plausible version of sociobiology that views human nature as fundamentally selfish from the biological point of view. According to Miles, these sociobiologists believe that the moral goodness found in so many human beings is purely a matter of cultural conditioning and has no roots in our biology. In contrast to their version of sociobiology he talks about "evangelical" sociobiology, which views morality as a product of natural selection. This is the sort of sociobiology advocated by Michael Ruse and E.O. Wilson as well as others. Miles presents various criticisms of "evangelical" sociobiology. In what follows I will briefly explain these criticisms and consider how they bear on Ruse's sociobiological account of morality.

Miles develops a critique of "evangelical" sociobiology by taking points from each of the three sociobiologists mentioned above. From John Maynard Smith he takes the point that "human societies change far too rapidly for the difference between them to be accounted for by genetic differences between their members" (Miles 1998, 601). From Dawkins he takes the point that the astonishing variety of human societies suggests "that man's way of life is largely determined by culture rather than by genes" (602). From Williams he takes the point that rather than promoting kindness natural selection promotes gross immorality (603–04). The first two of these points are directed towards human sociobiology generally. Since sociobiological accounts of the origin and nature of morality are a part of human sociobiology, they militate against any such accounts. The third point is directed toward sociobiological accounts of morality in particular. How do these points bear on Ruse's sociobiological account of morality? It is to this question that I will now turn.

I will deal with the first two points together. I do not think that these points will do much to undermine Ruse's sociobiological account of morality, because he leaves so much room for culture in the shaping of moral systems from biologically given foundations. Considering the point taken from Dawkins about the variety of human societies, Ruse would agree that human societies do admit of astonishing variety, but he would insist, and I think warrantedly so, that there is an equally astonishing similarity in the fundamental moral principles that are accepted across almost all cultures. Here I am reminded of the cross-cultural points made by Singer mentioned earlier. Ruse would respond similarly to J.M Smith's point. Of course, culture allows for changes in beliefs and attitudes that cannot be accounted for simply in biological terms. But again Ruse's biological understanding of morality allows for this. The basic moral principles that are ingrained within us from our biology have been present for thousands of years, but their different cultural expressions have shifted over time.

The third point derived from G.C. Williams is developed by Miles in the following way:

> Human decency is not 'animal'. Decency does not, *cannot*, exist in nature. The traits that the Darwinian philosopher Daniel Dennett is about to introduce you to are not *by-products* of natural selected behavior, they are the *dynamics* of natural selection: When a lion acquires a new lioness who is still nursing cubs from an earlier mating, the first order of business is to kill those cubs, so that the lioness will come more quickly into estrus. . . . langur-monkey males often kill the infants of other males to gain reproductive access to females . . . This dark message about our furry friends is often resisted.

Williams expands this message. All other animal populations are *thousands* of times more likely to kill than are humans from even the most murderous of American cities. "Simple cannibalism . . . can be expected in all animals except strict vegetarians." Infanticide is a commonplace. Take our cousins, the monkeys: "If she loses her infant, the mother quickly comes into estrus and accepts her infant's killer as the father of her next offspring" (Miles 1998, 604).

Miles goes on to present some more examples of horrific animal behaviors. And then he states:

> Yet these are the programs for *all* animals. There are not some male primates out there who will rape, and others who will not. There are not some male and female chimpanzees who will tear apart the male infant of a mother who has recently joined their group, and some who will not . . . Darwinism tells us about the universal nature of a species. The mistake evolutionary psychologists make is in trying *directly* to extend this understanding to man. They speak of a 'universal human nature' while simultaneously denying that they would ever dream of tearing apart their step-children of course. (Miles 1998, 604–05).

Now how does all of this bear on the theories of Ruse? Let me begin by noting that at some level Miles seems to be arguing that because of all these instances of horrific animal behavior that he and Williams and Dennett cite, there cannot be decency in nature. But this conclusion just does not follow. The fact that there is a lot of 'bad' behavior among animals does not mean that there is no 'good' behavior. Even if that 'bad' behavior is adaptive, as the examples from Dennett certainly suggest, it does not mean that 'good' behavior, such as a number of altruistic behaviors, are not adaptive. To this extent Miles's argument does not show that decency cannot exist in nature nor that it cannot be a product of the forces of natural selection.[5]

---

[5] Since I acknowledge that certain 'bad' behaviors, like male lions killing the cubs of their mates sired by another male, are adaptive and that certain 'good' behaviors, such as a lioness risking her life to protect her cubs, are also adaptive, it might be wondered whether I have just turned the evolutionary account of morality into the triviality that everything is adaptive. This worry can be resolved by keeping in mind the importance of context. The lioness whose cubs are threatened with danger really should risk her life and limb to protect them. This is a

Perhaps the stronger point that Miles makes comes in the second passage I quoted above. The point there seems to be that, given the universal nature of species, you will not find tendencies for 'good' behavior in some chimps and 'bad' behavior in others. Rather, you will find these 'good' and 'bad' tendencies in every chimp. Thus, if the evangelical sociobiologists are going to infer that our morality is evolved from our common ancestry with chimpanzees and other primates they must concede that we have likewise inherited the tendencies for the bad behaviors as well. But Miles does not think that the sociobiologists are willing to acknowledge this. Hence, the point about how sociobiologists would deny that they "ever dream of tearing apart their step-children."

A couple of points are in order here. First, I am not convinced that someone like Ruse would say that he would never "dream of tearing apart his step-children." (My apologies to Ruse here.) According to Ruse, we have morality to keep us from doing things that we might otherwise be naturally inclined to do. Notice what he says about incest taboos:

> We have such a strong drive to copulate, particularly with any member of the opposite sex who is almost literally thrown at us, that (biologically) we need something really strong to steer us away. Morality does the trick. (Ruse 1998, 222)

The idea here is that many of us do at some level have the desire to have sex with our kin, but since such sex is maladaptive moral prohibitions have arisen that discourage us from engaging in such behaviors. If Ruse is willing to admit to a human drive to have sex with kin, then I suspect he might also admit to the human drive to "tear apart" step-children. But of course this is the whole reason for morality. It leads human beings away from engaging in behaviors that are for the most part maladaptive.

'good' behavior that is adaptive. A lioness that is unwilling to offer such protection will not do well reproductively compared to other female lions. Thus, not all behaviors, "not everything," is adaptive. Certain contexts call for certain sorts of action. In some of these contexts 'good' behavior is called for and failure to perform it is maladaptive. In some other contexts 'bad' behavior is called for and failure to perform it is maladaptive. So, again, not everything is adaptive.

Miles might want to press the point here by arguing that a significant problem remains. In particular he might note that Ruse's point about the need for incest taboos works nicely because incest is maladaptive. But a male killing his step-children *is* adaptive if it means more resources and attention being devoted to his own children. Thus, a sociobiological explanation for the prohibition against killing step-children is going to be found wanting.

But are all sociobiological explanations for such a prohibition wanting? I don't think so. In *Taking Darwin Seriously* Ruse argues that the basic moral principles, promote the general happiness and treat others as ends and not as means, are both adaptive. If his arguments to this effect are sound, it is clear why he would be led to say that natural selection has led us to view the killing of step-children as wrong. For the killing of step-children would be a violation of a general principle the adoption of which is adaptive. In particular this seems clearly to violate the principle of ends. So the question arises as to just why adoption of the principle of ends is adaptive. Ruse explains in the following manner:

> That Darwinism is sensitive to the Kantian emphasis on individual rights is obvious. From the biological viewpoint, we are all persons in society, interacting in such a way that aims to maximize our share of society's goods. But, for each and every one of us, there must be a point beyond which the price of the acquisition of society's goods becomes too high. It is just not worth the cost. And the bottom line clearly is when we are used merely for the benefit of others. Thus, as Darwinians we want to stop this happening to us. The most obvious way to prevent this happening, particularly when the chief underlying causal mechanism for social functioning is reciprocal altruism, is to agree that we will not use others as means either. But how is this 'ideal' to be enforced? Natural selection serves it up under the guise of morality! We have the Categorical Imperative, or something very much like it, embedded in an epigenetic rule. We feel we ought to treat others as ends. They feel the same way about us. Hence, Darwinism and Kantianism are each satisfied. (Ruse 1998, 244)

Since Ruse offers up a plausible account of the adaptive reasons for adopting the principle of ends, and since killing step-children would be a violation of this principle, he can give a plausible sociobiological account of why we view such behavior as wrong. Thus, before Miles can make the point he develops from Williams and

Dennett count against "evangelical sociobiology" he must develop some critique of Ruse's account of the adaptive basis for adopting the Kantian principle of ends.

6. THE PROBLEM OF NON-ADAPTIVE ALTRUISM: SINGER'S WORRIES

In *The Expanding Circle: Ethics and Sociobiology* (1981) Peter Singer argues that sociobiologists would have us understand all altruistic behavior, including that of humans, as driven either by the forces of kin selection or reciprocal altruism. However, he notes that this cannot be correct, because of the phenomenon of anonymous, unpaid blood donation. In Britain the National Blood Transfusion Service takes blood from voluntary donors and does not pay them, and the donors' blood is then given to patients that need it and the donors have no idea who is receiving their blood. Singer states that such systems of blood transfusion,

> are working refutations of the contention that altruism can only exist among kin, within small groups or where it pays off by encouraging reciprocal altruism. There are other instances of equally altruistic behavior, though the lack of contact between donor and recipient makes this one unusually clear-cut. Anyway, one widespread practice involving people helping others without hope of reward is enough. Genuine, non-reciprocal altruism directed toward strangers does occur. (Singer 1981, 134)

This sort of criticism might work well against certain other sociobiological accounts of the origin and nature of morality, but it does not hold up against Ruse's version. Again I will remind the reader that Ruse believes the principle which says "promote the general happiness" is one that we have good adaptive reasons to adopt. If that is true, then from the perspective of his sociobiological theory it will be no surprise to find such anonymous blood donation to be commonplace. For giving blood is a way to promote the general happiness. But here the question to raise is how the adoption of this utilitarian principle can be adaptive.

In *Taking Darwin Seriously* Ruse writes:

> Since happiness is something which we all crave, what is more natural than that we should have a sense that *we ought to promote the happiness*

of others? Our general inclination is to look to our own ends. However, (unbeknown to us) our biological fitness is increased if we have urges to expend effort on promoting the ends that others (consciously) want. Since the ends of others are analogous to our ends—we are, after all, members of the same species—our urges are directed towards promoting the general happiness of our fellows, as well as ourselves. Given that the genes work through epigenetic rules—biases which incline (or, more precisely, direct) us towards or away from certain courses of action—the Darwinian argues that we have such rules to make us think that we have obligations to increase the happiness (and decrease the unhappiness) of all.

In broad outline, therefore, the utilitarian perspective on the nature of morality meshes comfortably with the Darwinian approach to such thought and behavior (Ruse 1998, 237).

Earlier in the book Ruse makes the point that the pursuit of our own happiness is adaptive insofar as what pleases us often contributes to our reproductive success. He notes that it is no biological accident that copulation is pleasurable (Ruse 1998, 236)! The point of the passage cited above is clarified further later on. Ruse believes it is adaptive for us to adhere to a principle which encourages the promotion of the general happiness. If we accept this principle it will encourage helping behavior. Each one of us is inclined to need the help of others from time to time, even if we are very well off right now. So, while this principle and the corresponding sense of obligation to those in need might lead me to give up more than I really want to, it is still a principle the acceptance of which is adaptive on the whole. To illustrate the point consider Singer's example of blood donation. If people believe that we ought to promote the general happiness this may lead them to donate blood. And since each one of us stands to benefit from this should we ever be in need of blood, it is easy to see how the principle in question promotes each of our chances at reproductive success. This is just one of numerous examples that could be given illustrating this point.

Ruse does admit that there are biologically based limitations to the kinds and amount of help that we can expect everyone to give to others. Those utilitarians who think that we are obligated to give equal consideration to the interests of the starving poor of distant Third World countries right along side of our own families are misguided. For, according to Ruse, our biology ingrains in us a sense that our own families deserve more of our concern and resources. And this does make biological sense because our own families share our genes.

Nonetheless, while it would be a mistake to look at Ruse as a full blown act-utilitarian, he does believe that there are adaptive reasons for our accepting a principle which tells us to promote the general happiness. And this also means that the sort of example Singer provides in his critique of sociobiological accounts of morality does nothing to undermine Ruse's approach.

7. The Prevalence of Maladaptive Behaviors: Jacquette's Critique

Dale Jacquette (1989) has argued that sociobiology cannot give adequate explanations of human behavior because there are too many instances of maladaptive human behaviors. Jacquette cites several examples of cultures that have engaged in maladaptive behavior and maintains that sociobiologists cannot explain the maladaptive behavior of such cultures because sociobiologists try to explain human behavior in terms of the reproductive function that it serves. Jacquette continues:

> This might be dismissed as an insignificant criticism of sociobiology, involving only a handful of unsuccessful societies. It does not count much against a scientific theory that there are obscure recalcitrant phenomena which it cannot satisfactorily explain. But the trouble with sociobiology is deeper, and becomes especially acute in the effort to provide a sociobiological reduction of ethics.
>
> If I want to know why I behave socially as I do, or why my neighbors do not practice incest or cannibalize their little children, it will not avail to consult sociobiological theory, since for all that I know the phenomena I wish to have explained may be reproductively self-defeating for the social group to which my neighbors and I belong. The best that sociobiology enables me to conclude is that, hypothetically, if the social behavior in question is not contributing causally to a decrease in the genetic continuity of the members of a society, then the teleological or teleological-reductive reason why the behavior exists is because it promotes the reproductive self-interests of those individuals. But this "explanation" borders dangerously on empty tautology, for it is much like saying that if the behavior promotes rather than diminishes reproductive self-interest, then it exists because it promotes rather than diminishes reproductive self-interest. (Jacquette 1989, 691)

Here Jacquette is arguing that, insofar as sociobiologists cannot explain the existence of maladaptive behaviors, this infects their attempts at explaining any human behaviors, including ethical behaviors, whether they are adaptive or not. The point seems to be that if sociobiologists are to explain some behavior, A, they must first know whether A promotes the reproductive self-interests of those who engage in it. If they find the behavior promotes reproductive self-interest, then they say A exists to promote reproductive success. If they find the behavior does not promote reproductive self-interest, then they suggest looking for some other explanation. Jacquette seems to point to two different problems with this. First, sociobiological theories of human behavior will be problematic because often times inapplicable. For oftentimes we will not know whether a given behavior promotes reproductive success, so that we oftentimes won't be justified in explaining behaviors in sociobiological terms. Second, even when we do know that a behavior promotes reproductive success and the sociobiologist subsequently says it exists to promote reproductive success, the explanation is problematic. Here Jacquette claims that the problem is one of "tautological" explanation. I am not sure what he is getting at here. For it seems to me rather that the problem is that sociobiologists are engaged in some kind of illicit *post hoc ergo propter hoc* reasoning. Regardless, what are we to make of this? Does the Rusean sociobiological explanation of the origins and nature of morality run into these problems?

As Jacquette presents it, this argument cannot as stated serve as a refutation of Ruse's sociobiology. The problem is that the examples of maladaptive behavior that Jacquette cites do not necessarily raise problems for Ruse. Of course this raises the question as to what the examples are. Jacquette writes:

> Consider the following examples of reproductively unsuccessful, self-defeating social mechanisms. In nineteenth-century Russia there existed for a time a religious sect that practiced total celibacy. This society was not fated for long-term genetic continuity. But sociobiology cannot begin to explain teleologically why the members of the group refused to reproduce. The vow of celibacy was presumably made on moral grounds with the deliberate intention of frustrating what sociobiology regards as the only scientific reason for social behavior. The Catharic Albigenisan heretics in fourteenth-century Languedoc, France, similarly instituted the *endura*, a rite of pro-

longed celibacy and suicidal starvation fast. Predictably, this would have had the same negative outcome, had it not been for the intervention of the Catholic Church and Inquisition. Anthropological evidence suggests that tribal societies on Easter Island in the South Pacific, and the Chaco Indians in the American southwest, declined to extinction or near extinction because of social problems involving over-population. (Jacquette 1989, 689–690)

In responding I would note again that Ruse believes human behavior is guided by biologically based general principles that place constraints on what we can regard as acceptable modes of conduct. He believes that this leaves a lot of room for cultural determination. In fact I think Ruse would be willing to admit that adaptive principles which we accept as a matter of our biology can be put to maladaptive ends depending upon cultural input. Just as someone who believes we ought to maximize the greatest happiness for the greatest number may be led to create much misery for others because he is confused about what would create the greatest happiness, so too someone acting with general adaptive principles might employ them in a way that is maladaptive, depending upon the factual beliefs he is led to have through his culture. Thus, it may well have been that the celibate religious sects mentioned by Jacquette might have been practicing and encouraging the practice of celibacy believing that this would lead to the greater happiness for the members of their community, a happiness they believed to be found in God's salvation. But this is adhering to a perfectly adaptive general principle! Thus, it is my suspicion that the examples of the celibate religious sects are *not* going to be inexplicable from the perspective of Rusean sociobiology. Similar sorts of points could be made with respect to the examples of over-population. Thus, for Jacquette's argument to carry any weight against Rusean sociobiology we would have to hear more about what the motivations for these maladaptive behaviors are and check to see if there is no reasonable way for the motivations to be rendered consistent with Ruse's vision of the biological constraints on human behavior. I suspect that such cases are going to be extremely rare.

In effect, the sort of thing that one would have to do to refute Ruse is give an example of someone who, say, rejects either or both the principle of promoting the general happiness and the principle of treating people as ends. Ruse regards these as adaptive principles that we humans find intuitive. When someone acts in maladaptive ways as a consequence of rejecting these principles for some other principles, like promote the general misery and use your neighbor as mere means, then you really have got something that the sociobiologist will have a hard time explaining as anything other than a sickness (perhaps caused by genetic abnormality). Ruse states:

> I, like you, have forty-six chromosomes. I, like you, have a shared moral sense. People who do not have forty-six chromosomes are considered abnormal, and (probably) sick. People who do not have our moral sense are considered abnormal, and (probably) sick. (Ruse 1998, 255)

For the reasons I have given, then, I do not think that Jacquette's critique works against Rusean sociobiology nor do I think it would be likely to work even if one went looking for the kind of data that would be needed to refute Ruse.

Conclusion

In this chapter I have shown that Ruse does provide a plausible sociobiological account of the origins and nature of morality. I have done this by presenting in a summary way the central elements of his view and by showing how his views are immune to a variety of the criticisms of sociobiological accounts of morality that have appeared in the philosophical literature. I do not intend to suggest that Ruse's theory is beyond any reasonable criticism. However, I do believe that the critics of sociobiology need to devote more attention to the specifics of Ruse's approach if they are to undermine significantly the plausibility of his view. Perhaps one fruitful line of criticism would be to examine carefully whether or not Ruse's argument for the adaptiveness of our intuitive acceptance of utilitarian and Kantian principles is really justified or plausible. I say this in part because several of my defenses of Ruse depended on the plausibility of his arguments on these issues. As of now I find the explanations he gives of these matters to be plausible.

Additionally, if Ruse's sociobiological explanations of the origins and nature of morality are plausible, then his argument that morality can have no objective foundation cannot reasonably be dismissed on the ground that it rests on a misguided sociobiology. Rather, it may be that his arguments for that view must be dealt with on their own terms. For that matter it also strikes me that the sort of sociobiological account of the origins and nature of morality that Ruse provides could also serve as the underpinning for the arguments of those philosophers who think sociobiology gives us the basis for an objectively justified system of ethics. Thus, if the arguments I have presented in this chapter are sound, then the views of this latter group of philosophers cannot be easily dismissed on the grounds of a misguided sociobiology. In the next chapter I will examine Ruse's nonobjectivist evolutionary ethic and in Chapter 3 I will consider objectivist theories.

2

Nonobjectivist Evolutionary Ethics

Michael Ruse has argued that moral claims about how we ought to live and act are incapable of rational justification and that this conclusion follows from the discoveries of sociobiologists.[1] He writes that

> in ethics once we see that moral claims are simply adaptations, there is neither place for nor need of rational justification. (Ruse 1993, 152)

And:

> [T]here is no foundation to ethics at all! This is not to say that substantival ethics does not exist, but, it is to say that the supposed underpinning is chimerical in some sense or another (Murphy 1982; Mackie 1977; Ruse 1986). What these thinkers argue is that sometimes, when one has given a causal explanation of certain beliefs, one can see that the beliefs, themselves, neither have foundation nor could ever have such a foundation. The claim of this kind of evolutionary ethicist, therefore is that once we see that our moral beliefs are simply an adaptation put in place by natural selection, in order to further our reproductive ends, that is an end to it. Morality is no more than a collective illusion fobbed off on us by our genes for reproductive ends. (Ruse 1993, 151)

Ruse does several things to support the claims cited above. First, he offers an argument from analogy. Second, he tries to

---

[1] See Ruse 1986; 1990; 1993; 1998. Ruse makes the same basic argument in each of these publications. In explaining his argument I will cite passages from his 1993.

explain away our natural resistance to his thesis. Third, he responds to an argument against his position. In what follows I will briefly summarize each of these three steps in his attempted justification of ethical skepticism and later will go on to assess his arguments.[2]

The Argument from Analogy

In defense of ethical skepticism Ruse writes:

> Many people turned [after World War I] to spiritualists for solace and comfort after their loved ones were killed. Moreover, they did not come away disappointed. Through the ouija board or other channels would come the comforting messages: "It's all right, Mom! I'm happy now! I'm just waiting for you and Dad!"
>
> Of course, we see that there was no justified foundation for a claim such as this. Excluding obvious cases of fraud, and I suspect that these were a lot fewer than cynics maintain, we know full well that the successes of the seance were due exclusively to the capacity of people under stress to deceive themselves. They wanted to hear (or if you like "hear") the comforting messages—and so they did. Once the causal analysis is given, we see that there is no place for rational justification. Likewise, in ethics once we see that moral claims are simply adaptations, there is neither place for nor need of rational justification. (Ruse 1993, 152)

Here Ruse is arguing that just as the causal explanation for the spiritualists' beliefs that they have heard the messages of their dead children leaves no room for a justification of such beliefs, so too does the causal explanation of moral beliefs leave no room for a justification of those beliefs. I will assess this argument later. For now, let us consider the next step in Ruse's defense of ethical skepticism.

Explaining Away Our Resistance

Ruse notes that many people will be reluctant to accept his claim that morality lacks foundation. According to Ruse there is a socio-

---

[2] For other critical assessments of Ruse's case for ethical skepticism, see Rottschaefer and Martinsen 1990 and Woolcock 1993. For a reply to Rottschaefer and Martinsen, see Barrett 1991. For a rebuttal to Barrett, see Rottschaefer and Martinsen 1991. For a reply to Woolcock, see Waller 1996.

biological explanation for this reluctance which gives further credence to his view. Ruse maintains that it is adaptive for us to believe that morality is susceptible to rational justification. For if we did not believe it is rationally justified we would be less inclined to obey it, and obeying moral rules *is* generally adaptive for human beings. Thus, according to Ruse it is perfectly consistent with his theory that there should be a strong and widespread resistance to its conclusion that morality cannot be rationally justified (Ruse 1993, 152–53).

An Objection Considered

In further defense of his position Ruse considers an objection derived from Nozick's *Philosophical Explanations* (1981). The objection runs as follows:

> To the claim of ethical skepticism, there is an obvious objection which runs somewhat like this: The fact that our ethical sense is a product of evolutionary processes in no way denies the reality of its referent. Take an analogy from the world of the epistemologist. If a speeding train is bearing down on me, I am inclined to jump out of its way. How is it that I am aware of this train? Obviously through my evolved capacities of sight and hearing and so forth. My awareness of the train comes to me through adaptations which selection has put in place. Yet, no one would want to claim that the train does not have a reality in its own right. Why, therefore, should one feel able to deny that ethics or morality has a reality in its own right? The fact that awareness comes through adaptations is quite irrelevant to matters of ontology. There is, therefore, a blatant fallacy, right in the middle of the evolutionary ethical position. (Ruse 1993, 155–56)

Now in arguing that morality lacks rational justification Ruse has taken himself to be saying that there is nothing "out there" external to consciousness to serve as the referent of our moral claims and in virtue of which they can be rationally judged as true or false. However, as Nozick argues, the mere fact that beliefs are adaptive or the products of adaptive capacities does not suggest that there is nothing "out there" external to consciousness to which they refer.

In response to Nozick's argument Ruse writes:

To counter this objection, the evolutionary ethicist must show that the analogy is not a true one. How can this be done? Start with the fact that the argument about the train goes through because and only because the existence of the train is assumed independently. Suppose, for instance, one had two worlds identical except that one has a speeding train and the other does not. There would be no reason to think the evolutionist is committed to a belief in speeding trains in both worlds. One is aware of the speeding train only because there is such a train. Now consider two worlds, one of which has an objective morality, whatever that might mean (God's will? Non-natural properties?), and the other world has no such morality. If the evolutionist's case is well taken, the people in *both* worlds are going to have identical beliefs—subject to normal laws of causation and so forth. The existence of the objective ethics is in no way necessary for a derivation of our belief in an objective ethics from an evolutionary perspective. So, at the very least, what we can say is that an objective ethics is redundant to the evolutionist's case. (Ruse 1993, 156)

Ruse finds Nozick's analogy to be weak because it assumes the existence of the train at the outset and yet we have no need to assume there are moral facts to serve as the referents of our moral claims. For our beliefs in the objectivity of ethics can be explained just as well without making any appeal to moral facts.

At this point a critic of Ruse might note that just because the *belief* in objective ethics can be explained just as well without appeal to the *existence* of an objective ethics or moral facts, it does not mean that there are *not* any. Being aware of this potential reply Ruse continues by noting:

If what has been said earlier about the nonprogressionist nature of evolution is well taken, then there was absolutely no guarantee that evolution would have led us to the point that it has. Perhaps, to make us cooperators, evolution might have filled us with other sentiments entirely opposite from those about the worth of altruism and so on and so forth. Perhaps, for instance, we might have been led to some kind of reverse morality, where we feel an obligation to hate each other. But, we know that others feel the same way about us and so consequently social interactions are kept in place in this way. This is not so implausible, when one thinks of the emotions operative in the 1950s during the Cold War. The situation, therefore, seems to be that not only is objective morality redundant but it might be something entirely different from that which we think that it is! (Ruse 1993, 156–57)

So Ruse views the belief in an objective ethics as not only redundant or unnecessary for explaining our belief in such objectivity, but he also views such a belief as incompatible with the fact that we might have evolved quite differently.

Assessing the Arguments

Having explained Ruse's evolutionary argument for ethical skepticism I will now subject it to critical scrutiny. In doing so, I will focus on his argument from analogy to spiritualism and his reply to Nozick. I will not discuss his evolutionary explanation for our resistance to his thesis. For if his argument from analogy and his reply to Nozick are both weak then the mere fact that he can give an evolutionary explanation for our reluctance to embrace ethical skepticism will not by itself make the case for his position.

(I) REFLECTIONS ON THE ANALOGY WITH SPIRITUALISM

In his argument from the analogy with spiritualism, Ruse maintains that once we've explained the experience of those who claim to have heard from their dead relatives as a mere wish fulfillment, then there is no place for a rational justification of their claims. Ruse writes:

> Excluding obvious cases of fraud . . . we see that we know full well that the successes of the seance were due exclusively to the capacity of people under stress to deceive themselves. They wanted to hear the comforting messages—and so they did. Once the causal analysis is given, we see that there is no place for rational justification. (Ruse 1993, 152)

The problem with Ruse's argument here is that we cannot warrantedly conclude that these people hear what they hear as a matter of *mere* wish fulfillment or "due *exclusively* to the capacity of people under stress to deceive themselves" until we first have independent evidence that their beliefs that they have heard the voices of the dead are not rationally justified. Ruse's argument falls prey to certain excellent points that Gary Gutting (1987) has made against certain criticisms of arguments for God's existence from religious experience. In reply to the Freudian critique of such arguments, which says that religious experiences are not evidence of God's existence because they are mere wish fulfillments, Gutting writes that

> to be entitled to assert the actual operation of wish fulfillment mechanisms, we must first have good reason to think that the experiences they explain are nonveridical. So the Freudian attempt to explain away religious experience is inevitably question begging. . . . It is not sufficient to show just that such causes *could* produce the experiences and beliefs. It must also be shown that they are in fact operative in given cases; and it is very hard to see how this can be done without assuming ahead of time that the experiences are nonveridical. (Gutting 1987, 133–34)

Perhaps another way of seeing the error in Ruse's thinking is to consider the following. Suppose I am Pythagoras working on a proof for the Pythagorean theorem. Suppose that I have just completed the proof and I bring it to you and try to show you how it works. But now suppose you know that I have wanted to complete such a proof for some time now and you lend no credence to my proof regarding it as mere wish fulfillment. Were one to accept Ruse's views on the claims of the spiritualists (or Freud's views on religious experiences) one would have to regard your refusal to consider my proof as evidence as a rationally warranted refusal. But this is absurd!

For all of the above stated reasons I find Ruse's argument from analogy flawed. In addition to this, the errors I have found in the argument are actually suggestive of a problem in Ruse's contention that "in ethics once we see that moral claims are simply adaptations, there is neither place for nor need of rational justification." All of the errors in Ruse's thinking about the early twentieth-century spiritualists are actually carried over into his thinking about ethics. Ruse cannot warrantedly maintain that moral claims are *simply* adaptations and not rationally justified until he first gives independent reason for the claim that they are not rationally justifiable. Insofar as Ruse's reasoning about the spiritualists really *is* analogous to his reasoning about the objectivity of ethics, and insofar as his reasoning about the spiritualists is flawed, his reasoning about the objectivity of ethics is also flawed.

(II) Reflections on Ruse's Reply to Nozick

In discussing Ruse's reply to Nozick I will raise three main objections.

Point 1: Ruse's reply to Nozick rests on the claim that the belief in the objectivity of ethics can just as well be explained without reference to objective moral facts existing "out there" external to consciousness. But what is this equivalent explanation? All that we are told is that we believe ethics is objective because this will get us to obey the moral rules, obedience to which is adaptive.

Three observations are in order here. First, for the belief in the objectivity of ethics to be adaptive it should be fairly widespread, since its adaptiveness will contribute to the reproductive success of those who have it, meaning that it should have spread widely within the population through inheritance. But is this belief widespread? I am not sure that it is. Many, perhaps most, of my students do not believe in the objectivity of ethics. While the fact that many of my students do not believe in the objectivity of ethics does not prove that the belief is not widespread, it does at least raise some doubts. My point is simply that it would certainly help if Ruse supplied some statistical data which show that the belief in the objectivity of ethics is widespread.

Second, even if many or most people did not believe in the objectivity of ethics they would probably go on engaging in the sorts of behaviors regarded as moral out of fear of the repercussions of wrongdoing or due to conditioned positive reinforcement. This suggests that the belief in the objectivity of ethics is more likely to be some aspect of human nature which, from the point of view of evolutionary biology, is extraneous to the reproductive success of human beings.[3]

---

[3] Bruce Waller, who is generally more supportive of Ruse's position than I am, seems to share with me in the critique I make of Ruse here. He argues that Ruse's proposed "illusion" of moral objectivity is superfluous. According to Waller, folks would go on acting morally even if it was widely believed that morality lacked objectivity. See Waller 1996 and 1986. In Lemos 2000, I challenge Waller's contention that a widespread belief in ethical skepticism would not result in moral backsliding.

Third, the belief in objective morals also seems unlikely to have been an adaptation when so many other possible and more successful avenues to ensure cooperative behavior could have been put in place. Perhaps we might have all been instilled with an innate enjoyment in doing what is regarded as moral. This would have led many of us to obey the moral rules, possibly more of us than have been so inclined by possessing a "false belief" in the objectivity of morality. After all, how adaptive can this "false belief" be if it is so easy for Ruse and others to see through it?

For all of the above stated reasons we have reason to doubt that our beliefs in the objectivity of ethics can be explained just as well without making reference to objective moral truths. But perhaps Ruse *is* right that you can explain the belief in objective ethics equally well without reference to objective moral truths. Even so, and as he is aware, this itself would not suggest that there are no objective moral truths. After noting this Ruse goes on to make a separate argument wherein he appeals to the fact that humans could have evolved rather differently with a rather different set of moral beliefs and practices and says that this fact is incompatible with the existence of objective moral truth. What are we to make of this argument?

Point 2: Let me begin by noting that I do not see what is so paradoxical about saying that there are objective moral truths while at the same time admitting that human beings might have evolved quite differently in such a way that our moral beliefs might have been quite the opposite of what they are. Had we evolved differently the objective moral truth would have or might have been quite different from what it is, being something more properly suited to our differently evolved human nature. The mere fact that human nature could have been otherwise than it is does nothing to suggest that there is no objective moral truth. Why does Ruse think differently? Examining more closely what he says about this may tell us.

After noting how paradoxical it is to say that morality is objective and that humans could have evolved to have quite different moral beliefs, Ruse writes:

> Certainly, it is unacceptable on traditional notions, for instance that morality is endorsed by God's will or a function of non-natural prop-

erties or some such thing. There is something distinctly peculiar about saying that God wants certain things of us, but that not only is our behavior in no way predicated on God's wishes but that what we do might be something quite different because our biology has led us thus wise. (Ruse 1993, 157)

This passage suggests what might be leading Ruse to his claims of paradox. Notice what Ruse regards as traditional notions of objective moral truth. He lists as possibilities objective truth as governed by the will of God and objective truth as governed by non-natural properties. If one overlooks the possibility that objective moral truth is grounded in the facts of human nature (albeit evolved and evolving human nature) and views the objective grounding in divine or non-natural properties wholly divorced from the facts of evolved human nature, then one would reasonably be led to view the marriage of evolutionary theory and objective morality as paradoxical. However, there is a long standing tradition which views the objectivity of morality as being grounded in the facts of human nature. I have in mind here the Aristotelian and Thomistic traditions among others.[4]

Point 3: Thus far I have argued that there are some reasons to doubt that our belief in ethical objectivity is adaptive (Point 1). I have also argued that grounding objective moral truth in human nature, as Aristotle and St. Thomas did, is not given consideration by Ruse in his argument that the idea of an objective ethics is paradoxical (Point 2). But Ruse also argues that objective moral truth is redundant. His point here is that we don't need to appeal to any objective moral truths to explain why we have the moral beliefs we have. Thus, there is no reason to think objective moral truth exists. This argument for redundancy is basically the same kind of argument that Gilbert Harman (1977) has made against ethical objectivism. Further, insofar as Ruse's argument shares such kinship with Harman's argument, it can be subjected to the same kind of criticism that Nicholas Sturgeon (1998) has made against Harman's argument.

---

[4] Rottschaefer and Martinsen (1990) also criticize Ruse for failing to give adequate consideration to the prospect of objectively grounding morality in the facts of human nature.

Like Ruse, Gilbert Harman argues that the belief in objective moral truth is redundant since we do not need to appeal to any moral facts to explain why people hold the moral beliefs they hold. In the case of Ruse it is clear that he thinks sociobiology would play an important role in any account of the moral beliefs a person has. In reply to this line of argument Sturgeon has argued that moral facts *do* play a role in explaining the moral judgments we make. One of his more famous examples concerns the moral depravity of Hitler. Sturgeon argues that the moral fact of Hitler's depravity plays an essential role in explaining our belief that he *is* depraved. We say that he is depraved because he initiated a world war, he ordered "the Final Solution," and so forth. According to Sturgeon, in the closest possible world in which Hitler was not depraved he would not have done this, and consequently we would not believe he was depraved. However, this just means the fact of Hitler's depravity plays an essential role in our believing that he is depraved. Thus, he concludes, contra Ruse and Harman, that moral facts do play an essential role in explaining at least some of the moral beliefs we form.

In defense of Harman and Ruse one might say this argument assumes there is something which in fact *is* moral depravity which explains why Hitler did what he did. In reality Hitler's *beliefs* lead him to do what he does. He *believes* Jews are inferior and consequently not worthy of equal moral consideration. This is a fact about what he believes. It is *not* a moral fact. And it this nonmoral fact which explains his actions and our moral observations. In response to this Sturgeon will say that Hitler's depravity supervenes on his beliefs about the Jews. Thus in the closest possible world in which he is not depraved he will not hold such beliefs and consequently will not order the Final Solution and, thus, we will not believe him to be depraved. Thus, any reference by Harman or Ruse to Hitler's beliefs as the cause of his actions will do nothing to undercut Sturgeon's critique.

Before drawing conclusions here I would like to consider two other possible replies. First, Harman and Ruse might balk at the concept of supervenience, arguing that this is some sort of occult relation, having no objective validity, which ethical naturalists of the objectivist stripe refer to in hopes of escaping the naturalistic fallacy. Second, they might also argue that there can be no objective truth where rational observers can disagree in the face of all evidence, and assessments of depravity are a case in point. They might note that every rational observer can be shown that Hitler believed Jews were inferior, but not every rational observer can be shown that he is depraved, since not every rational observer accepts this as a sign of depravity. And since judgments of depravity depend upon one's perspective in this way, there is no good reason to think there is a moral fact about Hitler's depravity which plays a role in explaining our moral observation that he is depraved.

David Brink (1998) has given a good reply to the claim that the supervenience of moral truth is an occult or mysterious relation. Brink defends the supervenience view in reply to part of J.L. Mackie's argument from queerness (Mackie 1977). The relevant part of the argument from queerness focuses on the allegedly puzzling or mysterious nature of the relation between moral facts and natural facts. Mackie notes that if moral facts exist they must depend in some way upon the existence of natural facts. For we justify claims about what is right and wrong with reference to claims about natural facts, for instance, this is right because it causes greater happiness, that is wrong because is causes greater misery, and so forth. Mackie says that it is a puzzle or mystery as to how such natural facts give rise to moral facts. In reply Brink says that moral facts supervene on natural facts. He goes on to define the concept of supervenience and he argues that there is nothing mysterious about it.

Brink defines supervenience as follows:

> A supervenient relation obtains between two properties or sets of properties just in case the one property or set of properties is causally realised by the other property or set of properties; the former property or set of properties is the supervening property or set of properties, and the latter property or set of properties is the base property or set of properties. Supervenience implies that no change can occur in the supervening property without a change occurring in the base property, but it also asserts a claim of ontological dependence. (Brink 1998, 534)

In response to the charge that there is something odd, strange, or *queer* about there being supervenient moral properties, he states:

There is nothing strange and certainly nothing unique about the supervenience of moral properties on physical properties. Assuming materialism is true, mental states supervene on physical states, yet few think that mental states are metaphysically queer (and those that do do not think that supervenience makes them queer). Social facts such as unemployment, inflation, and exploitation supervene upon physical facts, yet no one supposes that social facts are metaphysically queer. Biological states such as being an organism supervene on physical states, yet no one supposes that organisms are queer entities. Macroscopic material objects such as tables supervene on microscopic physical particles, yet no one supposes that tables are queer entities. In short, it is difficult to see how the realist's use of supervenience in explaining the relationship between moral and physical properties makes his position queer. (Brink 1998, 534)

In reply to those who might balk at the notion of moral truth supervening on natural facts it is reasonable to defer to Brink. He makes the right kinds of points, and, while there no doubt are objections that can be made to Brink's position, it should at least be clear from the preceding comments that for Ruse to make his case for ethical skepticism much more would need to be said.

In reply to the second point that morality does not admit of objective truth because rational observers could disagree about moral truth in the face of all evidence, I again would disagree. While this might occur in the case of some moral disputes, it will not occur in all of them. Additionally, I would argue that the case of Hitler's depravity is a case in point *for* the objectivist and *not* the skeptic.

Like Brink and, for that matter, Aristotle, I view moral properties as functional properties. Moral properties, the virtues in particular, are "those which bear upon the maintenance and flourishing of human organisms. Maintenance and flourishing presumably consist in necessary conditions for survival, other needs associated with basic well-being, wants of various sorts, and distinctively human capacities" (Brink 1998, 534). It is in an individual's rational self-interest to possess virtues, such as justice, courage, or temperance. Possessing them enables one to act in ways that preserve friendships and the kinds of healthy community relations that best serve one's interests in the long run. Since Hitler's actions are incompatible with the possession of the virtues, there is no basis upon which a rational observer can view his ordering of the final solution as anything other than immoral and a sign of his depravity.

While it might be objected here that injustice sometimes benefits the individual, I would contend that this is true only about individual acts of injustice. However, my point, as was Aristotle's, is that in starting out in life and in choosing what traits it would be best for one to have, justice is rationally preferable to injustice. While an occasional unjust deed might benefit a person, a life lived in accordance with injustice is not nearly as likely to promote flourishing as a life lived in accordance with justice. And since acts should be judged as right or wrong in accordance with whether or not they conform to the virtues, there is then no rational basis upon which Hitler's actions can be viewed as ethical.

Again there are possible replies to this conception of how to resolve moral disputes rationally, but my sense is that they will be answerable. Regardless, my point here is to show that Ruse's case for ethical skepticism is weak. My discussion here does that by showing how much more one would need to consider in making such a case.

Conclusion

For all of the reasons stated, we have good reason to regard Ruse's evolutionary defense of ethical skepticism as inadequate. His argument from analogy to spiritualism is flawed and reveals that before he concludes that moral beliefs are *mere* adaptations and before using this point to infer that justification of moral beliefs is out of place he must first establish on independent grounds that moral beliefs are incapable of justification. His response to Nozick is also problematic. He does not do enough to show that evolutionary theory offers a better account of our belief in objective ethics than do accounts which appeal to the existence of objective moral truth. More importantly, in arguing that evolutionary theory is incompatible with objective moral truth he does not give any consideration to the prospect that an evolved and evolving human nature could serve as the objective grounding for the truth of our moral claims.

Ruse might not consider the prospect of grounding objective moral truth in human nature because he may believe that doing so will necessarily involve one in the naturalistic fallacy.[5] However, as Alasdair MacIntyre has argued in *After Virtue* (1981) not all moves from 'is' to 'ought' are fallacious. MacIntyre maintains that since we can rightly view human nature teleologically, we can justifiably derive moral norms from facts about human nature. To this Ruse might respond that teleological views of human nature are incompatible with evolutionary thinking. Even so, there are various kinds of teleological theories of human nature, some of which may be incompatible with evolutionary thinking and others of which may not be. At any rate, before accepting Ruse's arguments such teleological theories or the naturalistic fallacy need further consideration. For Ruse to argue convincingly that any attempt at grounding an objective morality in the facts of human nature is bound to fail he must do more than appeal to the naturalistic fallacy. The best attempts at bridging the 'is-ought' gap need to be confronted individually. Among these attempts there are even a number which argue that, contrary to the claims of Ruse, evolutionary biology provides the keys to an objective grounding of morality.[6] In the next chapter I will consider the merits of these various attempts to bridge the 'is-ought' gap with evolutionary biology.

---

[5] Indeed this seems to be the very sort of move that Ruse makes in *Taking Darwin Seriously*. See also Rottschaefer and Martinsen 1990. They do a nice job of clarifying the significance of the naturalistic fallacy for Ruse's argument for ethical skepticism.

[6] Rottschaefer and Martinsen (1990) distinguish between the definitional version of the naturalistic fallacy and the derivational version. They also argue contra Ruse that evolutionary thinking can play a role in the objective grounding of moral discourse without committing either form of the naturalistic fallacy. For an interesting critical reply, see Barrett 1991. For other evolutionary approaches to providing an objective grounding to moral discourse, see Richards 1986a; 1986b; 1989; and Campbell 1996. For a critique of Richards's view, see Williams 1990. For a neo-Aristotelian defense of the objectivity of morality which employs the concept of a human *telos*, see MacIntyre 1981.

3

Recent Objectivist Approaches to Evolutionary Ethics

Evolutionary ethics can be categorized as either objectivist or nonobjectivist. The previous chapter provides a fairly detailed exposition and critique of Ruse's nonobjectivist evolutionary ethic. In this chapter I will explain and critically engage with a variety of recent objectivist approaches to evolutionary ethics. Each of the advocates of the objectivist approach believes that if sociobiological explanations of human behavior, including moral behavior, are true, then these facts can be used to give a naturalistic justification of normative claims. They believe that the truths of sociobiology would enable rationally justified inferences from biological facts about human nature to moral facts about how we ought to live and act. In what follows I will examine a number of these recent attempts at bridging the "is-ought" gap, arguing that each of them commits some version of the naturalistic fallacy.

The Good Is the Desirable: Arnhart's Definitional Attempt at Bridging the "Is-Ought" Gap

In his recent book, *Darwinian Natural Right: The Biological Ethics of Human Nature* (1997), Larry Arnhart argues that:

> There are at least twenty natural desires that are manifested in diverse ways in all human societies throughout history: a complete life, parental care, sexual identity, sexual mating, familial bonding, friendship, social ranking, justice as reciprocity, political rule, war, health, beauty, wealth, speech, practical habituation, practical reasoning,

practical arts, aesthetic pleasure, religious understanding, and intellectual understanding. (Arnhart 1997, 29)

He says that these are natural because they are so deeply rooted in human nature that they will manifest themselves in some manner across history in every human society. He wants to show that:

> The universality of these natural desires supports universal standards of moral judgment, so that we can judge societies as better or worse depending upon how well they satisfy those natural desires. (Arnhart 1997, 17)

Thus, Arnhart believes that the biological facts of human nature can be used in bridging the fact-value gap and in providing an adequate naturalistic justification of moral claims.

Arnhart believes that there is no gap between facts and values because the good *is* the desirable and what is desirable is a matter of fact. Here he would have us understand that "the desirable" is not simply whatever *can* be desired. Rather it is what is truly to be desired in the sense of promoting human flourishing, which Arnhart regards as promoting the fullest satisfaction of desires over a complete life (Arnhart 1997, 18). He also argues that his conception of the good is neither culturally nor individually relative since our biological natures as human beings shape what is truly desirable for us.

Rather than simply asserting that there is no gap between facts and values and that the good is what promotes the fullest satisfaction of desires over a complete life, he defends this view by responding to G.E. Moore's charge of "the naturalistic fallacy." In doing so he points out that Moore would object to any definition of the good as the desirable. Arnhart says that according to Moore something is good only if it is acceptable to desire it. Since some things that *can* be desired ought not to be desired, Moore believes the good cannot be defined as the desirable. Arnhart thinks his understanding of the desirable as that which promotes the fullest satisfaction of desires over a complete life allows him to escape this argument, since working with this conception of the desirable we no longer view just *anything capable of being desired* as good. According to Arnhart desiring things incompatible with one's own achievement of the fullest satisfaction of desire over a complete life is not desiring what is truly desirable, and so it is to desire something that is not good. For instance, sleeping with my students may in some sense be desirable but not truly desirable in the sense that interests Arnhart. For I love my job and my wife and my children very much and sleeping with my students would then for obvious reasons jeopardize my chances of a fully satisfying complete life. Thus on Arnhart's view not just anything desirable, such as sleeping with my students, is truly desirable or, in other words, good.

Arnhart also argues that to insist on a logical gulf between facts and values as Moore and Kant do "would render all normative judgments impotent, because we would have no factual reasons to obey them" (Arnhart 1997, 85). To illustrate this point he considers the judgment that "we ought to be just." He says that unless we understand the good as the truly desirable we will have no way of explaining why we ought to be just.

> If "we ought to be just" is an example of a normative judgment, then we could ask, "Why ought we to be just?" If the answer is "because it is right for us to be just," this would still beg the question of why this is right for us. Eventually, we must answer that "we ought to be just because justice satisfies some of our deepest desires and thus contributes to our happiness." A Kantian separation between *is* and *ought* would render all normative judgments impotent, because we would have no factual reasons to obey them. (Arnhart 1997, 82–83)

Again the idea here is that we must define the right or good in terms of the desirable if we are ever to explain to people why they should be just.

(1) REPLY TO ARNHART'S FIRST POINT

Simply switching the naturalistic definition of the good from (a) the desirable to (b) that which promotes the fullest satisfaction of desire over a complete life does not by itself allow Arnhart to escape Moore's argument. For Moore might still say that something is good only if it is acceptable to desire it or pursue it, and the mere fact that something promotes the fullest satisfaction of desires in a complete life does not mean that it is acceptable to desire it or pursue it and thus does not mean that it is good. Arnhart overlooks the fact that some things which promote the fullest satisfaction of desire in a complete life are things that are bad and ought not to be pursued. Referring back to my earlier example I noted that I love my job, my wife, and my children very much. They are some of the most cherished things in my life. It is quite conceivable that circumstances could arise in which to preserve these things for myself I might need, and therefore desire, to do any number of unjust deeds. Desiring such things might well promote the fullest satisfaction of my desires over a complete life, but would such things be good? Moore's criticism still holds against Arnhart's revised definition of the good.

(II) REPLY TO ARNHART'S SECOND POINT

Is it true that separating fact and value as Moore and Kant do would "render all normative judgments impotent, because we would have no factual reason to obey them"? This seems to me to be false. Moore's point is that you cannot define "good." Even if this is so there may be any number of factual reasons why someone should pursue the good. I suppose Moore's view might leave open the possibility that on some occasions pursuing the good might have no connection to the satisfaction of human interests, but these would indeed be rare circumstances. What is the alternative? According to Arnhart it is defining the good as that which promotes the fullest satisfaction of desires over a complete life. Certainly this would mean that we could *always* give factual reasons for doing what is good, since doing what is good is defined with reference to what in fact promotes satisfaction of desires. But it only makes sense to define the good in this way if it first gives you an accurate characterization of what *is* good. And for reasons given in the preceding section Arnhart's definition fails this test.

Should we really be motivated to define the good in a way which connects it definitionally to human interests so that we will *always* be able to give interested reasons to pursue it even though this definition has serious drawbacks, or should we just admit that conceivably on some rare occasions the pursuit of the nonnatural and perhaps indefinable good may not be justified by appeal to human interests? Arnhart gives no reason to think one approach is superior to the other.

Overwhelming Mutual Advantage and the "Is-Ought" Gap: A Reply to Campbell

Richmond Campbell (1996) argues that evolutionary biology can play a role in giving an objective justification for morality. He notes that in giving an objective justification for morality one might try either to give an objective justification for possessing some morality or other or for possessing some particular morality. Campbell is skeptical that there can be any objective justification for possessing some particular morality, such as say Mill's utilitarianism or Kant's Categorical Imperative, but he does think that evolutionary biology can play a role in giving an objective justification for possessing some morality.

Campbell's argument might be outlined in the following way:

(1) The biological explanation for the existence of morality implies that having some morality rather than none overwhelmingly improves the life prospects for every member of the group that possesses a morality.

(2) If (a) having some morality rather than none overwhelmingly improves the life prospects for every member of the group that possesses a morality, then (b) having some morality rather than none is justified for every member of the group.

So, (3) having some morality rather than none is justified for every member of the group (Campbell 1996, 24).

In support of the first premise Campbell tells us that moral beliefs are dispositions to think, feel, and act in accordance with certain norms. And he states:

Suppose that these dispositions are heritable and fitness enhancing. Then we have the basic ingredients for a Darwinian story of how natural selection favors the preservation and refinement of such dispositions from one generation to the next—in short, the evolution of morals. Would such dispositions be fitness enhancing? The moral prohibition against incest is perhaps the most frequently cited example where this assumption seems reasonable, since avoidance of incest (at least prior to the advent of sophisticated methods of birth control) is biologically adaptive in strict Darwinian terms. But prohibitions against murder, assault, stealing, and breaking one's word are arguably fitness enhancing as well, for humans have on average more to lose in terms of fitness when they are subject to these wrongs than they have to gain as perpetrators. In sum, natural selection would appear to favor what we can call a common core of moral inhibitions, which we now express in the form of general moral beliefs about what we ought to do and not do. (Campbell 1996, 21–22)

Campbell takes this to be the typical account of how morals have evolved. Further, since morality enhances fitness by improving the life prospects of the members of groups of organisms, it follows that having some morality rather than none improves the life prospects of every member of the group that possesses a morality.

In explaining the second premise of his argument Campbell must explain why (a) implies (b). Why is it that if (a) having some morality rather than none overwhelmingly improves the life prospects of every member of the group that possess a morality, then (b) having some morality rather than none is justified for every member of the group? In answer to this Campbell states:

> Since humans are naturally moved by considerations of overwhelming mutual advantage, the fact that having some morality rather than none is overwhelmingly mutually advantageous (OMA), carries normative force, justifying morality. (Campbell 1996, 26)

According to Campbell, then, in the second premise of his main argument (a) implies (b) because humans are naturally moved by considerations of overwhelming mutual advantage.

As with Arnhart's argument, in thinking critically about this argument we must ask whether it commits the naturalistic fallacy. Campbell does not believe he commits this fallacy. In response to the claim that he has unwarrantedly reasoned from facts to values he states that

> my argument proceeds directly from a normative premise about what should count as justification in this context. Whatever the merits of that premise, there is clearly no attempt to deduce "ought" from "is". Nor, I should add, is the argument circular, for the "ought" implicit in this premise is not a moral "ought" but the "ought" of rationality. (Campbell 1996, 25)

This reply to worries about the naturalistic fallacy is misguided. For in the justification he provides for premise (2) it is clear that he has unwarrantedly moved from an "is" to an "ought." The mere fact, if it is a fact, that humans are naturally moved by considerations of overwhelming mutual advantage, does not mean that they ought to be so moved. Social scientific studies have shown that many people are naturally inclined to regard certain fallacious forms of inference as legitimate.[1] Does this mean that these people are reasoning as they ought? To provide an objective justification for possessing some morality Campbell needs to give a defense of premise (2). For otherwise his argument is question-begging. The defense he provides commits the naturalistic fallacy. Thus, Campbell has not shown how evolutionary biology can be used in giving an objective justification of morality.

Richards's Revised Version of Evolutionary Ethics

In a number of publications Robert Richards (1986a, 1986b, 1987, 1989) has defended what he calls "the revised version of evolutionary ethics (RV)." He summarizes this position in the following way:

> RV stipulates that the community welfare is the highest moral good. It supposes that evolution has equipped human beings with a number of social instincts, such as the need to protect offspring, provide for the general well-being of members of the community (including oneself), defend the helpless against aggression, and other dispositions that constitute a moral creature. These constitutionally imbedded directives are instances of the supreme principle of heeding the community welfare. Particular moral maxims, which translate these injunctions into the language and values of a given society, would be justified by an individual's showing that, all things considered, following such maxims would contribute to the community welfare. (Richards 1986a, 286)

In his writings Richards endeavors to give a justification for the supreme principle of morality—promote the community welfare

---

[1] For an extensive discussion of this social scientific data, see Stich 1990.

or act altruistically. In what follows I will briefly summarize his justifications for this principle and then subject them to critical assessment.

Richards does not try to justify the sociobiological foundations of RV. Rather, in providing a justification of it and the supreme principle of morality he wants us to work on the assumption that the sociobiological account of the evolution of morals is true. His project is not to defend these sociobiological accounts of the origins of morality but to show that if true, then they give justification for moral claims, providing the objective grounding for a system of ethics. He claims to provide three justifying arguments for the supreme principle of morality. I take the first two arguments to amount to the same thing. Richards acknowledges this himself. The following passages make this point clear. In expressing his first justifying argument he writes:

> [T]he constructive forces of evolution impose a practical necessity on each man to promote the community good. We must, we are obliged to heed this imperative. We might attempt to ignore the demand of our nature by refusing to act altruistically, but this does not diminish its reality. The inability of men to harden their consciences completely to basic principles of morality means that sinners can be redeemed. Hence, just as the context of physical nature allows us to argue "Since lightening has struck, thunder ought to follow," so the structured context of human evolution allows us to argue. "*Since each man has evolved to advance the community good, each ought to act altruistically.*" (Richards 1986a, 288)

And in expressing his second justifying argument he writes:

> The justifying argument, then, amounts to: *the evidence shows that evolution has, as a matter of fact, constructed human beings to act for the community good; but to act for the community good is what we mean by being moral. Since, therefore, human beings are moral beings—an unavoidable condition produced by evolution—each ought act for the community good* (Richards 1986a, 289)

A glance at the preceding passages makes it plain that the first two justifying arguments amount to the same thing. Richards is arguing that just as we can reasonably infer that thunder ought to occur from the fact that lightening has struck, so too can we reasonably infer that humans ought to act altruistically from the fact that each man has evolved to advance the community good. Thus, he believes that how we ought to act can be logically deduced from the facts of human nature.

Richards's third strategy for justifying the supreme principle of morality involves showing how RV must be "warranted because it grounds other of the known strategies for justifying moral principles" (Richards 1986a, 291). He argues that to get agreement on the basic principles of the ethical systems of Moore, Kant, and Spencer requires that human beings "must resound to the same moral cord, acting for the common good" (Richards 1986a, 292). RV provides an explanation for this. Richards writes:

> for the vast community of men, they have been stamped by nature as moral beings. RV, therefore, shows that the several strategies used to support an ultimate ethical principle will, in fact, be successful, successfully showing, of course, that the community good is the highest ethical standard. But for RV to render successful several strategies for demonstrating the validity of the highest ethical principle is itself a justification. (Richards 1986a, 292)

In assessing Richards's position I am most interested in determining whether he has adequately justified his claim that we have a moral obligation to act for the community good. Given that this is my interest, it strikes me that what he calls his first "two" arguments are more important than the third. For the third does not really show that we ought to act for the community welfare so much as it shows that different systems of ethics, like Moore's, Kant's, and Spencer's, can reasonably expect agreement on their principles only because evolution has constructed us to value the community good. Just because evolution has constructed us in this way it does not obviously follow that we have a moral obligation to value or act for the community good. Richards thinks it does follow, but the only argument he gives for this is expressed as his first "two" arguments. Thus, in short, we need to ask whether the following bit of reasoning demonstrates why we are morally obligated to act for the community welfare:

> Just as we can reasonably infer that thunder ought to occur given that lightening has occurred, so too can we reasonably infer that we ought to act altruistically given that we have evolved to do so.

What are we to make of *this* argument? A natural and legitimate reply is to argue that Richards has not demonstrated that we are morally obligated to act for the community good because the "ought" employed in the argument above is not a moral "ought." Rather it is a predictive "ought." This point has been made by at least two critics of Richards's work.[2]

Richards has published a reply to this sort of objection . He insists that the "ought" used in his derivation is a moral "ought."

> The "ought" is a moral "ought," not because of its logical character, but because of the nature of the causal context to which it is applied—namely, man's moral nature (i.e., his altruistically disposed nature). The case of thunder is precisely the same: it is the physical process of 'lightening-producing thunder' that makes the "ought" a physical-process ought. So the moral process of acting according to the evolutionarily derived disposition to altruism makes the "ought" a moral ought. (Richards 1989, 340)

The idea here is that since humans are led to act altruistically because of their evolved disposition to so act, and since this disposition just *is* a moral disposition, it follows that the "ought" used in his derivation is a moral "ought." Richards' point is that human beings are morally obligated to act altruistically because of their moral nature, their evolved disposition to act altruistically.

The legitimacy of this reply rests on the assumption that our evolved disposition to act altruistically just is a *moral* disposition. But one might wonder why this is true. Richards states:

> The "ought" derived from the structured context of man's evolutionary formation, then, will be a moral ought precisely because the activities of abiding the community good and approving of altruistic behavior constitute what we mean and (if RV is correct) must mean by "being moral." (Richards 1986a, 290–91)

So, the disposition to act altruistically is a *moral* disposition because this is what we do and must mean by "being moral."

This reply lays Richards open to the charge of circular reasoning. For clearly "being moral" also means disposed to act as one

---

[2] See Bart Voorzanger 1987 and Patricia Williams 1990.

ought. But it is an open question as to whether one should act altruistically or egoistically. Consequently, if one says "being moral" means disposed to act altruistically, then one is not simply defining "being moral" but is also telling us how we ought to act. And if Richards's argument for the supreme principle of morality rests on a claim about how we ought to act then he is not deriving an "ought" from an "is" as he claims. Rather, he is providing a circular argument to the effect that we ought to act altruistically.

In reply Richards might object to my claim that the question of how we ought to act is an open question. He says that if RV is true then by "being moral" we *must* mean acting altruistically. However, this will still not save his argument. Richards's original argument was that, "Since we have evolved to act altruistically, we ought to." Now even if by "being moral" we must mean acting altruistically, he has argued that the "ought" in his original argument is a moral "ought" on the grounds that acting altruistically is what is meant by "acting morally." But to argue in this way means that his original argument really says "Since we have evolved to act morally, we ought to." Now if the "ought" of this argument is a moral "ought", the argument is vacuous. For of course we morally ought to act morally. The question to be answered is not whether we morally ought to act morally, but which of the various acts we might perform that could be called "moral" we have a moral obligation to perform. And if the "ought" in his argument is not moral but, say, predictive, then Richards is not deriving the relevant kind of "ought" from "is" and, consequently, he gives no justification for how we morally ought to act.

Rottschaefer's Teleological Reworking of Richards's Evolutionary Ethics

William Rottschaefer (1991) has argued that indeed there is a problem with Richards's justification of the supreme principle. He takes the problem to be the same as the one noted in the previous section. Referring to Richards's justification of the supreme principle, he states, "Isn't Richards confusing causal and moral 'oughts'?" (Rottschaefer 1991, 344) Despite this, Rottschaefer believes the problems encountered by Richards's evolutionary ethics can be solved by (1) drawing a distinction between mechanistic and teleological causal laws and (2) noting how teleological laws are at work in the evolution of man's moral disposition.

According to Rottschaefer mechanistic causal explanations explain phenomena with reference to their antecedent conditions. Teleological explanations explain phenomena with reference to their consequences. The traits of human beings, including the disposition to act altruistically, can be explained teleologically by referring to them as traits that have the consequence of promoting reproductive success.

> [W]hile both mechanical and T/T [teleological/teleonomic] causal laws can provide explanations only the latter can provide justifications. Appeals to ends set the marks to be achieved and enable the formulation of criteria of success. Appeals to ends can provide, therefore, justificatory explanations; appeals to antecedents can provide only explanations. Therefore, RV's mere appeal to a relevant causal context fails to discriminate between the two and thus blurs the logic of NJ [naturalistic justification]. Thus it is precisely because evolutionary, behavioral, and cognitive explanations are sometimes in terms of consequences that they can be candidates for justificatory explanations. (Rottschaefer 1991, 345)

Clearly Rottschaefer finds Richards's RV, revised version of evolutionary ethics, problematic. But he also thinks the problems with it are solved once we recognize that teleological causes are at work in the evolutionary explanation of the human tendency towards altruistic behavior.

One might wonder just how the appeal to the teleological aspects of evolutionary explanations helps matters. Rottschaefer is not especially clear about this. The point seems to be the following: Richards's inference, "Human beings have evolved to act altruistically, so they ought to," justifies a moral "ought" only because the evolved disposition to act altruistically exists *for* benefiting reproductive success. In the passage quoted above Rottschaefer says, "Appeals to ends set the marks to be achieved and enable the formation of criteria of success." The idea seems to be that since as biological organisms we all share the goal of reproductive success and since the disposition to act altruistically can correctly be explained as existing *for* this common goal of human existence, it follows that we ought to act altruistically to achieve this end. According to Rottschaefer, moral "oughts" are practical "oughts," meaning they must be justified with reference to the consequences of human action (Rottschaefer 1991, 345). Thus, it is not until the teleological character of evolutionary explanation is explained and related to Richards' argument that we can recognize the argument as justifying the supreme principle.

Another way of looking at Rottschaefer's point that "Appeals to ends set the marks to be achieved and enable the formation of criteria of success" would involve stating that since we have the biologically given goal of reproductive success, and since goodness is to be judged with respect to achieving goals, and since acting altruistically increases chances at reproductive success, the good human being acts altruistically. Further, since we ought to act as the good human being does, we ought to act altruistically.

In response to Rottschaefer's reasoning here it could be argued that he begs the question. Pointing out that altruism exists for reproductive success, thereby explaining its existence teleologically, does not provide the keys to determining how we ought to act. The biologically determined goal of reproductive success only helps us prove that we ought to act altruistically if that goal is itself good. Is it good? That's an open question. Thus, without an argument as to why reproductive success is good Rottschaefer's revision of Richards' revised evolutionary ethics begs the question.

In an earlier article by Rottschaefer and David Martinsen (1990) one can find what would seem to be Rottschaefer's most likely response to the criticism above. In this article they give an argument to the effect that human survival and reproductive success are good.

> [O]ur claim about the value of human fitness and S/R [survival and reproduction] are not, it seems to us, completely unwarranted. For their value is supported both by the fact that they are necessary conditions for the achievement of what we deem to be intrinsically, or, at least, independently valuable, and because they are often valued in themselves. (Rottschaefer and Martinsen 1990, 168)

Their point is that since human survival and reproduction are (1) necessary for the attainment of other things that we deem to be intrinsically valuable and (2) often valued in themselves, human survival and reproduction are good. On the same page that this argument appears Rottschaefer and Martinsen list science, math, and art as some of the other things that we deem to be intrinsically valuable.

In reply to this it should be noted that while the premises of this argument are true the conclusion just does not follow. For the mere fact that we deem human survival and reproduction as good or that we deem art, science, and mathematics as good does not mean that they *are* good. Rottschaefer wants to provide a naturalistic justification for the claim that we ought to act altruistically and, given that he wants to do this by arguing that altruism serves the goal of human survival and reproduction, he does need some argument to show that human survival and reproduction are good. The argument he provides will not suffice for the reason given above. Thus, we have still not seen an evolutionary ethic that has adequately bridged the "is-ought" gap.

Informed readers might feel that I have missed something important in my understanding of Rottschaefer's position. In Rottschaefer and Martinsen 1990 the authors argue that moral properties are not reducible to nonmoral properties; rather the former supervene on the latter. And they additionally maintain that it is because moral properties supervene on nonmoral properties that moral claims can be given adequate naturalistic justifications. This aspect of Rottschaefer's thinking has been criticized by Jonathan Barrett. He challenges the contention that moral properties supervene on the nonmoral. (See Barrett 1991. For a reply to Barrett, see Rottschaefer and Martinsen 1991.) I have not engaged in any discussion of Rottschaefer's views on supervenience simply because I think that even if we grant him his points about supervenience, there are other more significant problems with his naturalistic approach.

It might be argued that the claim that human survival and reproduction are good is *self-evident*, meaning that Rottschaefer does not need to give an argument in its support. However, such a retort to my criticism raises questions about the nature of self-evidence. What does it mean to say that something is self-evident? On one conception of the self-evident it would seem that only tautologies—definitional truths, like "All bachelors are male," and logical truths, like "For any proposition, P, either P or not P"—and reports of sense data, like "It seems to me that X" are self-evident. But, the claim that human survival and reproduction are good fits into neither of these categories. Perhaps, this conception of the self-evident is overly stringent, and maybe we would do better to understand self-evident propositions as simply any propositions that are taken as obviously true by all rational adult human beings. But, do all rational adult human beings believe that human survival and reproduction are good? This is not obvious to me. Someone might look at the human tendency to overpopulate and to destroy the natural environment and come to the conclusion that the world would be better off if human beings did not thrive. Consequently, even on this weaker conception of self-evidence, it cannot plausibly be argued that the claim that human survival and reproduction are good is self-evident and thereby in no need of support.

Collier and Stingl and the Problem of Species Relativism

Like Rottschaefer, John Collier and Michael Stingl believe that with a minor adjustment the basic idea behind Richards's RV could be turned into a workable evolutionary ethic. They argue that Richards's RV suffers from a problem of species relativism. They provide a solution to this problem and maintain that their revision of Richards's position will allow for an adequate naturalistic justification of morality.

Richards has argued that "Since human beings have evolved to promote the common good, to act altruistically, they ought to." Collier and Stingl maintain that, depending on the contingent circumstances of human existence, for instance had the environmental conditions in which we live been significantly different, human beings might not have evolved to act altruistically. Rather we might have evolved to act in ways quite different from what we now regard as moral. Because of this Richards' conclusion about how we ought to act only gives justification for a species relative conception of how we ought to act. Depending on the environmental conditions in which they find themselves, intelligent non-human creatures from other planets (if there are any) would not necessarily be justified in drawing the same conclusions about how they ought to act. According to Collier and Stingl, "A satisfactory naturalistic morality needs a way to connect our moral capacities and behaviors to nonrelativistic moral values" (Collier and Stingl 1993, 54).

It is really not clear just what the problem is that Collier and Stingl are getting at. Are they trying to point out the absurdity in saying that fictional creatures so very much like us, such as seen on *Star Trek*, might be justified in acting in ways we regard as horrific? Are they making a point similar to Plato's critique of the divine command theory of value? Just as God's commands would arbitrarily designate what is right, so too would the dictates of evolutionary processes? Maybe the point is captured in both of these ways. In any case, Collier and Stingl provide what they regard as a solution to this problem, a solution which they think will make a naturalistic justification for morality workable. In what follows I will explain their solution and then critically examine their approach.

In their article Collier and Stingl note that Richards is not alone in falling into the trap of species relativism. Michael Ruse (1998) also falls into this trap. Collier and Stingl write:

> On our view, the species relativism that both Ruse and Richards fall into results from their implicit assumption that our evolved moral sense is as good as it could be. If evolution is not optimal, this opens up the possibility of studying the sorts of conditions that could produce creatures with more optimal moral instincts. The conditions for this hypothetical optimality will be determined by the general conditions governing evolution for the sorts of creatures to which morality applies: intelligent social creatures. Optimal moral instincts will ground fundamental moral principles that are absolute for our world and nomologically similar worlds, but contingent on evolution. These principles are the basis of objective morality. (Collier and Stingl 1993, 55)

The point here is that evolution is not optimal. The traits of organisms that have evolved to perform certain functions could have been even better than they are at serving their function. For instance our eyes and ears could be better than they are at detecting images and sounds. Consequently, we have reason to believe that our moral principles could be better than they are. According to Collier and Stingl, evolutionary thinking actually runs counter to Richards's assumption that our evolved moral sense is as good as it could be.

Further, Collier and Stingl believe that we can deduce objective moral principles that are "absolute for our world and nomologically similar worlds" by reflecting on "the sorts of conditions that could produce more optimal moral instincts."

The world does . . . naturally produce creatures that have ends. Given the contingencies of evolution and the various demands for survival, in any intelligent creature the ends are likely to have a certain amount of consistency and harmony. Given the need of any organism for nutrients, and the advantages of sensitivity, avoidance of harm, and anticipation of the environment, it seems reasonable to expect that pleasure, avoidance of pain, and intelligence will be natural values. In highly evolved social creatures, true altruism is also likely to evolve, for a variety of well-known reasons. This function can be enhanced in intelligent creatures if it is cognitive. We should expect, therefore, that highly evolved intelligent and social creatures will have, in some more or less distorted fashion, common welfare and other mutual projects as fundamental goals. The convergence of theoretically expected natural values and our evolved moral intuitions suggests that at least sometimes our moral intuitions direct us towards objective and general values. (Collier and Stingl 1993, 56)

What Collier and Stingl seem to be getting at is that by reflecting on the general sorts of conditions in which evolution occurs in this world and nomologically similar worlds and by reflecting on how highly evolved, intelligent, and social creatures might best survive in the face of these broadly conceived conditions, we might come to discover moral principles that would be reasonable for any intelligent, social creatures facing these conditions to adopt. Thus, by reflecting on the general conditions that give rise to evolution and how intelligent, social creatures, whether human or extra-terrestrial, might best cope with these conditions, we can discover moral values that are not merely relative to human beings.

In short, Collier and Stingl think Richards's attempted justification for the supreme principle, "Act for the common good / Act altruistically," is flawed because it appeals only to the fact that *human beings* have evolved to act this way to justify the claim that we ought to. According to Collier and Stingl, an objective justification requires showing that *any* evolved, intelligent, social creatures ought to act altruistically. They also believe that reflecting on how any evolved, intelligent, social creatures will best cope with the conditions that give rise to evolution will reveal that any such beings ought to act altruistically. This is part of the point in the passage cited above.

It is time to ask whether their recommendations really improve the chances for a naturalistic justification of morality. Do they? I don't think so. Collier and Stingl are arguing that (1) any evolved, intelligent, social creatures facing the circumstances that give rise to evolution will evolve a disposition to act altruistically. So, (2) any such creatures ought to act altruistically. Putting the argument in this way certainly helps get around the problem of species relativity, but it does not give a satisfactory naturalistic justification of any moral obligations because (2) does not follow from (1), or at least not obviously so. Thus, for the inference from (1) to (2) to work more needs to be said to justify this inference.

Collier and Stingl seem to want to say that any social, intelligent creatures faced with the relevant sort of conditions will have "common welfare and other mutual projects as fundamental goals" (Collier and Stingl 1993, 56). They would also refer to these as "natural goals." And since acting altruistically serves these natural goals we ought to act altruistically. But here it only really follows that we ought to act altruistically if the goal is good. Thus, to complete their naturalistic justification of the claim that we ought to act altruistically they need to argue that the "natural goals" of the common welfare, etc. are good. Yet they provide no clear argument for this.

The general tone of the passage I cited earlier suggests their view is that the natural goals that any evolved, social, and intelligent creatures have are goals that any such creature must possess as a product of its evolutionary development. They also think any such goals must be common to all such creatures, thereby establishing their *objective* value, merit, or goodness. But the mere fact that all such creatures possess some goal in common does not thereby entail the objective goodness of the goal. Suppose that the world were radically different from the way that it is such that in it and in all nomologically similar worlds such creatures were led to value, to have as a goal, torturing, killing, and eating their first born child. The mere fact that all creatures living in such worlds must have this goal does not thereby make the goal objectively good. Does it? It certainly seems not.

Conclusion

As the preceding discussion makes clear, I believe that none of the recent attempts by evolutionary ethicists to give a naturalistic justification for moral claims is adequate. I hope that I have made it sufficiently clear why these attempts fail. Assuming that I am justified in my claims, one might be led to wonder where all of this leaves us.

First, my arguments by no means demonstrate that there can be no adequate naturalistic justifications for moral claims. Rather, all I have done is show that recent attempts by evolutionary ethicists are flawed. It may be that some other approaches to giving a naturalistic justification from either the evolutionary perspective or some other one may work.

Second, I do not intend to suggest that all of the justifications considered in this chapter are beyond any hope of working, though I do believe they can never work as *naturalistic* justifications. To be *naturalistic* they must exclude any normative claims from their premises, moving strictly from nonmoral premises to a moral conclusion. None of the approaches to justification I have considered will work as long as they remain naturalistic justifications. However, it seems to me that some of them would have promise were they to import some intuitive normative claims into the premises. For instance, Richmond Campbell's argument might work if he just included the premise "Policies and practices that are overwhelmingly mutually advantageous ought to be adopted." Or Rottschaefer's argument might work if he just included an intuitive premise to the effect that "Human survival and reproduction are good." But of course once these moves are made the justifications are no longer naturalistic.

4

Sketch of an Aristotelian
Evolutionary Ethics

As we have seen in the previous two chapters, it is my view that neither the recent nonobjectivist nor the recent objectivist approaches to evolutionary ethics are satisfactory. In this chapter I want to sketch an objectivist approach to evolutionary ethics which would be able to overcome the problems faced by the recent objectivist approaches noted in the previous chapter. The approach I will defend is an Aristotelian virtue-centered approach.

Aristotelian Ethics

In the *Nicomachean Ethics*, Book 1, Chapter 7, Aristotle presents his famous function argument. Here he argues that the function of each thing, whether an artifact or a living thing or the parts of such, can be determined by its characteristic activity. The characteristic activity of a knife is to cut. So its function is to cut. The characteristic activity of the heart is to circulate blood. So its function is to circulate blood. Aristotle maintains that the characteristic activity of human beings, the activity that distinguishes them from other animals, is rational activity. So he concludes that the human function is rational activity.

According to Aristotle, the determination of the function of things has very significant implications for the correctness of our evaluative judgments. He recognizes that things are good when they perform their function well. So, for instance, a knife is good when it cuts well. A heart is good when it circulates the blood well. And so too human beings are good when they do well at rational activity. Aristotle holds that when something does well at performing its function we have criteria for making objective judgments about its merit. This in turn provides objective criteria for determining what qualities the thing must have in order to be good. So, for instance, the good knife must cut well, and since this is the nature of the good knife, this enables us to determine that the good knife must have certain qualities, such as a sharp, durable blade or a comfortable, stable grip. These qualities are what Aristotle would refer to as the excellences or virtues of a knife. They are the qualities which enable a knife to perform its function well. As noted, Aristotle says the human function is rational activity so that the human virtues will be those qualities which enable humans to reason well.

Aristotle distinguishes between two kinds of rationality—practical rationality and theoretical rationality. Practical rationality is reason employed in the pursuit of *eudaimonia* (flourishing or happiness). This is the reasoning we use in deciding what to do so that we might lead happy lives. Theoretical reason is the reasoning we use to acquire knowledge. It is the reasoning used in historical, mathematical, and scientific inquiry. Since reason can be divided into these two main categories, there is some question as to what role each of these is to play in the Aristotelian conception of a good life. Does the good human being need to do well at both of these? Does doing well at one of these suffice? And so forth. In Book 10 of the *Nicomachean Ethics* it is clear that Aristotle thinks the life of theoretical reason is the best kind of life for a human being. Among other things, he says that it is the kind of life that enables us to be most like the gods. This, however, does not mean that a life spent engaging only in practical reasoning is a bad one. Rather, Aristotle seems to think ordinary people can have good lives too by doing well at practical reasoning. We must all engage in practical reasoning. We all need to make decisions in our lives, taking into account how we will be affected by the different choices we make. We do not all need to engage in theoretical reasoning. Since Aristotle regards doing well at practical reasoning as essential to any good human life, and since we typically regard the moral life as intimately involved with decision making and doing well at this, in what follows I will focus my discussion of the Aristotelian virtues on their contribution to a good life understood as a life of good practical reasoning. Since doing well at practical reasoning is necessary for living a good (though not necessarily the best) human life, we can discern those qualities necessary for any good human life by determining what qualities are necessary for good practical reasoning. According to Aristotle, possession of the moral virtues is necessary for the good life.

Aristotle believes that doing well at practical reasoning involves reasoning in a way that is best suited to the satisfaction of one's own long term self-interest. But this is not to say that good practical reasoning is performed in an egoistic mode. Rather, Aristotle seems to think that we should have a genuine non-selfish interest in the well-being of others. Here it might be wondered how living as a virtuous person best serves one's self-interest. Don't unjust deeds often profit the person who commits them? The best Aristotelian reply to this question would admit that unjust deeds can sometimes profit a man, but a life lived in accordance with injustice rarely does so. Rather, in contemplating lives lived in accordance with justice and injustice, we see that the life of the just person is more likely to lead to happiness, since a life of injustice is more likely to lead to loss of friends, social ostracism, and retribution, whereas a just life is more likely to lead to the preservation of friendships, social acceptance, and other benefits.

In Aristotelian ethics the focus is on what traits of character possessed over a lifetime would best serve one's interest. The sorts of considerations noted in the previous paragraph make it reasonable to think possession of the virtues is most likely to serve one's interests over a lifetime. Thus, according to Aristotle, the good human being engages in practical reasoning in accordance with virtue. His virtues lead him to decide as he ought, and this will in the long run best serve his pursuit of *eudaimonia*.

Self-perfection, Social Animals, and the Darwinian Connection

In considering this sketch of the Aristotelian ethic one might wonder why things are so focused on providing for the happiness of the individual agent. While it is true that Aristotle does not encourage self-interested decision-making in the mode of the calculating egoist, he does at bottom suggest that one ought to be virtuous because it is in one's long-term self-interest. It might also be wondered why this kind of self-interested focus is at the core of his justification for living the life of virtue. In answering this question I want to focus on two main points. First, I note that Aristotle believes every human being, indeed every living thing, strives toward its own perfection, flourishing, or *eudaimonia*. Since this is a fundamental drive built into us as a consequence of our biological nature, Aristotle would not see the point in telling us to act virtuously for any other reason than this. Second, for Aristotle humans are by nature social animals. We live together in groups because this affords each of us the best opportunity at achieving our natural goal of *eudaimonia*. Since he views our individual happiness as only achievable through social living and since the virtues help us achieve social acceptance, Aristotle sees no conflict between the rational pursuit of *eudaimonia* and the moral life. So, again, the focus on the attainment of personal happiness in Aristotle's ethics is perfectly natural.

The Darwinian theory of evolution by natural selection enhances our understanding of the conception of human nature that underlies and serves as the justification for the Aristotelian ethic. The innate human drive to live well, to flourish, an innate drive which, according to Aristotle, is possessed by all living things, is explicable in terms of the Darwinian concept of reproductive success. Those organisms that are more fit to survive and reproduce in their environments are the ones that are more likely to pass on their genes to future generations. Adaptive traits or characteristics are traits that well serve the goals of survival or reproductive success. Changes in species occur over time when certain physical or behavioral characteristics become more adaptive than others. The human drive to live well, to flourish, is explicable as an adaptive trait. By seeking out what I can find to provide for myself, to better myself, I increase my chances at reproductive success. By making myself smarter, stronger, more virtuous, by perfecting myself, I make myself a more valued member of my community, enhancing my own standing within it. Each of these consequences is likely to increase my own chances at reproductive success.

The Darwinian theory also makes sense of the fact that we are social animals. According to Darwinism, social living is natural to us because it enhances our chances of reproductive success. Human beings simply don't have the physical characteristics and abilities that allow them to survive and reproduce well living on their own. But we do have the characteristics and abilities that make communal living adaptive. Because we are very good communicators we can organize ourselves into cooperative units that are very effective at providing the food, clothing, and shelter necessary for our survival and reproductive success. Providing these necessities is much easier in a group setting than it is by an isolated individual. For the above reasons, it is reasonable to conclude that the Darwinian theory of evolution *does* enhance the Aristotelian conception of human nature which underlies and justifies his virtue ethics. Indeed, were someone to doubt the Aristotelian conception of human nature and thereby the legitimacy of the Aristotelian ethic, a contemporary advocate of the Aristotelian approach would be well-served by explaining how the Aristotelian view is supported by the Darwinian theory. Given the tremendous explanatory and predictive success that the Darwinian theory has had in the biological sciences in general, its contribution to explaining the Aristotelian view of human nature should lend significant credence to the latter view.

Overcoming the Weaknesses of Other Recent Objectivist Theories of Evolutionary Ethics

The Aristotelian evolutionary virtue ethic I have just described escapes various problems encountered by the objectivist approaches considered in the previous chapter. In what follows I will illustrate some of the merits of my view by showing how it avoids the problems with these other approaches.

ARNHART'S VIEW

The chief problem with Arnhart's approach (1997) was that he defined the good as that which "promotes the fullest satisfaction of desire over a complete life." In reply to this I argued that something can promote this end and not be good. Thus, the conception of the good that underlies his ethical theory is problematic. In contrast to Arnhart's approach, my view does not depend upon providing a definition of the good. Rather, it holds that things are good when they do their function well, so that humans are good when they do their function well. To assert this is not to define the good; it is simply to claim that functioning-well is one of the ways in which something can be good. This claim also has the merits of being quite plausible, since we generally do not regard the poorly functioning watch, car, heart, or employee as good, and we *do* regard them as good when they are functioning well. Additionally, if things are good by doing their function well, then we have a basis for making objective assessments about which characteristics are good for them. Those characteristics which contribute to the functioning-well of the thing are good.

CAMPBELL'S VIEW

Richmond Campbell's evolutionary ethic (1996) required a justification of the following proposition: If having a morality improves the life prospects of every member of a group, then having a morality is justified for every member of the group. Campbell tries to justify this crucial tenet of his approach by arguing that we are naturally moved by considerations of mutual advantage and having a morality *is* mutually advantageous. In reply to this I argued that the mere fact that we are moved by such considerations does not justify being moved by them. After all, many people are naturally led to engage in certain forms of illogical inference but that does not make it rational to engage in such forms of inference. My approach does not require giving any justification of crucial tenets by appeal to what humans are naturally inclined to accept. I am not saying that we should possess the virtues because we are inclined to think that they serve functioning-well or that we should pursue the goal of functioning well because we naturally accept that doing so is good. Rather, I claim that the virtues *do* serve functioning-well and that functioning-well *is* good.

It could be argued that my defense of the claim that functioning-well is good relies on the view that what we accept as good is good, since I justify my judgment by appealing to our acceptance of watches as good when functioning-well, hearts as good when functioning-well, and so on. But this move constitutes a distortion of my argument. I am not saying that functioning-well is good because we *accept* that a variety of things are good when functioning-well. Rather, I am saying that the fact that things are good when functioning-well implies the truth of the statement that things in general are good when functioning-well. Mine is an inductive inference from particular cases. The relevant cases are not cases of what we accept, cases about our inclinations, but are cases about the merits of watches, hearts, and other entities. In this way, then, my theory is immune to the problems faced by Campbell's approach.

In the preceding paragraph I argue that things are good when functioning well. It might be argued that this is false because some cancer cells function well but are not thereby good. Or it might also be argued that a person could serve well as a part of an evil organization, such as the Nazi S.S. or an early twenty-first-century terrorist group, and yet not be good. These are important points and they deserve a fairly detailed response.

In reply to the point about cancer cells, it is unclear as to whether it makes any sense to speak of well-functioning cancer cells. Parts of the body, such as cells, get their function from serving some role in the health and maintenance of the body of which they are a part. Since cancer cells detract from the health and maintenance of the body, there is no sense in which they can be said to be functioning-well. Consequently, to speak of them as good because of their functioning-well doesn't make sense.

The problem of the well-functioning Nazi or terrorist calls for a different kind of response. In contrast to the case of cancer cells it does make sense to speak of the well-functioning Nazi or terrorist. The alleged problem with this is that by the logic of my argument, it follows that such a well-functioning Nazi or terrorist is good. But, I am not convinced there is a problem here. Well-functioning Nazis and terrorists are good *qua* Nazis and *qua* terrorists. This does not mean that they are good human beings nor that they possess the moral virtues necessary for human goodness. I see no problem in saying that one can be a good Nazi but a terrible human being.

However, it could be said that there really is a problem here because we are not just human beings. Rather, we are members of different social groups as well. For instance, I am not just a human being; I am also a family member, a faculty member, a U.S. citizen, and so forth. Other people will be members of other groups, such as the 4-H Club, or the Catholic Church, or the American Medical Association (AMA), or, in some cases, the KKK or some terrorist organization. If we are not just human beings but also members of such other groups and if we can be good *qua* functioning well as a human being or *qua* functioning well as a member of the 4-H Club or some other group, such as a terrorist organization, then upon what basis can it be said that we ought to favor the pursuit of human goodness and the moral virtues necessary to it? Presumably, when I argue that human goodness involves doing well at practical reasoning and that possession of the moral virtues is necessary to this, it is my intent to suggest that we ought to have these virtues and we ought not to live and act in ways that are incompatible with such human goodness and the moral virtues necessary for such. But if we are equally members of other groups whose values might conflict with those constitutive of human goodness, then it might reasonably be wondered why the pursuit of human goodness should take precedence over the pursuit of one of these other forms of goodness, such as (and most problematically) being a good terrorist.

The proper reply to this problem involves noting the primacy of human goodness. Human goodness and the human flourishing which is constitutive of it is primary in the sense that these different social organizations, such as the 4-H Club, the AMA, or university faculty, which generate their own distinct criteria of goodness, exist to provide for, to support and maintain, the human good. What I mean is that, while social organizations do exist and while one can do well or poorly as members of these groups and, consequently, be good or bad with respect to how one functions within them, these groups are ultimately established to provide for the support and maintenance of human flourishing, the human good. Even groups that we regard as immoral, like the Nazi S.S. or the KKK or various terrorist organizations, exist to serve and support the human good. It's just that these groups unjustifiably attempt to serve the good of certain human beings at the expense of other human beings.

In any case, since we form different social groups to ultimately provide for human flourishing or human goodness, it follows that human goodness has a primacy to it which warrants the conclusion that the pursuit of it and the moral virtues necessary to it should be favored over the pursuit of any socially constructed conception of the good which conflicts with it. Thus, being a good human being is more important than being a good terrorist or good Nazi, so I ought to forgo the latter pursuits if they conflict with the more important pursuit of human goodness.

As noted earlier, the logic of my argument does imply that one can be a good Nazi or a good terrorist, since one can do well at serving one's function within one of these groups. But it does not follow from my argument that one should pursue such forms of goodness. For I have just argued that there is a primacy to human goodness and the virtues necessary to it which gives it a greater value. Thus, conflicting forms of goodness, such as that of the good Nazi, ought not to be pursued.

Richards's View

Robert Richards (1986a, 1986b, 1987, 1989) argues that since human beings have an evolved, adaptive disposition to act altruistically, they ought to do so. This is the central argument of his evolutionary ethics. In supporting this argument he maintains that just as it is reasonable to infer that thunder ought to occur given that there is lightning, so too we can reasonably infer that human beings ought to act altruistically given their evolved disposition to do so. As we have seen, however, this argument is problematic because of its confusion of the moral "ought" with the predictive "ought."

In contrast to Richards's theory my own approach does not involve this sort of confusion. My point is that our rationality is determinative of our function, so that we are good insofar as we reason well. Consequently, since the virtues are essential to doing well at practical reasoning throughout the course of one's life, one ought to possess them. Additionally, I have argued that the Darwinian theory of natural selection can help us understand why the pursuit of our own perfection and the preservation of friendships and community are goals natural to us and that recognizing this in turn helps us understand why the virtues are needed to help us do well at practical reasoning.

But I do not argue that we have innate drives to act altruistically and that consequently we can say with some degree of predictive certainty that we ought to do so. Nor do I try to infer any moral "oughts" from such predictive "oughts." Rather, while I do want to suggest that the goals of self-perfection and the preservation of community are natural to us, I do not want to suggest that the moral virtues are natural. Rather, along with Aristotle I would say that we are naturally malleable to a life of virtue and that a life of virtue helps us to achieve goals natural to us. But since we are not *naturally* virtuous but require moral training, I do not argue that since we are naturally disposed to act altruistically (or virtuously), we ought to do so.

Notice that I say the goals of self-perfection and the preservation of community are natural to us. In addition my view is that human goodness involves doing well at attaining such natural goals and the moral virtues are to be defined and understood as those qualities of character which enable us to achieve those goals. It might be objected that in allowing these natural goals of self-perfection and the preservation of community to shape my conception of the human good and the virtues, I am doing the same sort of thing which Campbell did and for which I criticized his position. That is, Campbell talks about how we are naturally moved by considerations of overwhelming mutual advantage (OMA), and he argues that since having a morality is overwhelmingly mutually advantageous we ought to have one. In criticizing Campbell I said that the mere fact that we are moved by such considerations does not mean that we ought to be moved by them. Here it might be wondered why it is legitimate to ground moral claims upon the natural *goals* of human beings, as I do, but not to ground moral claims upon *considerations by which we are naturally moved*, as Campbell does.

The difference between these has to do with teleology. My claims about the human good and the moral virtues hinge upon the fact that there is a defining activity, rationality, of human beings and that certain conditions must be met to do well at this sort of thing. The idea here is that the objective criteria of human goodness are shaped by the natural ends of human beings. In contrast, Campbell makes no reference to there being a shared end, or *telos*, of human beings which provides the criteria of goodness and the virtues. Rather, he moves from the fact of there being certain considerations which naturally move us to the conclusion that we ought to be moved by these. But when the point is made in this way, as Campbell does, we have grounds to reject this argument. For as I have noted earlier human beings are naturally moved to accept certain forms of reasoning that are fallacious. Thus, being naturally moved by a consideration does not justify being so moved.

In contrast when the distinctive activity, end, or purpose of something, such as, in this case, a human being, is clarified this sets objective standards upon which judgments of goodness can be made. My approach to the justification of moral norms appeals to such a distinctive activity, or end, found in human beings. In this way my appeal to the natural goal of human beings in justifying normative conclusions differs in significant ways from the approach taken by Campbell.

None of my comments here should be taken to suggest that Campbell could not modify his position in a way that is amenable with my own. If it turns out that being moved by considerations of OMA is part of what is involved in doing well at practical reasoning, part of what's involved in achieving or living the good life, then this should be clarified by Campbell. Once it is clarified then the objective grounding for the claim that we *ought* to be moved by such considerations can be established. In the end, I think this can be done. Thus, in a certain sense, what I am saying is that I accept the conclusion Campbell draws. We *should* be moved by considerations of OMA. But I do not believe Campbell does an adequate job of explaining why we ought to be so moved. To do this he would need to say some things about the human *telos* and how being moved by considerations of OMA is part of what is involved in any flourishing human life.

ROTTSCHAEFER'S VIEW

Of all the views considered in the previous chapter Rottschaefer's seems to come closest to my own. I say this because of the emphasis he places on teleology and the role of moral behavior in helping human beings to achieve their natural goals. This emphasis upon teleology in determining what is moral is where the kinship with my own Aristotelian approach lies.

In defending his position Rottschaefer (1991) argues that since we all have survival and reproduction as a goal, and since altruistic behavior serves this goal, we ought to act altruistically. In support of this conclusion he also argues that the goals of survival and reproductive success are good because: (1) they are valued in themselves and (2) they are necessary for attaining other things that we value. In reply to this I argued that the fact that we value these things does not mean that they are valuable. There is a subjectivity to Rottschaefer's determination of the valuable that consists in his determining the valuable from what we value. This perspective-dependent notion of value constitutes a subjectivism that I find objectionable, since, again, the mere fact that we value something doesn't make it valuable.

In contrast to Rottschaefer I argue that when a thing performs its function or characteristic activity well it is good. That is why we all know and agree that a watch is good when it tells time well, eyes are good when they let us see well, and so forth. Since this is clearly a way in which things can be good, and since humans have the function or characteristic activity of rationality, we can determine that humans are good when they do this well. From this notion we can go on to determine objectively what the virtues are. This characterization of my position should remind us that it relies upon no perspectivalism or subjectivism about value.

One could argue that this characterization of my position just masks a hidden subjectivism. For in the end my assertion that things are good when they perform their function well is just another way of saying that we value things that perform their function well, so that statements of the form "X is good" are expressions of a personal, cultural, or human perspective. In this way Rottschaefer might be viewed as saying the same thing I say except that he does so in a manner that is more honest or, at least, more sensitive to the true nature of our evaluative judgments.

In response to this a couple of points are in order. First, it is doubtful that Rottschaefer would himself make this move, since it relies upon a subjectivist analysis of moral judgments that is antithetical to his project of providing an objective justification for moral claims. Despite this it is still an objection that could be made by a subjectivist who finds my approach no better than Rottschaefer's.

Second, and perhaps more importantly, the subjectivist analysis of moral judgment that this objection is based on is highly controversial and is one that I reject. If claiming that "X is good" simply means "I value X" then we could not make sense of claims of the form "X is good but I don't like (value) it." The latter sort of claim is both commonplace and intelligible, yet the subjectivist analysis would suggest it is internally inconsistent and thereby unintelligible. For, according to the subjectivist analysis "X is good but I don't like it" means "I like X but I don't like it." For this reason and others I reject such a subjectivist analysis of moral judgments.[1]

---

[1] This subjectivist theory of the nature of moral judgment has been given a lot of attention in the literature over the years. One of the more famous defenses of this theory is that of C.L. Stevenson. See his 1941. For criticisms of the theory see, for instance, Rachels 1999, Chapter 3; and MacIntyre 1991. For criticisms of MacIntyre's attack on emotivism, see Waller 1986 and Unwin 1990. I have defended MacIntyre against their criticisms. See Lemos 2000.

Another possible objection to my discussion of Rottschaefer might take note of the fact that I give a goal directed, or teleological, justification of the moral life just as Rottschaefer does. Consequently, just as it could be demanded of Rottschaefer, it might also be demanded of me to give an explanation of the merits of the goal. As indicated above, Rottschaefer gives an objectionable reply. But it might be wondered whether my own theory is any better since the same question could be raised of it. In other words, it might be asked of my own theory why we should acquire the virtues of doing well at practical reasoning if we do not know why well performed practical reasoning is good?

I have argued that things are good when they perform their characteristic activity or function well. Assuming that rationality is characteristic of human beings it is reasonable to conclude that we are good when we reason well. So, if someone wants to know why good practical reasoning is good, I would say that it is not good *per se* but in human beings it is good because practical reasoning is definitive of being human in such a way that doing it well makes them good. Analogously, clocks engage in the definitive activity of keeping time, so that they are good when they do this well.

In pressing this issue a critic might want to know why things are good when they perform their characteristic activity well. In raising this question the critic might want to know whether I can also answer this in a way that will still allow me to avoid subjectivist conclusions. I think this can be done. Some well functioning things would seem to be good only as a means to some other end, whereas the well functioning of some things would seem to be good in itself. For instance, a well functioning guitar produces beautiful music, which is something good in itself, as well as the pleasures that come from hearing or playing such music, which is also something good in itself. In contrast, the well functioning tree, the tree that does well in the activities characteristic of trees of its kind, seems to be good in itself. That is, the tree that does well at absorbing nutrients from the soil, engaging in photosynthesis, and so forth, and doing well at these makes the tree a good tree whether or not that tree ever produces any other goods such as beauty, pleasure, or knowledge.

Well functioning artifacts are good because their functioning well leads to other goods such as pleasure, beauty, and knowledge. But the functioning well of biological organisms is good in itself.

Thus, the well-functioning human being is something good in itself. A man or woman who lives well, does well at practical reasoning, is good even if she is miserable and even if she can do little to help others. In humans living well is a question of character, a question of possessing dispositions to act in the right ways, and one can possess these dispositions even if one lacks the power to bring about the good consequences—more happiness, knowledge, or beauty—that typically result from the engagement of these dispositions. My views here depart somewhat from their Aristotelian origins and have some kinship with Kant's concept of the good will, which is good in itself regardless of its efficacy.

The merits of artifacts are extrinsic to them because they are made by humans to serve certain ends. In contrast, biological organisms have ends that are granted them not by human beings but by nature itself. That is, there is internal to biological organisms a developmental plan the fulfillment of which and the living in accordance with which provide objective criteria for determining the intrinsic value of the organism. These ideas have Aristotelian roots going back to Aristotle's vision of biological organisms as possessing an innate drive toward their own perfection. For Aristotle this involves self-actualization in accordance with the formal cause of the organism. These Aristotelian ideas can be made sense of today in terms of the organism's drive to fulfill the genetic blueprint of the organism found in its DNA.

Since the well-functioning organism does well at living up to the goals intrinsic to being an organism of its kind as opposed to living up to any goals imposed upon it by humans, it makes sense to say that well-functioning organisms have an intrinsic value that is not dependent in any way upon humans valuing them. Since the functioning-well of things is determined by their doing their characteristic activity well, human beings are good by doing their characteristic activity well. And doing this (rational activity) well would be good whether we value it or not. In these ways, then, I think my views depart somewhat from Rottschaefer's in such a way as to avoid certain subjectivist elements in his position that I find problematic.

COLLIER AND STINGL'S VIEW

Collier and Stingl (1993) believe that an objective justification of the injunction "Act altruistically" requires not just showing that human beings have evolved to act this way but also showing that *any* evolved intelligent creatures ought to act this way. They are concerned about a certain sort of species relativism which would suggest that, for instance, evolved intelligent creatures from different but nomologically similar worlds might have radically different moral views which might not require any respect for human rights. To circumvent this problem they argue that promoting the common good is a value that any evolved intelligent creatures will have because of its adaptive value in this and any nomologically similar worlds. Due to the universal acceptance of such a value not just by humans but by any evolved intelligent creatures across nomologically similar possible worlds, they believe "Act altruistically" is objectively justified. In reply to their view I argued that the mere fact that a value is shared by all rational beings across nomologically similar worlds does not make it good. It could be that something quite bad could be valued by all such creatures. The quest for objectivity through intersubjectivity across nomologically similar worlds is still too subjectivist for comfort.

My view escapes the problems with this position in the same way in which it escapes the problem with Rottschaefer's. Since there is something intrinsically good about the good performance of our characteristic activity, there is an objective goodness about this and the virtues necessary for it. My view makes no problematic appeals to intersubjective agreement across possible worlds in determining objective values. In this way I avoid the problems of Collier and Stingl's approach.

In reply to this Collier and Stingl might say that I avoid the problem of subjectivism here but only by falling into the trap of species relativism. That is, since I define the virtues relative to the specifically human good of doing well at practical reasoning, this leaves it open that there may be evolved intelligent social creatures in other worlds that have rather different values but are objectively justified in holding them. One possible consequence of this is that were we to encounter such beings they might have no objective reason to respect our rights or values. I suppose that this *is* a problem, since it would be strange to think that rational alien beings, such as those seen on *Star Trek*, who could understand and communicate with us might have objective moral reasons for disregarding our rights. This issue does puzzle me. At some level I feel that it is possible that such beings could conceivably be justified in disregarding our rights, but I am not sure what conditions would justify this. Also, and perhaps more importantly, it may be that any creature with the capacity of rationality will have as at least one of its goals the functioning-well of its rationality. If this is so, then at least part of any good life for any rational creature will involve doing well at reasoning. But, if this is so, and since any such creature will employ at least practical rationality if not also theoretical rationality, and since the moral virtues are needed to do this well, any rational creature whether human or otherwise will need to possess the virtues to be good. If the possession of the virtues is required for any rational creature to be good, then there is an objective justification for any rational creature, even alien ones, to exhibit the virtues in their relations with us, in which case they would be obligated to be respectful of our rights.

It could be objected here that in the case of humans well-performed practical rationality is good because it is definitive of us. The rationality possessed by aliens might not be definitive of them, since there might be other kinds of extraterrestrials from their home planet that also possess reason. In such cases it is hard to see how doing well at practical reasoning would be morally required of them, and so it is hard to see why they should exhibit virtue in their interactions with us.

First, it does not seem unreasonable here to speak of primary and secondary senses of goodness. Human beings are good primarily by doing their characteristic activity (practical reasoning) well. But we are not only rational. We are animals too. Perhaps part of a good life also involves doing well at the things characteristic of animals too, like finding food and mates. These would be good in a secondary sense, and doing well only at this would not be considered a good life for human beings *qua* human beings. If this makes sense, then it might be reasonable to say that any being that is rational but not defined by rationality would still have as part of its good the functioning- of its rationality. If this is so then any such creature, even if not defined by its rationality, would need the virtues so as to do well at that part of its good which is comprised of rational activity.

Second, the concept of a person might be relevant to the discussion at this point. It could be argued that creatures, whether humans, extraterrestrials, or angels, that possess rationality are persons. Since rationality is definitive of persons, doing well at reason is necessary to their being *good persons*. Since possession of the moral virtues will be necessary to their doing well at reasoning any such person will need the virtues to be good.

Each of these replies seems plausible. Consequently, I think I have shown how my own Aristotelian evolutionary ethic can escape the problems with Collier and Stingl's approach, while avoiding the problem of species relativism. However, I am led to express my reply in a rather tentative mode here, as the sorts of issues raised here by the consideration of alien life forms is especially hard to theorize about. Since we have never encountered any such beings, it is hard to know just what to say about some of these issues.

Concluding Remarks and Some Objections

In this chapter I have described an Aristotelian evolutionary virtue ethics. This view is Aristotelian because it determines the goodness of human beings with reference to the good performance of their characteristic activity or function and defines the virtues with reference to the successful performance of this function. It is an evolutionary ethic insofar as it envisions evolutionary biology as playing an important supporting role in its defense. Two important elements of the Aristotelian conception of human nature are that (1) we have a natural impulse towards our own self-perfection and (2) we are social animals. I argued that the Darwinian theory of natural selection can be used to defend each of these fundamental aspects of human nature by pointing out how each of these are adaptive traits which from the Darwinian perspective we would expect humans to have. Defending these two points about human nature is important because each of them plays an important role in understanding what counts as a virtue. For instance, because we are social animals it will be important for us to reason in such a way as to preserve community relations. Thus, justice is a virtue we must possess in order to live well. In support of this theory I have also reviewed various flawed approaches to objectivist evolutionary ethics. I argued that my own Aristotelian approach escapes the various flaws of these other approaches. In doing so I hope to have provided some support for my own position or, at least, to have provided some reason to think it worthy of serious consideration.

Before moving on I should note again that this chapter seems to provide only an outline for the development of a complete system of Aristotelian virtue ethics. Various points could no doubt profitably be developed further, and I suppose there are various objections that would need to be given consideration. For instance, it might be objected that evolutionary biology is incompatible with the Aristotelian understanding of human beings as rational animals. Since Darwinism views the differences between species as differences in degree and not in kind, it follows that we cannot clearly differentiate human beings from the other animals with reference to their rationality, since on the Darwinian view we have to recognize that other animals possess this characteristic to some degree.

The second half of the next chapter will consider this aspect of the Darwinian view in some detail and it will examine its relevance to the controversial issue of our obligations towards nonhuman animals. For now let me just say that I do not find this to be an especially troubling objection. Even if it is conceded that other animals besides humans possess rationality it is clear that the typical human being possesses a different kind of rationality from the other animals. Consequently, the Aristotelian ethic could define the human *telos* with respect to the good performance of this more advanced rationality, thereby making sense of the distinctly human good and the virtues relevant to its achievement.

Besides the alleged problem of shared rationality, it might also be argued that Aristotle viewed species as fixed and permanent, whereas Darwin saw them as evolving over time. For this reason it might be argued that an Aristotelian evolutionary ethic is indefensible. However, while it is true that Aristotle viewed species as permanent, I do not see this as presenting any problem for an Aristotelian evolutionary ethic. Moral truth is objectively grounded in human nature as it exists today. If there are significant changes in human nature brought about in the future by evolutionary development, then there might need to be adjustments made to our theory of the virtues In any event, the mere fact that Aristotle viewed species as fixed and permanent gives us no grounds for rejecting an Aristotelian evolutionary ethic.

Another possible worry is that my Aristotelian ethic harbors a progressionistic view of evolution that runs counter to Darwin's own anti-progressionism. Progressionism is the view that in the struggle for survival species are constantly bettering themselves over time, exhibiting progress. One of the earliest defenders of an evolutionary ethic, Herbert Spencer, based his views on such a mistaken view of the nature of evolution. However, my own approach to evolutionary ethics involves no such commitment to progressionism. I am *not* arguing that we ought to act to allow the inevitable progress of human nature to occur through the process of evolutionary development. Rather, my point is simply that we are at a point in the history of life on this planet (and have been for some time, thousands of years at least) in which humanity can be defined, as Aristotle did, with respect to its distinctive rational capacities, and because of this there are certain goals of normal human development that provide objective justification for the Aristotelian virtues. Where is the progressionism in this? There is none.

A final point that deserves consideration here concerns the naturalistic fallacy and the relationship between what I have said in this chapter and the previous chapter. In Chapter 3, I explained and critically discussed the work of several contemporary philosophers who appeal to evolutionary biological facts about human nature and who then appeal to these facts in an attempt to justify moral claims. In many of these cases I criticized their arguments on the grounds that they committed the naturalistic fallacy. That is, they unwarrantedly derived moral conclusions from nonmoral, or natural, facts about human nature.

It might be argued that the Aristotelian evolutionary ethic outlined in this chapter is inconsistent with the kinds of criticisms I have made in the previous chapter. After all, I am arguing for a certain conception of human goodness and the moral virtues by appealing to the natural fact that rationality is a distinctive feature of human beings. It might be argued that my own approach to normative ethics is just as guilty of committing the naturalistic fallacy as the approaches considered in Chapter 3. Hence, it might be alleged that there is a significant inconsistency here.

However, I don't think that there really is an inconsistency. My view is that some moves from 'is' to 'ought' are rationally defensible whereas others aren't. When such moves aren't, they are instances of the naturalistic fallacy. The move from 'is' to 'ought' endorsed in this chapter is based on a teleological conception of human nature which warrants the move from 'is' to 'ought'. Since the inferences made from 'is' to 'ought' in the previous chapter are not grounded in such a teleology they commit various versions of the naturalistic fallacy.[2]

The kind of point I am making here is inspired to some extent by the work of Alasdair MacIntyre. In *After Virtue* (1981) he acknowledges that inferences from 'is' to 'ought' will appear as various manifestations of the naturalistic fallacy, unless human beings are understood as having a *telos* that provides the basis for objective determinations of how they ought to be or act. According to MacIntyre, it is not until we see that human beings have such a *telos* that we can see how objective determinations of normative standards can be derived from facts about human nature.

The naturalistic justifications for moral claims countenanced in the previous chapter don't make reference to the human *telos*. Consequently, they commit various versions of the naturalistic fallacy. Since my own Aristotelian evolutionary ethic appeals to a teleological conception of human nature in grounding its normative claims, it does not commit this error.

---

[2] Of all the philosophers considered in the previous chapter, Rottschaefer seems to be the most sensitive to this point. He sees the important place of teleology in providing for objective naturalistic justifications of moral claims. However, for reasons given in this and the preceding chapter, I reject his approach on other grounds. See Rottschaefer 1991.

5

Evolutionary Biology and the Moral Status of Animals

The philosophical study of ethics can be broken down into theoretical ethics and applied ethics. Theoretical ethics can in turn be broken down into the study of normative ethics and metaethics, metaethics dealing with questions about the objectivity of morality and normative ethics dealing with questions about the criteria of right action and morally good personhood. The previous three chapters dealt with the possible relationship between evolutionary biology and theoretical ethics. In this chapter I will focus on a particular issue in applied ethics—the question of animal rights.

More than any other, this issue in applied ethics seems to have an important linkage with issues in evolutionary biology. A number of authors have argued that evolutionary biology plays an important role in making the case for animal rights, but none does so more forcefully, coherently, and thoroughly than James Rachels (1990).[1] In this chapter I will explain and critically engage with Rachels's argument. In doing so I will argue, contra Rachels, that evolutionary biology does not play a significant role, if any, in making the case for animal rights.

The General Structure of Rachels's Argument

In *Created From Animals: The Moral Implications of Darwinism* (1990) Rachels says that the idea of human dignity is that human beings are different in kind from other animals and that this dif-

---

[1] For other treatments of animal rights focusing on the importance of evolutionary biology, see Rodd 1990 and Petrinovich 1995.

ference makes human beings deserving of moral considerations that need not be extended to nonhuman animals. For instance, it is believed that humans alone have rights to life, liberty, and the pursuit of happiness that nonhumans do not possess. Thus, it is generally considered acceptable to keep animals constrained in zoos and on farms and to kill and eat them and to run painful scientific experiments on them, even though we would never think of doing these things to human beings.

Rachels believes this idea of human dignity has led to a lot of mistreatment of nonhuman animals by human beings. He argues that the idea of human dignity, which supports this mistreatment of animals, lacks rational justification. In arguing that it lacks such justification he holds that there are two main supports for the idea of human dignity, neither of which he thinks is rationally defensible. These two supports are the image of God thesis and the rationality thesis. The image of God thesis is the view that human beings alone are made in the image of God. The rationality thesis is the view that human beings alone are rational. Rachels believes that Darwinism undermines these two theses, and thus that Darwinism plays a crucial role in making a case for animal rights. In what follows I will examine Rachels's case against each of these theses. I will begin with his views on the image of God thesis and then turn to a discussion of his views on the rationality thesis.

Rachels on the Image of God Thesis

Rachels gives a detailed argument for the view that the Darwinian theory of evolution by natural selection undermines the view that human beings are made in the image of God. According to Rachels, to undermine a view is to take away the support for it. Thus Rachels believes Darwinism makes matters such that there is no longer any good evidence for thinking that human beings are made in the image of God. He is not the only contemporary thinker to hold this view. Both Richard Dawkins (1985) and Daniel Dennett (1995) also seem to hold it. However, Rachels gives a detailed argument for it which is very different from anything in the works of Dawkins and Dennett. They are primarily interested in giving a Darwinian account of the origins of life and the variety of living things in the world today. They actually do little more than this in making their case for the view that Darwinism undermines religion. In contrast, Rachels gives a detailed argument that Darwinism undermines religion and in doing so responds to those who think God created human beings and the diversity of life today through the process of evolution.

In what follows I will show that Rachels does not sufficiently consider all the options open to the theist in defending the view that human beings are made in the image of God, so that his argument is flawed in significant respects. I should also note here that Rachels's case for the view that Darwinism undermines the "image of God thesis" is probably about the best case that can be made for this view. Thus, if it fails, then we have good reason to think the view is indefensible, so that Dawkins and Dennett are open to justified criticism on this issue as well.[2]

In making his case that Darwinism undermines the notion that human beings are created in the image of God, Rachels develops three main points and responds to possible objections. I will explain each of his three main points and then examine the objections he considers and his replies.

THE PROBLEM OF EVIL

Rachels begins by discussing the problem of evil. He provides five traditional replies to the problem and gives standard criticisms of the first four. He believes that the standard criticisms are telling but are not grounded on any Darwinian assumptions. The fifth reply to the problem of evil states:

---

[2] For criticisms of Dawkins's views on the religious implications of Darwinism, see Sadowsky 1988. For criticisms of Dawkins's Darwinian account of the origins of life, see Gallagher 1992; 1993. For criticisms of Dennett's views on the religious implications of Darwinism, see Harris 1999. The critique of Rachels I make in this chapter is more in line with the sort of critique that Sadowsky makes of Dawkins than it is with the critiques of Dawkins and Dennett made by Gallagher and Harris. I am not as skeptical of the success of Dawkins's and Dennett's biological accounts of the origins of life and new species as they are. What differentiates my work in this chapter from that of Sadowsky is that I am responding to the more detailed and philosophical argument that Rachels makes. As noted in the text above, Dawkins and Dennett do not do as much as Rachels in supporting their case for the negative religious implications of Darwinism.

> [I]f all else fails the theist can always fall back on the idea that our limited human intelligence is insufficient to comprehend God's great design. There is a reason for evil; we just aren't smart enough to figure out what it is. (Rachels 1990, 104)

Rachels believes that Darwinian considerations can be very useful in developing a good reply to this point. He argues that Darwinism gives us a way of understanding why evil exists. He says that according to Darwinism pain, a type of evil, exists to motivate creatures to act in adaptive ways.

> In order to survive, an animal must be motivated to act in ways conducive to its self-preservation. Pain and pleasure are the motivators. In the absence of food, we suffer hunger; and when we eat, we enjoy it: together, these ensure that we eat. When enemies are nearby, we suffer fear; when we flee, we feel relieved; together, these ensure that we keep safe. (Rachels 1990, 106)

Rachels believes that if we look at divine creation and natural selection as alternative ways of explaining why nature is as it is, we will find that the latter hypothesis does a better job of making sense of things. Were we products of the creative activity of a supremely perfect being it would be hard to make sense of why pain and other forms of evil exist. The idea here is that were there a supremely perfect creator He surely would be able to encourage wise and good action on the part of human beings in some way other than the threat of physical or emotional pain. But the Darwinian theory of natural selection does, as explained above, offer a quick and easy explanation. In this way it seems more reasonable to think that we are products of the blind forces of natural selection rather than of a supremely perfect being's creative activity.

The Ultimate Origin of the Universe

After discussing the problem of evil Rachels next makes a general criticism of any attempt to understand God as the first cause of the universe. He cites a letter that was written by Charles Darwin in which Darwin makes a standard criticism of the idea that God exists as the original creator of the universe. After quoting from the letter Rachels writes:

> Here, incidentally, Darwin alludes to the standard traditional objection to the first-cause argument. The argument is motivated by the

thought that nothing can exist without a cause, so we posit God as the cause of the universe. But this only invites the further question: what caused God? And if we are willing to think of God himself as uncaused, why not think of the universe as uncaused? Thus the argument fails, even on its own terms: the craving that motivates the argument (the craving to have everything causally explained) cannot be satisfied even if the argument is accepted (because we are still stuck with at least one thing, God, that is left uncaused). (Rachels 1990, 108).[3]

THE DESIGN ARGUMENT

As an introduction to his discussion of the Darwinian implications for the design argument Rachels writes:

> Darwin's great contribution to the debate about religion was not, however, his discussion of the argument from evil, or the first cause argument, or any of the other arguments that have been mentioned thus far. His great contribution was the final demolition of the idea that nature is the product of intelligent design. When we turn to this aspect of Darwin's thinking, it becomes clear why he believed that 'the gradual illumination of men's minds, from the advancement of science' leads to the abandonment of theism. (Rachels 1990, 110)

In a section entitled "Darwin and Paley" Rachels explains how Paley's famous early nineteenth-century design argument for the existence of God was very persuasive to educated people. Paley focused his attention on the complex workings of biological organisms, how they have many parts that are very complex in their organization and that work together to provide for the survival of

---

[3] This argument completely overlooks the traditional conception of God as a necessary being, a being whose existence is explained by its essence. If God were a necessary being, then His existence would not need to be explained with reference to the creative activity of any other being. In contrast, the universe is a contingent being. Its existence is not explained in terms of its essence. Hence, its existence requires explanation in terms of something external to it. The standard explanation of God's necessary existence comes through reflection upon the definition of God as a supremely perfect being. Presumably, such a being would have to exist to be supremely perfect. Two of the more famous discussions of this idea come to us from St. Anselm and René Descartes. See Anselm 1961 and Descartes 1997, especially Meditation V. For more contemporary discussions of the issue, see Hartshorne 1967; Plantinga 1974.

organisms. Paley argued that these complex biological phenomena give us ample evidence for the existence of a powerful and intelligent designer of nature.

Rachels rightly notes that the design argument had existed for centuries and that, consequently, Paley's presentation of it is not revolutionary. He also notes that the criticisms of the design argument expressed in Hume's *Dialogues Concerning Natural Religion*, while reasonable and seemingly devastating, are not enough to refute it. The reason for this is that it is not until the development of Darwin's theory of natural selection that we have an adequate naturalistic alternative account of the complex design of living things that could serve as a reply to the design argument. Until the publication of the *Origin of Species*, people who were familiar with Hume's criticisms of the design argument could still reasonably accept it on the ground that there was no better way to explain the complex design of living things than to postulate the existence of an intelligent and powerful creator. Darwin's theories changed all that.[4]

OBJECTIONS AND REPLIES

Before concluding his discussion of how Darwinism undermines the notion that man is created in the image of God, Rachels goes on to consider some possible objections and to respond to them. The two main objections are (1) that the theory of evolution by natural selection is not incompatible with the theory of intelligent design and (2) that even if Darwinism has shown that the design hypothesis is false, this does not mean that theism is false. I will discuss each of these points and Rachels's replies to them.

(I) DARWINIAN EVOLUTION AND INTELLIGENT DESIGN AS COMPATIBLE

In developing the compatibility thesis Rachels cites the work of George Mavrodes (1987).

Is Darwinism really incompatible with the idea that the world, and all its inhabitants, are the products of intelligent design? The philosopher

---

[4] For similar views on the implications of Darwinism for the design argument, see Dawkins 1985 and Dennett 1995.

George Mavrodes is one of many thinkers who have argued that there is no incompatibility here. Mavrodes distinguishes a 'naturalistic' interpretation of the evolutionary process, according to which the process is 'explicable entirely in terms of natural law without reference to a divine intervention', from a theistic interpretation, according to which 'there was a divine teleology in this process, a divine direction at each crucial stage in accordance with divine plan or intention'. Then he argues that there is no evidence that rules out the theistic interpretation. (Rachels 1990, 120)

The idea behind Mavrodes's point seems to be that Darwinism does not undermine the belief that God created nature nor the belief that man was made in the image of God. For it might be that God creates the diversity of living things, including human beings, through the process of evolution.

Rachels responds to this point in three ways. First he argues that if nature were the product of God's intelligent design then we would expect the design of organisms to be even better than they are.

> For example, we would not expect an intelligent designer to include useless parts in organisms; but, on the hypothesis of evolution by natural selection, we would expect to find such useless parts, because they would be the vestiges of once-useful structures. And things are, in fact, as the evolutionary hypothesis predicts: in humans we find muscles that can no longer move ears, useless body-hair, a vermiform appendix that serves no purpose, the remnants of a tail, and so on. (Rachels 1990, 121)

Rachels also argues that if we were the products of God's intelligent design we would expect to find "perfect, elegant adaptation" but instead we find "improvised, jury-rigged adaptation," which agrees more with the evolutionary hypothesis. Similar points are made in Gould's *The Panda's Thumb* (1980).

In developing his second reply to Mavrodes, Rachels begins by noting that the preceding points do not really work against Mavrodes's argument if he intends to suggest that God creates *through* the process of evolution. Rather, the preceding considerations really only seem to militate against the idea that God creates each species separately. To respond to the notion that God works through the evolutionary process, Rachels maintains that we must first have some proposal for how this happens.

At what point does God intervene in the process and how? The most obvious conjecture would be that God intervenes by providing the specific variations that he knows will confer advantages. If God wants to modify wolves in a certain direction, for example, he can arrange things so that as the climate grows colder some animals will have slightly thicker fur. If he wants that species to become extinct, he will not provide the thicker fur and let them be killed off by the cold. This is the most natural way to fill in the details of the theistic interpretation, and Darwin addressed it directly in *The Variation of Animals and Plants under Domestication.* (Rachels 1990, 122–23)

The idea here seems to be that if God works through the evolutionary process in producing the variety of life forms that exist today, then he must do so by providing the variations that allow for the survival of some creatures within a species and the death of other members.

But is this view reasonable to hold? Neither Rachels nor Darwin thinks so. In responding to this view Rachels endorses an argument that Darwin himself provided. In summarizing Darwin's argument Rachels writes:

If the variations utilized in natural selection are not simply random, but are directed by God, then this is no less true of the variations seized upon by breeders. But Darwin thinks it is impossible to believe that variations occur for the benefit of the breeders, and so he rejects the idea that the variations occur in order that natural selection can take a given direction. (Rachels 1990, 123)

A key part of this argument concerns why Darwin thinks it is impossible to believe that variations have been designed by God for the benefit of breeders. Darwin argues that since we cannot reasonably maintain that the rocks used by builders were shaped for the use of builders, we cannot reasonably maintain that the variations among species used by breeders were shaped for the use of breeders. Darwin writes:

[C]an it reasonably be maintained that the Creator intentionally ordered, if we use the words in an ordinary sense, that certain fragments of rock should assume certain shapes so that the builder might erect his edifice? If the various laws which have determined the shape of each fragment were not predetermined for the builder's sake, can it be maintained with any greater probability that He specially

ordained for the sake of the breeder each of the innumerable variations in our domestic animals and plants—many of these variations
being of no service to man, and not beneficial, far more often injuri-
ous, to the creatures themselves? (Darwin 1868, 515)

Darwin thinks that we can no more believe that the builders' rocks
were shaped by God for their use than we can believe that the variations of different species were shaped by God for the use of
breeders. Additionally, Darwin thinks that if God did not design
the variations of species for the benefit of breeders, then we can
have no good reason to think that he designs the variations of
species that are shaped by the process of natural selection. For all
of these reasons, both Darwin and Rachels would contend that we
cannot reasonably believe that God has created the diversity of life
forms through the process of evolution.

Rachels's third reply to Mavrodes is developed as a response to
an objection to the preceding discussion. Rachels notes that in
response to the preceding criticism of Mavrodes's position one
could contend that God created man and all other forms of life
through the evolutionary process, while refusing to specify how
God does this. The preceding criticism is directed at a particular
conception of how God does this. If one refuses to offer such an
account then the criticism would not hold against one's position.

Rachels finds this approach to defending the notion that God
creates through evolution to be ultimately unsatisfying. He makes
two points here. First, when the theistic interpretation of the evolutionary process is construed in this way it guarantees compatibility with any possible evidence. Second, he argues as follows:

> Suppose God *is* somehow involved in the process that evolutionary
> biologists since Darwin have been describing. This would mean that
> he has created a situation in which his own involvement is so totally
> hidden that the process gives every appearance of operating without
> any guiding hand at all. In other words, he has created a situation in
> which it is reasonable for us to believe that he is not involved. But if
> it is reasonable for us to believe that, then it is reasonable for us to
> reject the theistic interpretation. (Rachels 1990, 125)[5]

---

[5] This argument problematically ignores the possibility that there might be
other grounds for belief in God. Were there such other grounds then the facts of
evolutionary biology would not warrant the conclusion that God is not involved
in the evolutionary process. I will return to this point later on in this chapter.

(II) Even if the Design Hypothesis Is False, Theism May Still Be True

As noted earlier, Rachels responds to two objections before ending his account of why Darwinism undermines the notion that man is created in the image of God. So far I have focused on his reply to the first objection, which states that intelligent design is compatible with Darwinian evolution. The second objection involves contending that Darwinism does not undermine theism because even if the intelligent design hypothesis is false theism can still be true.

In responding to this position Rachels contends that it amounts to a defense of deism. According to this view, "God is credited with designing the grand plan of the universe—the laws of nature—he is not seen as concerning himself with the details. On this view, we might say that although God created the mechanisms by which natural selection occurs, he did not design its products in any other sense" (Rachels 1990, 125). And such a deistic conception of God is "so abstract, so unconnected with the world, that there is little left in which to believe" (Rachels 1990, 125–26).

Rachels makes two other points. First, he says that to say God is the cause of the universe as the deists do is "mere speculation." "One can *say* that, but one can give no good reason in its support" (Rachels 1990, 126). Second, he argues that according to this deistic version of theism,

> There is now far less *content* to the idea of God. The concept of God as a loving, all-powerful person, who created us, who has a plan for us, who issues commandments, and who is ready to receive us into Heaven, is a substantial concept, rich in meaning and significance for human life. But if we take away all this, and leave only the idea of an original cause, it is questionable whether the same word should even be used. By keeping the original word, we delude ourselves into thinking that we are talking about the same thing. (Rachels 1990, 126)

In summary, Rachels argues that Darwinism undermines the notion that man is created in the image of God by arguing that: (1) the Darwinian hypothesis gives a better account of why evil exists than does theism; (2) saying that God created the universe explains nothing, because we cannot explain why God exists; (3) Darwinism demolishes the design argument; and (4) the best theistic defenses to these criticisms fail.

A Critique of Rachels's Views on the Image of God Thesis

As just noted, Rachels's argument has four main parts. However, in the critical examination that follows I will lump the third and fourth parts together, treating the claim that Darwinism demolishes the design argument and the theistic defenses and Rachels's replies to them together, since they are all part of his attempt to show that Darwinism demolishes the design argument.

CONCERNING THE ARGUMENT THAT TO SAY GOD CREATED THE UNIVERSE EXPLAINS NOTHING

As we have seen, Rachels thinks that if we explain the existence of the universe by appealing to the creative activity of God, we must be able to provide an explanation of the existence of God. And since there is no adequate explanation of the latter, to say God created the universe explains nothing. Even if this were a good argument, which is doubtful, it would not show how *Darwinism* undermines intelligent design or the notion that man is created in the image of God.[6] When it is said that Darwinism undermines these ideas it is meant that Darwin's theory of evolution by natural selection does. The point made in this argument has no connection to the theory of natural selection. Even though, as Rachels notes in his book, Darwin used this argument himself, someone who rejects Darwin's theory of natural selection could also use it.

CONCERNING THE ARGUMENT THAT DARWINISM BETTER EXPLAINS EVIL THAN DOES THEISM

Rachels also argues that Darwinism undermines the concept of intelligent design because it better explains the existence of evil. But in making this argument he treats the intelligent design view as a rival to Darwinism. Admittedly Darwinism does give us an explanation for why at least some evils exist. This, however, undermines the concept of intelligent design only if we *assume* that these are rival hypotheses. Many people think that God created man and other living things *through* natural selection. Thus, many people

---

[6] See Note 3 above for some explanation of the potential problem with this argument.

do not view these as rival hypotheses. So, until it is shown that these *are* rival hypotheses Rachels's point about evil does nothing to show that Darwinism undermines the intelligent design view.

CONCERNING THE ARGUMENT THAT DARWINISM DEMOLISHES THE DESIGN ARGUMENT

The previous point makes Rachels's discussion of the design argument and his critique of the idea that Darwinian evolution and intelligent design are compatible seem all the more important. Recall that in defending the view that Darwinism undermines the design argument he is led to respond to objections which suggest that the Darwinian theory of natural selection is compatible with the concept of intelligent design. Rachels argues that the compatibility thesis is unreasonable. And if he is right about this it would mean that my proposed response to his argument about evil is weak. Thus, the important question to be considered here is whether intelligent design is compatible with the Darwinian theory of evolution by natural selection.

In the first stage of his reply to the compatibility thesis Rachels argues that the Darwinian theory of evolution by natural selection is incompatible with the theory of intelligent design because we find that the physical features of organisms are "jury-rigged" and include "useless" parts. Since this is not what we would expect from an intelligent all-powerful designer but is what we would expect according to the Darwinian view, it is not reasonable to think the views are compatible. However, as Rachels himself notes, this argument does not work against someone who thinks God creates *through* evolution. Jury-rigging and useless parts are perfectly consistent with the idea that God creates through evolution.

Since the evidence for evolution by natural selection is sufficiently strong, it seems to me that the only plausible compatibility thesis will have to be grounded on some idea of God creating through evolution. However, Rachels objects to this notion as well. In doing so he first endorses an argument of Darwin's own construction. Recall that Darwin argued that since we cannot reasonably think God shaped rocks to make them useful for builders, we cannot reasonably believe he provided varieties among domestic plants and animals for the sake of breeders. And if the latter is true we cannot reasonably believe God designed any of the other variations we see among life forms.

This is not a good argument. The fact that rocks and the variations of domestic species do not all come ready made for our easy use does not mean that God did not design them. It could be that the world is somehow better with things being as they are, even though it makes building and breeding more difficult. Additionally, it should be noted that while things do not come made ready for easy use, rocks and domestic species are nonetheless malleable and useful, and one might take this as some sign that they have been designed for us. While Rachels might respond by demanding an explanation for how the world could be better with things being as they are, with rocks and domestic species not being ready made for our use, such a demand seems inappropriate. The question at hand is whether one could reasonably think that the design hypothesis is compatible with Darwinism. And one can reasonably believe this without having a solution to the problem of evil. This is especially true if one is willing to concede that God is somewhat less than perfect.

I have not here explained just how God *does* create through evolution. Thus, I leave myself open to the criticism expressed in Rachels's third reply to Mavrodes, in which he argues that those who say God creates through evolution but give no explanation of how he does this make their compatibility thesis agree "with any possible evidence." Additionally, he argues that if God creates through evolution then "he has created a situation in which it is reasonable for us to believe that he is not involved. But if it is reasonable for us to believe that, then it is reasonable for us to reject the theistic interpretation" (Rachels 1990, 125). The "theistic interpretation" refers to the view that God creates through evolution.

The first point above seems to be a charge of unfalsifiability. Rachels contends that if one alleges that God creates through Darwinian evolution without explaining how, then one's view agrees "with any possible evidence"—it is unfalsifiable. He is right about this. When presented in this way the compatibility thesis *does* become unfalsifiable. But so what? This does not mean that one could not reasonably believe it. One might have reasons to believe that God, an intelligent designer, exists, reasons independent of Paley's specific version of the design argument. Thus, one might have reason to believe that God exists and even creates through the process of evolution. In this way one might have reason for holding unfalsifiable beliefs.

Rachels might contend that if beliefs are unfalsifiable, that if any facts would agree with them, then no facts can support them either. So, there is no way that one could reasonably believe in the compatibility thesis when it is construed in unfalsifiable terms. In reply to this I would say that the premise is false. From the fact that no facts can refute a proposition it does not follow that no facts can support it. Consider the claim that there is an intelligent and powerful designer of the universe. This strikes me as an unfalsifiable claim. But nonetheless facts might still support the claim. Consider for instance Richard Swinburne's (1991) version of the design argument. He presents an argument for the existence of an intelligent designer of the universe that appeals to facts about the nature and limits of scientific explanation. Whether his argument is a good one is not what is relevant here. Instead, the point is that it is at least conceivable that good reasons can be given in support of the truth of a claim that is unfalsifiable. Thus Rachels's point about the unfalsifiability of claims of the compatibility of Darwinian evolution with intelligent design does not establish their unreasonableness.

Let us turn now to his other point. He argues that if God creates through evolution then he has created a situation in which it is reasonable to believe he is not involved. But if it is reasonable to believe this then it is reasonable to reject the view that God creates through evolution. The problem with this argument is that the first premise assumes way too much and in this way it begs the question.

To appreciate this argument we need to remember that evolution is a process for which, thanks to Darwin, we have a perfectly good naturalistic explanation. Thus, according to Rachels, if God is involved in or in control of this process we have no good reason to think so. The problem with this is that he is assuming there is no other good reason for believing that God is at work in the creation of man and other species besides Paley-type design arguments. This is a huge assumption. As noted earlier, Richard Swinburne has provided his own type of design argument, an argument that is wholly compatible with Darwinian evolution. He explicitly acknowledges that Paley's design argument is sufficiently refuted by Darwin's discoveries (Swinburne 1991, 134–35). Nonetheless, he still believes that the structure of the universe gives us good reason to believe in the existence of an intelligent designer. In essence his argument is:

1. There are two and only two ways of explaining phenomena: (a) in terms of normal scientific explanation; (b) in terms of the free choice of a rational agent.

2. Normal scientific explanation of regularities of succession consists in explanation by reference to more fundamental (general) regularities.

So, 3. the operation of the most fundamental regularities of succession in nature cannot be given a normal scientific explanation.

So, 4. if these regularities are to be explained at all it must be in terms of the free choice of a rational agent (or agents).

5. If the hypothesis of a rational agent or agents as the cause of natural laws is confirmed by the evidence, it should be adopted, since it is the only hypothesis available.

6. The universe in all parts we have observed exhibits fundamental regularities of succession (general laws of nature).

7. We observe that the free choices of rational agents (human beings) produce regularities of succession.

So, 8. (given that there is no more satisfactory explanation), it is probable in some degree (depending on the strength of the analogy) that the regularities of succession in nature are produced by an agent or agents similar to human beings in having free will and intelligence.

So, 9. the hypothesis that the universe was produced by a rational agent or agents with free will and intelligence should be adopted.[7]

When Swinburne talks about "regularities of succession" what he has in mind is the fact that physical objects move or behave in a way that is predictable and understandable through laws of nature. The most fundamental regularities of succession cannot, however, be explained scientifically because scientific explanation always involves explaining one phenomenon in terms of some more fundamental phenomenon. So that if the *most* fundamental regulari-

---

[7] This summary of Swinburne's argument is quoted from Doore 1980.

ties are to be explained at all they cannot be explained scientifically. Yet, since these most fundamental regularities cry out for explanation, the explanation must be given in terms of the free choice of a rational agent or agents. Swinburne goes on to give arguments to show that it is more reasonable to believe that there is but one agent, God, involved in the creation of these most fundamental regularities as opposed to several agents. It should be obvious from this reconstruction of Swinburne's argument that Darwin's theory of natural selection has no bearing upon its soundness, since the order Swinburne appeals to as evidence for the existence of God is not simply the order found in the design of biological organisms; rather it is the order found in the regularity of the behavior of *any* physical objects. Someone who embraces this kind of argument has reason, perhaps good reason, to think that God creates man and other forms of life through evolution. Thus, contra Rachels, it is not at all obvious that if God creates through evolution we can have no reason to think so.

Rachels's book and earlier sections of this essay suggest a possible reply to my argument. Remember that Rachels considers the views of those who think God designed "the grand plan of the universe—the laws of nature," that "God created the mechanisms by which natural selection occurs" but "did not design its products in any other sense" (Rachels 1990, 125). Rachels refers to this conception of God and His relation to creation as "deistic" and goes on to criticize such a view. Perhaps Rachels would regard Swinburne's view as a form of deism.

Recall that Rachels makes three criticisms of deism. First, he says that such a view provides a conception of God that is "so abstract, so unconnected with the world, that there is little left in which to believe" (Rachels 1990, 125–26). Second, he says that although the deist claims that God creates the universe, he can give no good reason in support of his claim (Rachels 1990, 126). Third, he writes:

> There is now far less *content* to the idea of God. The concept of God as a loving, all-powerful person, who created us, who has a plan for us, who issues commandments, and who is ready to receive us into Heaven, is a substantial concept, rich in meaning and significance for human life. But if we take away all this, and leave only the idea of an original cause, it is questionable whether the same word

should even be used. By keeping the original word, we delude our-selves into thinking that we are talking about the same thing. (Rachels 1990, 126)

The third point seems to be a way of spelling out what is meant by the first point. The second point is clearly different from the other two. In response to it let me just briefly note that some con-frontation with the arguments of people such as Swinburne is required before this point can reasonably be made. Concerning the first and third points, it is not clear how viewing God as cre-ating the universe and the natural laws which govern it is incom-patible with the concept of a God who knows and loves us. It is not clear how the former concept implies that God is an empty abstraction.

Contra Rachels, I have been arguing that perhaps one can rea-sonably believe that God creates man in his image through the process of evolution by natural selection. One final reply that he might have to my argument can be expressed as follows: According to the theory of evolution by natural selection the existence of man is contingent upon the occurrence of random mutations in pre-cursor species. According to this theory, human beings exist today due to the occurrence of random favorable mutations that enabled humans or human like precursors to survive and reproduce. Had these random mutations not occurred and/or had environmental conditions been different humans might never have existed. Rachels might argue that I need to pay closer attention to the importance of "random mutation" here. If, as Darwinism sug-gests, random mutation plays a crucial role in the story about how we came to exist then God could have no hand in our creation, for God acts intentionally not randomly.

The reply to this is that the random mutations that occur in nature are at least in principle capable of being explained, for they are material events governed by the laws of nature. If the laws of nature are a product of God's creation, as Swinburne maintains, then God could have set things up so that eventually human beings would have to come into existence. Thus there is no incompatibil-ity between the prevalence of random mutation in Darwinian nat-ural selection and the view that God creates human beings in his own image.

CONCLUDING REMARKS ON THE IMAGE OF GOD THESIS

For all of the above reasons, we have sufficient reason to conclude that Darwinism does not undermine the view that human beings are created in the image of God, or, at least, that Rachels has not shown that it does. I have argued that perhaps one could reasonably believe that God created human beings and the other species of animals through the process of evolution. I am not arguing that it *is* reasonable to believe this, but just that one *could* reasonably believe it. Whether it is reasonable to believe it will depend upon the strength of arguments for God's existence provided by people such as Swinburne.[8] Since it is the strength of arguments such as Swinburne's that must be examined in determining whether it is reasonable to believe that God creates us through evolution and since, as I have argued, Darwinism does nothing to undermine these kinds of argument, we have very good reason to think that Darwinism does not undermine the idea that we are made in the image of God.

Rachels on the Rationality Thesis

Rachels argues that according to Darwinism the difference between human beings and nonhuman animals is a difference in degree and not a difference in kind. Thus, we should expect to find rationality (though perhaps less of it) among nonhuman animals if we find it in humans. According to Rachels this is a significant point which if true would undermine the rationality thesis, one of the main supports for the view that human beings alone possess moral rights. I will argue that Rachels is, indeed, correct in thinking that many nonhuman animals are rational, but I will go on to argue that the difference in degree in the rationality of the typical adult human being and the typical adult of any other animal species justifies a difference in the moral standing between them, which in turn justifies a difference in the moral consideration we should extend to them.

---

[8] For critical assessments of Swinburne's argument, see Mackie 1982, 146–49; Priest 1981; Doore 1980; and Smith 1998. For replies to some of these criticisms, see Swinburne 1991, Appendix A; and Forrest 1983.

Rachels briefly considers the idea that possession of sophisticated linguistic abilities is essential to the possession of rationality and then goes on to consider a view that he finds more plausible. This is the view that a being possesses rationality if and only if it can engage in means-end reasoning to solve problems it faces in its environment (Rachels 1990, 140–41). He rightly notes there is ample evidence that both human and nonhuman animals engage in this kind of reasoning. So, he concludes that both humans and many nonhuman animals share in rationality. Thus, according to Rachels, the differences between humans and nonhuman animals with respect to rationality is a difference in degree and not in kind. In support of this view he provides three main arguments and responds to a couple of possible objections.

First, he argues that since we see our behavior as rational and observe somewhat similar behavior in animals, and since we share common evolutionary origins with them, it is reasonable to conclude that they are rational. Second, he argues that to say human beings alone are rational suggests there is a sharp break in evolutionary development between humans and their closest relatives. But such sharp breaks are not to be expected, according to Darwinism. So, if Darwinism is true it is unlikely that humans are the only rational animals. Third, he argues that experimental psychology runs tests on animals to understand the human mind and that this practice only makes sense if we assume animal rationality. So, to deny animal rationality is to deny the legitimacy of experimental psychology (Rachels 1990, 165–66).

The two objections that Rachels considers can reasonably be referred to as "the Skinnerian objection" and "the tropism objection." The Skinnerian objection states that since animal behavior can be adequately explained with reference to factors of classical conditioning alone, there is no good reason to ascribe beliefs and desires to animals. Thus, animal behavior cannot reasonably be described as rational. Rachels describes this objection as a red herring. His ultimate concern is to undermine the notion of human dignity. And if animal behavior can be understood in terms of classical conditioning without reference to beliefs and desires, then so can human behavior. Consequently, we could still understand both human and animal psychology as continuous rather than different in kind. And if there is no difference in kind between them then there is still no basis for the concept of human dignity (Rachels 1990, 141–43).

The tropism objection states that animal behavior is tropistic and not rational. According to this objection, it could be argued that since human behavior cannot reasonably be viewed as tropistic but must instead be viewed as rational, there is still good reason to accept the concept of human dignity. A tropistic behavior is an automatic or reflex behavior of an entire organism. As such, these behaviors are both the same as and different from someone jerking his leg when his knee is struck. Such jerkings of the leg are nonrational reflex behaviors, but they are movements of just a part of the organism as opposed to an activity of the entire organism. A classic example of tropistic behavior comes from the sphex wasp. Rachels quotes from the writings of Dean Wooldridge in describing this tropistic behavior.

> When the time comes for egg laying, the wasp *Sphex* builds a narrow burrow for the purpose and seeks out a cricket which she stings in such a way as to paralyze but not kill it. She drags the cricket into the burrow, lays her eggs alongside, closes the burrow, then flies away, never to return. In due course, the eggs hatch and the wasp grubs feed off the paralyzed cricket, which has not decayed, having been kept in the wasp equivalent of deep freeze. To the human mind, such an elaborately organized and seemingly purposeful routine conveys a convincing flavour of logic and thoughtfulness—until more details are examined. For example, the wasp's routine is to bring the paralyzed cricket to the burrow, leave it on the threshold, go inside and see that all is well, emerge, and then drag the cricket in. If, while the wasp is inside making her preliminary inspection the cricket is moved a few inches away, the wasp, on emerging from the burrow, will bring the cricket back to the threshold, but not inside, and will then repeat the preparatory procedure of entering the burrow to see that every thing is all right. If again the cricket is removed a few inches while the wasp is inside, once again the wasp will move the cricket up to the threshold and re-enter the burrow for a final check. The wasp never thinks of pulling the cricket straight in. On one occasion, this procedure was repeated forty times, always with the same result. (Rachels 1990, 144)

According to Rachels and Wooldridge, such behavior can be best understood using the language of computer science. Rachels states:

> [T]he insect's actions are controlled by a program with only a limited number of subroutines, with each subroutine called into play by a specific stimulus. The cricket-at-a-distance is the stimulus that triggers

the subroutine for dragging-to-the-threshold; the cricket-on-the-threshold is the stimulus that triggers the subroutine for checking-out-the-burrow; and so on for each item in the wasp's limited behavioural repertory. (Rachels 1990, 145)

According to the tropism objection, all animal behavior can be understood as the mindless carrying out of such programming. As such, all animal behavior can be viewed as nonrational. However, in contrast human behavior cannot be viewed as the product of such rigid programming and so it cannot reasonably be thought of as tropistic. So, according to this objection, there still is a basis for the concept of human dignity.

In reply to this, Rachels again maintains that a red herring has been introduced. He argues that if all animal behavior can be understood as tropistic, then so too can that of human beings. Our behavior might look like rational behavior, but it might well be the product of more sophisticated programming that takes into account more variables and allows for a greater variety of responses to the same stimuli. This would not mean that the behavior is any less tropistic nor any more rational than that of animals. As was the case with his reply to the Skinnerian objection, Rachels would remind us that his goal is to undermine the concept of human dignity. If we are going to argue that animal behavior is tropistic, this then opens the door to thinking that human behavior is also tropistic, suggesting that once again animals and human beings are on equal footing, meaning that the concept of human dignity still has no basis (Rachels 1990, 145).

For all of the above stated reasons, Rachels believes the rationality thesis is false. As noted earlier, he thinks this thesis and the image of God thesis provide the most common and plausible reasons to believe in human dignity, the idea that human beings as a class are different in kind from other animals and that because of this difference they are deserving of moral considerations that need not be extended to other animals. What I want to suggest is that although Rachels is indeed correct to maintain that animals share in rationality, this does not undermine the concept of human dignity. For the difference in the degree of rationality of the typical adult human being in contrast to the degree of rationality of the typical adult of any other animal justifies a difference in the moral considerations that we extend to human beings as opposed to the considerations that we extend to animals.

On the Significance of Differences in Degree

It might be wondered how a difference in degree, as opposed to a difference in kind, can possibly justify such a difference in moral consideration. But this seems to me to present no real worries. Take myself. Like top-flight amateur basketball players, I am a basketball player. The difference between their play and mine is a matter of degree and not a difference in kind. They dribble, shoot, pass, rebound, and defend and so do I, but they do all this a lot better than I do. Thus, top-flight amateur players are deserving of consideration for participation on professional teams that I am not deserving of. I cannot complain that I have been excluded from tryouts for NBA teams, because I am simply not good enough to deserve consideration. Similarly, we can say that the rational capacities of nonhuman animals are so stunted that they are not deserving of the same moral considerations and moral rights.

In reply Rachels might demand a better analogy. He might agree that I deserve no consideration for membership on an NBA team, but he might note that this is because of the characteristics I possess as an individual and not as the member of a group. He is arguing that it is wrong to exclude the *group* of nonhumans from equal moral consideration. He might note that a more fitting example would point out the wrongness of excluding Native Americans from consideration for membership on an NBA team on the ground that the typical Native American does not possess sufficiently sophisticated basketball skills. This would clearly be wrong to do, since it is irrational and racist. But it would more closely approximate my argument that it is acceptable to exclude animals because the rationality of the typical adult human being far surpasses the rationality of the typical adult of any other species.

This would be a good reply to the initial version of my argument. But let us suppose for a moment that due to certain factors inherent in the biology of Native Americans they are all slow, fat, and terribly uncoordinated. Now, if such were the case, then there would be nothing wrong with excluding all Native Americans from tryouts for NBA teams. For in this case none of them would be capable of possessing the kind of sophisticated basketball abilities that would make one suitable for membership on an NBA team. This is what I want to say about nonhuman animals. None of them is capable of possessing the level of rationality of the typical adult human being and for this reason they are not deserving of equal moral consideration and moral rights.

The Argument from Marginal Cases

At this stage of the argument Rachels is likely to maintain that mentally handicapped human beings are not capable of possessing the level of rationality of the typical adult human being either.[9] Yet we do not use this fact to exclude them from equal moral consideration or equal rights, nor should we. This move could be made to criticize my suggestion that it is the capacity for having the rationality of a typical adult human being that makes all human beings deserving of an equal moral consideration that need not be extended to nonhuman animals. The point is that if this is the direction of my argument then I cannot make sense of why we should grant equal moral consideration or equal rights to mentally handicapped human beings. In the literature on animal rights this kind of point has been referred to as "the problem of marginal cases" and I will refer to it as such here.[10]

One possible reply to this can be derived from the writings of Jane English. She has argued that there are good moral reasons to extend equal moral consideration to person-like nonpersons, such as late term fetuses and chimpanzees. She writes:

> An ethical theory must operate by generating a set of sympathies and attitudes toward others which reinforces the functioning of that set of moral principles. Our prohibition against killing people operates by means of certain moral sentiments including sympathy, compassion

---

[9] Rachels employs this kind of argument strategy. See Rachels 1990, 184–87.

[10] The name given to this kind of argument, "the argument from marginal cases (AMC)," was originally coined by one of the critics of the argument, Jan Narveson. See Narveson 1977. Two of the most well-known defenders of animal rights have both employed the AMC. See Singer 1975 and Regan 1983. For a very thorough discussion and defense of the AMC, see Dombrowski 1997. There have been various published critical replies to the AMC. Among these are: Becker 1983; Benson 1981; Devine 1978; Diamond 1978; and Francis and Norman 1978. Dombrowski explains and critically responds to the criticisms of these philosophers and others in his excellent book. While the reply to the AMC expressed in this chapter is influenced by the work of some of these earlier critics, it does, I think, bring something new to the table which is worth considering.

and guilt. But if these attitudes are to form a coherent set, they carry us further: we tend to perform supererogatory actions, and we tend to feel similar compassion toward person-like nonpersons.

It is crucial that psychological facts play a role here. Our psychological constitution makes it the case that for our ethical theory to work, it must prohibit certain treatment of nonpersons which are significantly person-like. If our moral rules allowed people to treat some person-like nonperson in ways we do not want to be treated, this would undermine the system of sympathies and attitudes that makes the ethical system work. (English 1997, 156)

What Jane English is arguing is that person-like nonpersons, such as late-term fetuses, new-born humans, and chimpanzees, should be granted equal moral consideration alongside of human beings because if we do not grant them this status then our sympathies toward persons would be in danger of deterioration. English uses this argument in supporting the view that late-term abortions are immoral, but it can also be used to show that mentally handicapped people should be afforded equal rights. They are so much like the typical human being that were we not to extend them equal rights this could lead to the erosion of the rights of those who clearly are typical.[11] (This argument is not intended to suggest that no mentally handicapped human beings are persons. I suspect that most of them possess the mental capacities that are sufficient for personhood, while some of them may be so badly off that they are not even persons. Regardless, the point is that even if they were not persons, we would still have very good reason to regard them as persons in our ethical thinking.)

While one could respond in this way, I do not find such an approach to be helpful. The problem is that English's concern for the erosion of our moral sympathies does not provide a sufficiently strong basis for prohibiting all mistreatment of the mentally handicapped. In particular, what concerns me is the fact that many of us would be quite capable of maintaining strong sympathies for normal healthy human beings while looking at the handicapped as substandard and thereby undeserving of equal rights. I say this

---

[11] This argument strategy is used by some of those authors who have published replies to the argument from marginal cases. For instance, see Devine 1978, 497.

because many white racists have been able to look at blacks as substandard human beings undeserving of equal rights while posing no threat to the rights of other whites. Similarly, I suspect that many Nazis, who looked at Jews as substandard human beings, were no threat to Aryans. For these reasons I believe it is all too easy for human beings to look at a segment of their population as substandard and to treat them as such, while becoming no threat to the rest of the population. Thus, I find approaches like that of English to be seriously flawed.

Another possible reply to the problem of marginal cases is that of Bonnie Steinbock. In dealing with this problem she writes:

> I am willing to admit that my horror at the thought of experiments being performed on severely mentally incapacitated human beings in cases in which I would find it justifiable and preferable to perform the same experiments on nonhuman animals (capable of similar suffering) may not be a moral emotion. But it is certainly not wrong of us to extend special care to members of our own species, motivated by feelings of sympathy, protectiveness, etc. If this is speciesism, it is stripped of its tone of moral condemnation. It is not racist to provide special care to members of your own race; it is racist to fall below your moral obligation to a person because of his or her race. (Steinbock 1997, 470)

Speciesism is the unjustified failure to give equal consideration to the interests of other species. In the animal rights literature this is viewed as wrong in the same way that racism and sexism are wrong. What Steinbock is getting at here is that she does not think it is racist to provide special care to members of your own race as long as you do not "fall below your moral obligations to a person because of his or her race." I suppose that she would, for instance, see nothing wrong with a black person devoting a lot of her time and attention to the causes of the NAACP, as long as she remains respectful of the basic rights of whites and other groups. Similarly, she does not think it is speciesist to provide special care to members of your own species as long as you do not fall below your moral obligation to members of other species because they are members of other species. For this reason she does not think there is anything wrong with experimenting on animals as opposed to the mentally handicapped because one feels a special sympathy and protectiveness towards members of one's own species.

In response to this it could be argued that it is not clear when providing special care to members of your own race entails falling below your obligations to members of other races. Consequently, appealing to the moral acceptability of such behavior to support favoritism of one's own species is not a workable solution to the problem of marginal cases. To develop this point further, consider a situation in which I am out boating and come upon a shipwreck where strangers of many races are in the water needing to be rescued. Suppose my boat can only hold myself and four passengers, and all the people in the water are in the same condition, and that it is no more trouble for me to rescue any one of them as opposed to any other. Now suppose upon my arrival at the scene and upon recognizing all these facts, I come to the conclusion that since I am white I will make a point of saving four whites before saving any blacks. This seems to me to be clearly irrational. For I can see no reason why the racial similarity between myself and the other whites should be any grounds for preferential treatment. To favor four whites simply because they are of the same race is irrational.

Now I can imagine other scenarios in which favoring four whites on other grounds might be justified. Suppose for instance that upon showing up at the scene of the wreck I see that four white friends of mine are there and I save them first. This would be morally acceptable, since the friendship relation presents a special case which justifies such preferential treatment. There are other situations in which preferential treatment could be justified on other grounds. Suppose I see my wife and three kids in the water along with all of the others. Or suppose that there are people of different nationalities in the water. Then I might be justified in favoring other Americans since I am an American. This last case is clearly more controversial. How one feels about it might have to do with one's attitudes towards nationalist sentiments, whether they are on the whole a good or a bad thing. My point here is that preferential treatment for a race based solely on the fact that they share your race is irrational, whereas certain other forms of preferential treatment are not.[12]

The preceding considerations suggest that Steinbock's argument is significantly flawed. She argues that showing special care

---

[12] For a different perspective on the ethics of showing special care or preferential treatment for members of one's own race, see Schmid 1996.

for members of your own species because they are members of your species is not necessarily wrong. She says this because she thinks showing special care for members of your own race because they are members of your race is morally acceptable. But the latter assumption, as I have just shown, is problematic. There *is* something wrong with favoring members of your own race just because they are members of your race. Consequently, Steinbock doesn't give adequate support for her claim that special care for members of one's own species is justified.

For all of the above reasons we have good reason to reject Steinbock's reply to the problem of marginal cases. Recall that both she and Jane English have offered possible replies to the argument from marginal cases. English says we should extend equal moral consideration to personlike nonpersons so as not to erode the system of sympathies necessary to a functional morality. Steinbock says there is nothing wrong with showing preference for members of one's own kind as long as one does not fail in his obligations to members of other groups. I have argued that neither of these solutions is adequate. Yet, I also believe that mentally handicapped human beings should be given equal moral consideration. Thus, insofar as my critique of Rachels's case for animal rights is open to the argument from marginal cases, it is still problematic. In the next section I propose an alternative reply to the argument from marginal cases.

Community, Virtues, Flourishing, and the Moral Life

To get at the problem with the argument from marginal cases we need to look at the human condition. Human beings are social animals that live in communities. The reason they do so is because it is the best chance individual human beings have at living well or flourishing. It is the recognition that our dependence upon others in the bonds of community provides the best hope of a good life that gives rise to and helps maintain communities over time. The moral virtues are those qualities of character that enable us to live well in these communities formed out of the recognition that we cannot go it alone, that we are dependent creatures. It is our dependence that makes sense out of the moral life, that is its *raison d'être*.

Being born of humans and raised by them, the severely handicapped are members of human communities and are some of the most needy members of such communities. As such their lives express in an exaggerated way the very dependence that is inherent in all our lives. The reason it would be wrong to kill and eat or to experiment upon the mentally handicapped is that in doing so we undermine the very reason for being of the moral life. The moral virtues—courage, justice, temperance, and so forth—exist to help us live well in community with others. We live in community with others because we are dependent creatures. Thus, to single out the most needy members of our communities for food or experimentation would tear away at the very foundation of the moral life. Since the virtues exist to help us live well in community with other human beings but not with other animals, the moral life is in no way undermined if we use nonhuman animals for food or scientific experimentation.

Objections and Replies

OBJECTION 1

The fact that the virtues originally arose to help us live well in community with other human beings and originally were traits guiding us in our conduct towards other human beings does not mean that we cannot nor should not alter our conception of the virtues. Perhaps it is time to rethink the concept of compassion. Perhaps we should now view the extension of it to animals as one of the requirements for its possession.

REPLY

The virtues not only arose to enable us to live well in community but still exist today for the same reason. While it might be a good thing to show compassion towards nonhuman animals, there is a danger in viewing such compassion towards animals as a requirement of the virtue. Compassionate interaction with nonhuman animals is not essential to our living well in human communities. But compassion showed to humans is essential. To require compassion for nonhuman animals when no such compassion stands in an essential relation to the *telos* for which compassion exists is to risk rendering the virtue meaningless. A likely negative consequence of this is that members of human communities might then become skeptical about the very point of living the moral life.

OBJECTION 2

I have argued that mentally handicapped people reflect in an exaggerated way the dependence of all human beings and that such human dependency is the reason for being of communities and the moral virtues which sustain these communities. Because of this I have said it would be wrong to treat such humans as mere means, using them for food or scientific experiments. In reply to my argument it could be argued that animals also reflect the dependence of human beings and for this reason we also should not use them as mere means.

REPLY

I agree that many animals do reflect the dependence of human beings. Watching young birds being fed worms and such from their parents or young pups sucking milk from the teats of their mother serve as reminders of this. But even though animals, like humans, are dependent, they are *not* part of the community for which the virtues are intended to serve. And so to suggest that justice and benevolence are owed equally to nonhuman animals runs the risk of robbing the virtues of their point.

OBJECTION 3

My argument involves an unwarranted inference from fact to value. I maintain it is a fact that virtues exist to help us live well in communities with other human beings. And from this alleged fact I infer that we have obligations to help needy human beings and no equal obligations to help needy animals. But since one cannot logically derive values from facts, my argument commits the naturalistic fallacy.

REPLY

While some inferences from facts to values might be illegitimate, committing the naturalistic fallacy, not all such inferences are.

When the facts referred to express the truth about the *telos*, the purpose, of a thing, this warrants certain normative conclusions. For instance, from the fact that a knife serves to cut, a fact about a knife's *telos*, one can reasonably conclude that its blade should be sharp, a normative conclusion. In my argument I derive normative conclusions about the different obligations we have to the mentally handicapped and to animals from facts about the *telos* of the virtues. Thus, I have not engaged in an illegitimate inference from facts to values.[13]

Objection 4

My argument makes much of the fact that the virtues exist to enable humans to live well in community with one another. Since this is the reason for being of the virtues, to suggest that we have an equal obligation to exhibit virtue in our relations with animals is to rob the virtues of their meaning. But suppose human space explorers encountered life on other planets and suppose these aliens were intelligent and communicative in the same ways that we are. Given the nature of my argument, humans would have no obligation to exhibit virtue in their interaction with these aliens since they are not human. But this is absurd, because it is intuitively obvious that such aliens would command our moral respect. It would be wrong to kill and eat rational, loving, communicative aliens just because they are not human beings.

Reply

While I am committed to the view that the virtues arose and function today to enable humans to live well in community with one another, I do not believe this means we would have no obligation to extend our moral concern equally to the kinds of alien beings just described. I have argued that membership in a human community is sufficient reason for thinking compassion, justice, and other expressions of virtue should be extended to a creature. And that is why the severely mentally handicapped should be protected

---

[13] For more defense of this teleological approach to avoiding the naturalistic fallacy, see Chapter 4, especially pp. 81–82.

and not preyed upon by us but that animals do not merit the same kind of protection. But there can be other reasons for thinking virtue ought to be exhibited to a creature.

What seems especially salient in the case of rational space aliens is their capacity and willingness to reciprocate. If such aliens were able and willing to reciprocate, exhibiting virtue in response to our exhibiting it in our relations with them, then we would be obligated to be virtuous in our relations with them. Since the nonhuman animals of our planet are neither members of human communities nor capable of such reciprocal relations, we have no such obligation to exhibit virtue in our interactions with them.[14]

Additionally, I should note the fact that my appeal to the capacity for reciprocation in reply to this objection can also be used to answer another kind of objection. It could be argued that there is nothing which is the "human community;" rather there are many different human communities that have been formed over the ages and which will be formed in the future. It could be said that my argument could be used to endorse racism or other illegitimate forms of discrimination on the grounds that people of a different race might not be a part of the community. For instance, in a white racist community black people might be viewed as lacking membership. Thus, according to my theory of the virtues we would then have no obligation to exhibit the virtues equally in our interaction with them. In reply to this, however, it seems to me that since membership in one's community is

---

[14] Here it might be wondered why the ability and willingness of rational aliens to reciprocate would obligate us to exhibit virtue in our relations with them. Keeping in mind that the virtues exist to enable us to live well in community with one another may help us to see why this is so. Where there is a willingness and ability in others to reciprocate—to show kindness in response to our kindness and honesty in response to our honesty—there is a chance to broaden our community to include those others. Broadening our community to include members of other groups who are capable of the kinds of reciprocal relations constitutive of communal living helps to increase the kinds of sharing and understanding that provides for peaceful coexistence. Peaceful coexistence between groups contributes to the goal of living well in community with one another. Thus, extending the moral community to those willing and able to reciprocate is a perfectly reasonable expectation given my conception of the nature and role of the virtues.

but one of the ways to account for the existence of an equal right to moral consideration and that the capacity for reciprocation is another, then the latter objection carries no weight. For, referring back to my example, blacks have an equal capacity for reciprocation and this can serve as the basis for an obligation to give them equal moral consideration, even if you are part of a white racist community[15]

Concluding Remarks on the Rationality Thesis

I do not intend to suggest that we have no obligations towards nonhuman animals. Their capacity for suffering should count for something in our moral considerations. But given that they are neither members of human communities nor capable of reciprocal relations of virtue, their capacity for suffering should not be considered on a par with the sufferings of human beings. To shoot dogs with B.B. guns to hear them squeal in pain seems clearly wrong, but at the same time raising animals under humane conditions to put food on the table or using animals for serious scientific research may well be justified for the reasons I have given.

Final Remarks

In this chapter I hope to have accomplished two things. I hope to have provided a clear and accurate account of Rachels's case for the view that Darwinism undermines the concept of human dignity, thereby making a case for animal rights. I also hope to have shown why it is that despite his arguments the Darwinian can still reasonably make sense of the concept of human dignity and thus be rationally justified in eating meat, supporting animal experimentation, or allowing the existence of zoos.

The discussion in this chapter has taken us into various kinds of issues—the rationality of faith (including the problem of evil and the plausibility of different kinds of design arguments), the nature of rationality, the criteria of equal moral standing, and the problem

---

[15] I am indebted to Bruce Waller for having raised this issue after his reading of an earlier draft of this chapter.

of marginal cases. In the next chapter I will move away from issues in evolutionary ethics, but will do so by delving deeper into issues pertaining to the rationality of faith. This move will enable us to examine further the possible relationship between evolution and the rationality of faith while at the same time allowing us to explore some of the alleged epistemological implications of evolutionary biology.

6

Faith, Reason, and
Evolutionary Epistemology

Ontological naturalism is the view that nothing exists other than spatio-temporal beings embedded within a space-time framework. As such, it denies the existence of abstract entities such as propositions and numbers, Platonic universals, disembodied minds, gods, and the like. Naturalized epistemology is a view about the nature of knowledge characterized by its commitment to externalism and the idea that knowledge consists in beliefs reliably generated by cognitive mechanisms operating in a suitable environment. Externalism is the view that to know that P one need not know that one's belief that P has been reliably generated.[1]

In recent years Alvin Plantinga (1993) has defended theistic naturalized epistemology. Among other things, theism includes the idea that there is an omniscient, omnipotent, and all-good creator of the universe who knows and loves us. As such, theism is incompatible with ontological naturalism. Plantinga argues that naturalized epistemology is the correct view on the nature of knowledge, but he contends that when combined with ontological naturalism it is an untenable position. In contrast, when combined with theism naturalized epistemology becomes tenable.

According to Plantinga, the problem with naturalistic naturalized epistemology (NNE), naturalized epistemology combined with ontological naturalism, is that for ontological naturalists the most plausible account of the existence of human beings and their cognitive capacities is the Darwinian account, which views human

---

[1] These definitions come from Fales 1996.

117

existence and human cognitive capacities as the products of the blind forces of natural selection. According to this Darwinian account, the cognitive capacities we have would exist as they are in us because of their tendency to enable us to survive and reproduce. Plantinga argues that there are any number of ways in which unreliable cognitive capacities could serve the ends of successful survival and reproduction. For this reason he concludes that if we are not the products of God's intelligent design, but instead are simply the products of Darwinian natural selection, then there can be no good reason for us to think that we possess cognitive capacities that are reliable producers of true beliefs. This in turn would mean that if NNE is true then we cannot really know anything, including whether or not NNE is true. In contrast, when naturalized epistemology is combined with theism, yielding theistic naturalized epistemology (TNE), we do not fall into this skeptical predicament because according to TNE we are the products of God's intelligent design. According to theism, we are made in the image of God. Since God is omniscient, we would then have good reason to believe that our cognitive capacities would be reliable producers of true beliefs.

Here it might be objected that Plantinga's argument that NNE leads to skepticism conflicts with his view that externalism is true. Recall that Plantinga embraces naturalized epistemology, which is committed to externalism, the view that to know that P one need not know that one's belief that P has been reliably generated. Plantinga goes on to argue that if ontological naturalism is true and we are simply the products of the blind forces of natural selection then we have good reason to doubt the reliability of our cognitive capacities, and he says that this means we could not really be said to know anything. It might be wondered why, if he embraces externalism, any of this should threaten our capacity to know. As long as our cognitive capacities are in fact reliable it shouldn't matter.

This objection overlooks the concept of a "defeater" and the role defeaters play in Plantinga's epistemology. Defeaters are reasons one might have for doubting the reliability of one's cognitive capacities. According to Plantinga, we do not have to know of the reliability of our cognitive capacities to know that P, but if there are defeaters of which we are aware that give us ground for doubting the reliability of our cognitive processes and if we cannot answer these defeaters, then we cannot justifiably believe that P, meaning we cannot know that P. Plantinga's point is that ontological naturalism, which includes the idea that our cognitive capacities exist as a consequence of the blind forces of natural selection, provides a defeater for our knowledge claims which the naturalist cannot answer. Thus, NNE leads to skepticism.

Plantinga's argument has drawn the attention of many philosophers in recent years. In what follows I would like to give it a little more attention, as I think it is sufficiently interesting and sufficiently well-articulated to deserve the amount of attention it has been getting. I will begin by discussing some of the relevant details of the argument. Then I will go on to examine two of the recent approaches to developing a critical reply to it, those of Michael Ruse and Evan Fales. I shall argue that Ruse's approach is flawed in significant respects but that Fales's approach is much more likely to be successful despite the recent replies to it from Plantinga.

Plantinga's Case Against Naturalistic Reliabilism

A central component of Plantinga's attack on NNE is his argument for the view that if we are simply the products of natural selection and not of intelligent design then it is unlikely that we have reliable cognitive capacities. In defending this thesis he presents us with five scenarios in which we could survive and reproduce sufficiently well even if our cognitive capacities were not reliable producers of true beliefs. He argues that since from the naturalistic perspective these scenarios are equiprobable alongside the scenario in which our cognitive capacities are reliable producers of true belief, it follows that from the naturalistic perspective it really is not very likely that our cognitive capacities are reliable.

Evan Fales provides a very nice summary account of these five scenarios. He writes:

(1) The first possibility is that there might be no causal connection between beliefs and action at all. Since the only thing survival and procreation demand are getting one's body parts into the right places at the right times, we can imagine creatures whose adaptive responses to their environment are handled in an entirely cognition-free way,

while their beliefs are on permanent holiday. In such creatures, the unreliability of belief-forming mechanisms would be no liability at all (nor would reliability confer a selective advantage).

(2) A second, related possibility is that beliefs are causally connected with behavior, but only by way of being effects of that behavior, or "side-effects" of the causes of behavior. Here again, the truth or falsity of a belief will play no role in the appropriateness of the behavior it is linked to; and so truth will confer no selective advantage.

(3) Beliefs might indeed causally affect behavior, but do so in a way that is sensitive only to their syntax, not to their content or semantics. Then once again, the *truth-value* of a belief would be irrelevant to its role in producing adaptive behavior.

(4) Perhaps beliefs could be causally efficacious, and their content materially relevant to the behavior they help generate, while the behavior thus generated is *maladaptive*. No organism, perhaps, is *perfectly* efficient, perfectly attuned to its environment. Maladaptive characteristics are a burden which can be borne provided they are not *too* maladaptive. Natural selection can even *favor* maladaptive traits, when these are closely linked on the genome with genes which confer strongly adaptive traits—so that the benefits of inheriting that region of a genome outweigh the costs. This can happen when the two genes lie closely adjacent on a chromosome, so that they tend to travel together during genetic reshuffling; or it can happen by way of pleiotropy—a single gene coding for two or more traits. Indeed, adjacency and pleiotropy can be invoked to provide mechanisms that would explain possibilities (1) and (2) as well. The present point is that an organism may be able to hobble along with lots of false beliefs and misdirected actions.

(5) Finally evolution might produce organisms in which false belief leads to *adaptive* action. As Plantinga points out, this can happen in several ways. Freddy the caveman may believe that saber-toothed tigers make great pets, may want

to tame the one that has just appeared, and believe that running away from it as fast as he can is the best way to corral it. Or Freddy may want to be eaten, believe correctly that this cat will eat him if given the chance, and believe falsely that shoving a firebrand in its face maximizes the chances for his desired fate. The general point is that when beliefs cause action, the action that results is the combined result of various desires and beliefs. Thus, a false belief can "cancel out" another false belief, or "cancel out" a destructive desire, to produce a beneficial action. Why should we suppose, then, that if nature selects for creatures whose actions are guided by their beliefs (and desires), it will be *true* beliefs that confer the greatest selective advantage? (Fales 1996, 438–39)

Again the idea here is that each of these scenarios is considered to be equiprobable alongside the scenario in which our cognitive capacities are reliable producers of true beliefs. Thus, from the perspective of evolutionary biology it is not very likely that our cognitive faculties are reliable producers of true beliefs. But, according to Plantinga, if this is so, then we cannot really be said to know anything at all, not even that NNE is true.

Michael Ruse's Reply to Plantinga

In Michael Ruse's recent publications, such as *Taking Darwin Seriously* (1998) and *Evolutionary Naturalism* (1995), he has advocated a certain sort of evolutionary epistemology and has argued that it implies a rejection of metaphysical realism (MR) in favor of a position that he calls "internal realism" (IR). Additionally he has maintained that since his evolutionary epistemology implies a rejection of MR in favor of IR, and since Plantinga's critique of NNE rests upon the assumption of MR, it escapes Plantinga's attack on NNE.

In what follows I will explain the kind of evolutionary epistemology Ruse advocates, briefly contrasting his evolutionary epistemology with that of David Hull.[2] I will also show that Ruse does

---

[2] See Hull 1982; 1988a; and 1988b.

indeed reject MR, replacing it with IR, and I will try to explain the difference between these views. Additionally, I will go on to examine the reasons Ruse gives for favoring IR over MR. I will argue that: (1) Ruse's case for rejecting MR has no essential connection to evolutionary considerations; (2) his case for rejecting MR depends upon internalist assumptions about the nature of knowledge that are in need of some kind of defense; and (3) given his implicit internalism and his commitment to IR, his argument for rejecting MR can be used against his IR.

Rusean Evolutionary Epistemology

In *Evolutionary Naturalism* Ruse distinguishes between two kinds of evolutionary epistemology and specifies which type he practices:

> there are two main approaches that people have taken in trying to bring evolutionary thinking to bear on philosophical problems of knowledge and epistemology. The first is to argue by analogy from the main evolutionary mechanism of natural selection to the supposed way in which knowledge, particularly scientific knowledge arises and develops. The second is to argue literally, from the way in which natural selection has shaped us humans as thinking beings to the kind of knowledge claims that we would make.
>
> Here, as elsewhere, I express a pretty strong preference for the second kind of approach, feeling that there are some major points of disanalogy between the growth of organisms and the growth of science. (Ruse 1995, 109)

Rusean evolutionary epistemology sees human cognitive capacities as an adaptation that has aided us in the struggle to survive and reproduce and examines the implications this has for traditional epistemological problems. In *Evolutionary Naturalism* this Rusean evolutionary epistemology is contrasted with the alternative version which has been advocated by David Hull. The alternative version tries to understand changes in our knowledge or scientific understanding as a result of something like Darwinian natural selective forces. So, for instance, on this view those scientific theories that have been prevalent for long periods of time will be understood as more fit for survival in the minds of humans as opposed to other theories. Thus, they tend to be reproduced more in the minds of humans through communication. Ruse explains the difference between these two types of evolutionary epistemology and explains why he prefers his brand to Hull's (Ruse 1995, 174–182).

According to Ruse's evolutionary epistemology the basic rules of mathematics, deductive logic, and scientific reasoning are things that we are innately disposed to accept into our thinking. He thinks that this is the case due to the principles of natural selection. In his writings he gives several examples illustrating how an innate tendency to think in accordance with some of the basic principles of mathematics and deductive logic would be adaptive and how failure to think in these ways would be maladaptive. For instance:

> Consider two would-be human ancestors, one with elementary logical and mathematical skills, and the other without much in that direction. One can think of countless situations, many of which must have happened in real life, where the former proto-human would have been at great selective advantage over the other. A tiger is seen entering a cave that you and your family usually use for sleeping. No one has seen the tiger emerge. Should you seek alternative accommodation for this night at least? How else does one achieve a happy end to this story, other than by an application of those laws of logic that we try to uncover for our students in elementary logic classes? (Ruse 1998, 162)

Ruse's evolutionary epistemology is primarily an attempt: (1) to support the view that such principles are innate within us and that they are the products of evolution by natural selection; and (2) to explain the philosophical significance of these facts.

In making the case for the view that we have such innate tendencies due to natural selection he makes three main points. First, he notes how different cultures, both Eastern and Western, have similar systems of logic, math, and causal reasoning. He says that this suggests the likelihood of innate tendencies to think in these ways. Second, he says studies of children show a number of mathematical and other reasoning skills develop in them without either formal or informal teaching. This again suggests the innateness hypothesis. Third, he states that "non-human and human animals show the kinds of overlap of formal reasoning ability which one would expect were natural selection at work, leaving its mark" (Ruse 1998, 166). He goes on to discuss experiments done with chimpanzees, demonstrating their capacities for rudimentary mathematical and deductive thinking.

Having briefly considered Ruse's reasons for believing that we have evolved innate dispositions to reason in certain ways, let us look at his thoughts on the philosophical implications of this. In particular let us examine what he thinks the Darwinian views imply about MR.

METAPHYSICAL REALISM AND RUSE'S REJECTION OF IT

While Ruse acknowledges that Hilary Putnam has criticized evolutionary epistemology, in rejecting MR in favor of IR he does to some extent align himself with Putnam.[3] Ruse is explicit about this in his writings. See Ruse 1995, 63-68; 193; 289 and Ruse 1998, 196; 202. In *Evolutionary Naturalism* he appeals to the writings of Putnam in order to define MR and IR. He quotes the following passages from Putnam:

> [According to MR], the world consists of some fixed totality of mind-independent objects. There is exactly one true and complete description of 'the way the world is'. Truth involves some sort of correspondence relation between words or thought-signs and external things and sets of things. I shall call this perspective the *externalist* perspective, because its favourite point of view is a God's Eye point of view.
>
> The perspective I shall defend has no unambiguous name. It is a late arrival in the history of philosophy, and even today it keeps being confused with other points of view of a quite different sort. I shall refer to it as the *internalist* perspective, because it is characteristic of this view to hold that *what objects does the world consist of?* is a question that it only makes sense to ask *within* a theory or description. Many 'internalist' philosophers, though not all, hold further that there is more than one 'true' theory or description of the world. 'Truth', in an internalist view is some sort of (idealized) rational acceptability—some sort of ideal coherence of our beliefs with each other and with our experiences *as those experiences are themselves represented in our belief system*—and not correspondence with mind-independent 'states of affairs'. There is no God's Eye point of view that we can know or usefully imagine; there are only various points of view

---

[3] For his critique of evolutionary epistemology, see Putnam 1982.

of actual persons reflecting various interests and purposes that their descriptions and theories subserve. (Putnam 1981, 49–50; See Ruse 1995, pp.64–65, for Ruse's quotation of this passage.)

Ruse also quotes the following passage:

> In an internalist view also, signs do not intrinsically correspond to objects, independently of how those signs are employed and by whom. But a sign that is actually employed in a particular way by a particular community of users can correspond to particular objects *within the conceptual scheme of those users.* 'Objects' do not exist independently of conceptual schemes. We cut up the world into objects when we introduce one or another scheme of description. Since objects *and* the signs are alike *internal* to the scheme of description, it is possible to say what matches what. (Putnam 1981, 52; quoted at Ruse 1995, 65)

When Ruse rejects MR he is rejecting the view that "There is exactly one true and complete description of 'the way the world is'," and the correspondence theory of truth. Instead, he embraces the idea that "'Truth' . . . is some sort of (idealized) rational acceptability—some sort of ideal coherence of our beliefs with each other and with our experiences."

Additionally in his own writings Ruse has said the following sorts of things:

> Thus, with Hume and Clark, I am led to reject the notion of a reality beyond our experience. (Ruse 1995, 192)

And

> . . . as an internal realist I think that everything is in the mind in some sense. (Ruse 1995, 289)

And

> This kind of reality—something outside the sensing interpreting subject—is meaningless. (Ruse 1998, 194)

While these passages from the text of Ruse's writings might make him look like he holds to some sort of metaphysical idealism *à la*

Berkeley, he doesn't. Along with his adoption of IR Ruse also embraces what he calls a "common-sense realism". He writes that

> at one (everyday) level we believe in the reality of chairs and tables and trees. They are not chimeras like Macbeth's dagger. This is common-sense realism, which the propensities inform and support. Chairs and tables and trees have a solid, ongoing existence. Today, we can include electrons, genes, and dinosaurs. (Ruse 1998, 192)

Ruse believes that tables and chairs and trees and cows and genes and electrons have an existence independent of consciousness. It is just that what ultimately makes our beliefs about the existence and nature of these things true is *not* the fact that our beliefs correspond with or accurately represent them. Rather, our beliefs in and about these things are true simply because of their coherence with our other beliefs and perceptions. A passage that reflects this Rusean position and his affiliation with Putnam follows:

> the Darwinian rejects a correspondence theory of truth. That is to say, he/she rejects the idea that his/her thought corresponds to true reality, where 'reality' in this context is some sort of absolute entity, like the thing-in-itself. Obviously, working within the common-sense level, the Darwinian is just as much of a correspondence thinker as anyone else. But at the final level, defending common-sense reality, as we have had to accept, the Darwinian subscribes to a coherence theory of truth, believing that the best you can do is to get everything to hang together. [*Ruse adds.*] (See Putnam 1981, for a similar point and Rorty 1980, for a powerful attack on the correspondence theory.) (Ruse 1998, 202)

In *Taking Darwin Seriously* and *Evolutionary Naturalism,* Ruse argues that when you take seriously the fact that human cognitive capacities are adaptations that exist in humans because they aid us in the struggle to survive and reproduce, and when you think through the implications of this you will come to see, as Hume did, that we simply posit the existence of objects existing external to consciousness in order to make sense of the coherence of our experience. For instance, to explain the continuous appearance of the desk in front of me and to explain that when I leave and come back and see a desk, I posit the existence of a table external to my consciousness. According to Ruse, evolutionary considerations lead us to recognize that humans are naturally led to posit or believe in the existence of such mind-independent objects, as doing so is adaptive. But, says Ruse, while we are naturally led to believe in the existence of objects external to consciousness, at the philosophical level there is a "justificatory void" (Ruse 1998, 192).

Ruse's view is that as long as we think that the truth of our claims about what things exist is governed by the correspondence of those claims with mind-independent facts, we will never be able to make sense of our knowledge of the world. Thus, Ruse is led to reject such a metaphysical realist theory of truth for the coherence theory. As a reflection of this point of view consider the following passage from *Taking Darwin Seriously*:

> Like the Darwinian, Hume emphasized that our knowledge of the world is based on propensities of the mind. This means that, with Hume, the Darwinian has to wrestle with the problem of scepticism. There is no guarantee that a philosophically satisfying answer will emerge. Fortunately, in real life this does not matter, for we have the world of common-sense reality. Moreover, natural selection has seen to it that we are psychologically inured against the torments of metaphysical doubt. In any case, the Darwinian epistemologist need not really fear even the deepest barbs of scepticism. Total deception of the kind that the metaphysical sceptic threatens is a far-from-plausible notion. So long as one recognizes that, ultimately, truth rests in coherence, not correspondence, all is well. (Ruse 1998, 206)

This passage shows quite clearly that Ruse views the coherence theory of truth as the way out of the skeptical difficulties which arise when MR is combined with evolutionary epistemology. According to Ruse, what in the end governs the truth of our claims about what things exist is simply the coherence of those claims with our other beliefs and experiences.

Having now shown what Ruse takes MR and IR to amount to, and having shown that he rejects MR in favor of IR, I will go on to consider in more detail just why he thinks an evolutionary epistemology should reject MR.

RUSE'S DARWINIAN CASE FOR REJECTING METAPHYSICAL REALISM

The clearest statement of why Ruse believes evolutionary epistemology implies a rejection of MR occurs in Chapter 6 of his book, *Evolutionary Naturalism*. He writes:

It is all very well to talk about reality, but it is clear—it is especially clear to the evolutionary epistemologist—that this reality is mediated as it were through our own perception and thought. Moreover, if you accept—as again the evolutionary epistemologist must accept—that there is something contingent about this perception and thinking, then even if the real world does exist it is at least one step removed from us. (Ruse 1995, 190–91)

The reality referred to in this passage is mind-independent reality, existing external to consciousness. Ruse wants to say that for an evolutionary epistemologist this sort of reality, if known at all, would have to be known "through our own perception and thought." Additionally, according to Ruse, our perceptions and thoughts about reality could have been radically different from what they are had evolution led our minds to operate in different ways from the ways they do operate. Hence the point about the "contingency" of our perception of reality. Ruse goes on to argue that the idea of such a reality existing external to consciousness in this way is incomprehensible.

What sense can we give to the idea of a reality that lies beyond our ken, and that necessarily must remain so? The answer seems to be that no sense at all can be given: to speak of a reality, we must in some way specify what it would be like to meet with this reality and, on the evolutionary epistemological position, this is precisely what we cannot do. (Ruse 1995, 192)

In short, Ruse wants to argue that if we know mind-independent reality at all, we must know it through our own perception and thought. But there is no way to make sense of such a reality existing outside of the ways in which it is perceived and understood. Therefore, the concept of mind-independent reality makes "no sense at all" and should be rejected. Notice in the preceding passage he says "no sense at all" can be given to "the idea of a reality that lies beyond our ken."

Now I can easily agree with and make sense of the view that we can only know of a mind-independent reality through our own perception and thought. However, what is not clear is why Ruse finds all of this so problematic. For how else could we know of reality except through our own perception and thought? The question is what is so problematic about this. The next to last passage cited above suggests an argument. Notice how Ruse states, "Moreover, if you accept—as again the evolutionary epistemologist must accept—that there is something contingent about this perception and thinking, then even if the real world does exist it is at least one step removed from us."

I suppose that at one level Ruse might want to say that since our ways of perceiving and thinking are contingent—they could have been different had we evolved differently—then our perception of reality does not necessarily reflect the true nature of that reality. Hence, no matter how we perceive reality to be the truth about it will always be "one step removed from us." According to Ruse, the problem is that as long as you think truth involves having your beliefs correspond with mind-independent facts, and given that our perception and thought do not necessarily reflect those facts, then there is not going to be a way for us to know the truth. In other words, MR conjoined with an evolutionary epistemology results in skepticism.

To overcome this skepticism Ruse rejects MR, replacing it with IR and its coherence theory of truth. If the truth of our beliefs is ultimately governed by nothing more than the coherence among them and with our experience, things we can witness because they are internal to our consciousness or conceptual scheme, then knowing the truth about reality will no longer require doing the impossible—transcending our own perception and thoughts to get an unbiased vision of reality.

A Critical Reply to Ruse: Three Points of Contention

What are we to make of this Darwinian argument for rejecting MR? First, Darwinian or evolutionary thinking is really inessential to the argument. Ruse makes much of the fact that because we could have evolved to perceive the world in radically different ways then reality (of the mind-independent sort) is "one step removed from us," meaning our perceptions don't necessarily reflect the true nature of reality. But this seems to be a fairly obvious point, and evolutionary considerations are hardly needed to see that our perceptions don't *necessarily* reflect the truth about reality. Reading Descartes's First Meditation will drive this point home quite clearly, for he gives some pretty good reasons to think that our perceptions don't necessarily reflect the true nature of reality, yet no evolutionary considerations are presented.

Second, is it true that because our perceptions do not necessarily reflect the truth about mind-independent reality we cannot be said to *know* that reality? Perhaps, I must concede that it means I cannot be certain or possess indubitable knowledge of that reality, but few people, besides Descartes, expect this from their criteria of knowledge. When I say I know that's a cow in the meadow, what I mean is that I have a justified true belief to this effect and that my belief about this can be 1) justified and 2) true even though I might be mistaken. Additionally, I can myself concede that I *might* be mistaken while justifiably and truthfully believing there's a cow in the meadow. For instance, I look down in the meadow and because I see a cow I believe there's a cow in the meadow, and my justification is that I see one in the meadow. Supposing there is, as a matter of mind-independent fact, a cow there, then I know the cow is there. But I *might* also concede I might be wrong, because I know that my senses sometimes mislead me or there might be an evil genie playing tricks on me.

In response to the preceding point Ruse might argue that I cannot know my beliefs correspond with a mind-independent reality unless I have good reason to think the method of justification for these beliefs is reliable. For instance, assuming MR for a moment, I cannot know there's a cow in the meadow unless I have good reason to think my seeing a cow gives me a reliable basis upon which to judge or believe that there's a cow. Additionally, Ruse might add that as long as there is no necessity that our thoughts and perceptions accurately represent reality there is no way to know whether they are reliable guides or not.

But this sort of response moves us into the realm of the debates in epistemology between internalists and externalists. While there is no easy way to characterize the difference between internalists and externalists about knowledge and at the risk of oversimplification, we might say internalists believe that to know that P one must know that one knows that P, whereas the externalists deny this. Having mentioned the debates between internalists and externalists here let me make a couple of points. First, it is difficult to characterize the internalist and externalist positions in this debate, because there are many different types of internalism Some internalists believe that to know that P one must simply believe that one knows that P, whereas others believe that one must know that one knows that P (as I have defined the view above), whereas others believe that one must justifiably believe that one knows that P to know that P.[4] Second, the internalism and externalism referred to here is not to be confused with the external and internal perspectives discussed in the passages quoted from Putnam earlier in this chapter. When Putnam says that the correspondence theory of truth found in MR reflects the externalist perspective, what he means is that it makes the truth of a belief dependent upon its relating to something external to consciousness. The coherence theory of truth that is associated with IR makes the truth of beliefs dependent upon their relationship to things internal to consciousness, namely other beliefs and perception. Hence, the internalism and externalism referred to by Putnam is not the same thing as the internalism and externalism referred to above.

It strikes me that Ruse's concerns with the fact that evolution could have led us to perceive the world differently and that, consequently, if we are metaphysical realists then we can never know whether our beliefs accurately reflect reality belie an underlying commitment to the internalist perspective. For it will only be by appeal to the sort of internalist considerations above that he can defend his argument against the critique I have made.

I agree that perception must be a reliable guide to the truth in order for the fact that I see a cow to justify my belief that I see a cow. But it is not at all obvious to me, nor should it be to anyone familiar with the debates in contemporary epistemology, that one must also be justified in believing in the reliability of perception for perception to justify beliefs. There are a number of counterintuitive consequences of this view which suggest that it is problematic.

On an intuitive level we would like to say that a child who doubts his mathematical abilities, but who consistently or reliably gives the right answers to a wide array of math problems after correctly working them out, knows mathematics. Such a person does not know that he knows math but he knows nonetheless. Additionally, we want to say two-year-olds know lots of things, but if we believe they can only know things when they are justified in their beliefs about the reliability of their faculties then they know

---

[4] For an introduction to the different ways of expressing the internalist position, see Dancy 1985, 130–35.

nothing at all, for two-year-olds have no beliefs about the reliability of their faculties at all. Other examples could be given, but this should suffice for now.

The preceding considerations are not necessarily damning criticisms of Ruse's position. It could be that there is some way for the internalist to escape the alleged counterintuitive consequences. Or, perhaps, the internalist and/or Ruse would just bite the bullet of intuition here, accepting these counterintuitive consequences, while arguing that the internalist perspective is superior on other grounds. Perhaps, externalism suffers from just as many, if not more, problems. However, having noted this, I do think (1) that before accepting Ruse's argument for rejecting MR one should think critically about the internalism that underlies it and (2) that for Ruse to make a more convincing case against MR some defense of his underlying internalist assumptions is called for.

The third point I want to make in response to Ruse's argument is that the IR he is replacing MR with is subject to the same sorts of problems he charges MR with. To see why this is so it will help to reconsider the conception of truth that IR embraces. According to IR, truth is "some sort of (idealized) rational acceptability— some sort of ideal coherence of our beliefs with each other and with our experiences as those experiences are themselves represented in our belief system." But having noted this, one might still wonder what exactly it means. To understand better the IR conception of truth consider the following passage taken from Putnam's *Reason, Truth and History*:

> Truth cannot *be* rational acceptability for one fundamental reason; truth is supposed to be a property of a statement that cannot be lost, whereas justification can be lost. The statement 'The earth is flat' was, very likely, rationally acceptable three thousand years ago; but it is not rationally acceptable today. Yet it would be wrong to say that 'the earth is flat' was *true* three thousand years ago; for that would mean that the earth has changed its shape. In fact, rational acceptability is a matter of degree; truth is sometimes spoken of as a matter of degree (for instance, we sometimes say, *'the earth is a sphere' is approximately true*); but the 'degree' here is the *accuracy* of the statement, and not its degree of acceptability or justification.
>
> What this shows, in my opinion, is not that the externalist view is right after all, but that truth is an *idealization* of rational acceptability. We speak as if there were such things as epistemically ideal con-

ditions, and we call a statement 'true' if it would be justified under such conditions. 'Epistemically ideal conditions', of course, are like 'frictionless planes': we cannot really attain epistemically ideal conditions, or even be absolutely certain that we have come sufficiently close to them. But frictionless planes cannot really be attained either, and yet talk of frictionless planes has 'cash value' because we can approximate them to a very high degree of approximation. (Putnam 1981, 55)

To preserve the intuition that truth cannot be lost but that justification can be, Putnam is driven to reject the idea that truth just *is* rational acceptability. Instead, he maintains that a belief is true if it would be rational to accept it under epistemically ideal conditions. This is the notion of truth that Ruse weds himself to in his own writings, but doing so is problematic given the nature of the argument he has made against MR.

None of us is in the situation of an ideal observer, and because of this the truth is once again "one step removed from us," just as Ruse has said of the metaphysical realists' conception of truth. Thus, even working under an IR conception of truth, it could be that, despite the coherence of my beliefs and experiences, they could be radically different from the beliefs and experiences that the ideal observer would have. This means that my beliefs, no matter how coherent and no matter how well justified, could still be mistaken in significant and numerous ways. So, the very skepticism that drove Ruse away from MR is not answered by his IR. Since he proposes IR instead of MR to escape those skeptical worries, he really gives us little reason to prefer IR.

In reply to this Ruse might argue that with respect to skepticism IR really is in a better position than MR. For, as noted in the passage cited above from Putnam, we can approximate epistemically ideal conditions (EIC). And because of this we can have good reason to think our beliefs are true when we see that a rational observer in the approximately ideal conditions would accept them. But how are we to know whether we have approximated the EIC? Whatever the EIC are we are not in them. Hence, they are external to us in some sense. This raises the same specter of skepticism which, according to Ruse, haunts MR.

In reply Ruse is likely to contend that indeed the EIC will be external in some sense, but they will not be external to our conceptual scheme. Thus, we can make sense of what better and better epistemic situations would be like, and so we can approximate these ideal conditions, meaning we can have good reason to think that many of our beliefs are true. However, this reply will not do. For we might wonder whether the conceptual framework we are working in even permits us to approach the EIC. I might wonder whether looking at and interpreting and analyzing the world as I do, using the conceptual scheme I do, somehow bars me from ever even approaching the EIC. And as long as this question can be meaningfully raised, and I think it can be, we will never really be able to know whether we have approximated the EIC. Thus, IR faces the problem of skepticism just as MR does, and because of this Ruse really gives us little reason to prefer IR over MR.

CONCLUDING REMARKS ON RUSE'S REPLY TO PLANTINGA

I conclude that Ruse has not shown why evolutionary epistemology calls for a rejection of MR in favor of IR. I do not intend to suggest that he could not make the case. Perhaps it could be done. Perhaps there are good replies to the arguments I have made. Perhaps some altogether different arguments could be made showing why evolutionary epistemology demands a rejection of MR. In any event, I do think I have shown that Ruse's case is inadequate.

One consequence of my arguments would be that Ruse's reply to the critique of naturalism by Plantinga is weakened. For, as noted above, Ruse believes that by showing how evolutionary epistemology implies a rejection of MR he can answer this critique. However, as I have argued, he really needs to do more to show that evolutionary epistemology implies a rejection of MR.

The Debate between Fales and Plantinga

Recall that Plantinga outlines five scenarios in which our cognitive faculties could be unreliable and yet we would be sufficiently well-adapted to survive and reproduce. Because he thinks these scenarios are equiprobable alongside the scenario in which we have reliable cognitive faculties, he concludes that if naturalism were true then the reliability of our cognitive faculties would be unlikely. In responding to Plantinga, Fales (1996) contends that these scenarios are significantly less probable than the scenario in which our cognitive faculties are reliable.

Fales deals with scenarios (1), (2), and (4) using one central argument. He notes that scenarios (1) and (2) suggest our cognitive faculties are adaptively irrelevant and scenario (4) suggests they are maladaptive. Fales argues that the cognitive faculties we possess are biologically expensive. Their biological expense is judged here in terms of the complexity of the genetic coding required for them and in terms of the energy needed for their growth and maintenance. Since, according to neoDarwinism, such biological expense is only likely to persist for the sake of adaptive traits, scenarios (1), (2), and (4) are, Fales argues, very unlikely.

Recall that according to scenario (3) beliefs would play a role in causing behavior but only in a way that is sensitive to their syntax, not their semantics. Thus, in this scenario it would also be the case that the truth or falsity of our beliefs would be adaptively irrelevant. From this point on and for the sake of clarity, I will refer to this scenario as "The Syntactic Control Scenario." In reply to this Fales argues as follows:

> [A]n entirely reasonable view, from a naturalistic perspective, is that mental representations get their content in virtue of being caused in the right way by items in the environment; and that this is a *conceptual* truth. Thus if a mental representation is caused in the right way by heat, then it is a representation of heat; and if it is not so caused, then it is not a representation of heat. So long as representations are causally linked to the world via the syntactic structures in the brain to which they correspond, this will guarantee that syntax maps onto semantics in a generally truth-preserving way . . . from a naturalistic perspective, the probability of (3) [or The Syntactic Control Scenario], while harder to assess, may well be no higher than that of (1), (2), or (4). (Fales 1996, 442)

Fales's point here seems somewhat obscure and one cannot help but wish that he had said more on this issue. But, regardless, the point seems to be that our mental representations, our beliefs, get their content by being caused by items in the environment. When items cause mental representations to occur in the right way the mental representations give an accurate portrayal of the environment. Thus, "so long as representations are causally linked to the world via the syntactic structures in the brain to which they correspond, this will guarantee that syntax maps onto semantics in a generally truth preserving way."

Even having paraphrased Fales's point in this way one cannot help but think "Yes, when items in the environment cause mental representations in the *right way* you get an accurate picture of the environment, but why from the naturalistic perspective should we expect items in the environment to cause representations in this 'right way'? After all, if adaptive beliefs and behavior are what counts, might it not be just as likely that items in the environment cause beliefs (representations) in the wrong way but which are nonetheless adaptive?" I will return to this issue later. For now let us consider Fales's reply to scenario (5).

Scenario (5) shows us how "evolution might produce organisms in which false belief leads to *adaptive* action" (Fales 1996, 430). From this point on I will refer to this as "The False Adaptive Beliefs Scenario." In reply to this Fales argues as follows:

Plantinga's examples, like my Freddy cases (see pp. 120–21), work only because the beliefs which supply the immediate doxastic input to Freddy's practical syllogism are perceptual—that is, non-inferential— beliefs, or simple inductive generalizations. That makes it easy to imagine a cognitive mechanism that takes input information, systematically reverses truth-value, and thereby produces *systematically* false beliefs. But what happens when deductive inference comes into play? *True* premises guarantee true conclusions: so a system that relies consistently upon true inputs to guide inference and action can employ general rules and hope to get things (i.e., action) right. But when deductive argument employs false premises, the truth-value of the conclusion is *random*. Thus there *cannot* be any set of *general* algorithms which get a creature to use the conclusions of such arguments in a way that reliably promotes successful action. A cognitive system which is not *extremely* limited in the inferential procedures it employs must either give up all hope of successfully directing action or become unintelligibly complex and *ad hoc* in its procedures for connecting belief to action.

But this conclusion applies *even when the beliefs in play* are non-inferential or based only on enumerative induction. Freddy, who is carrying a heavy rock he falsely believes to be light and soft, nearly steps on a Puff Adder. Believing that being hit by something light and soft will be fatal for the adder (also false), he quickly drops the rock on it, and lives to see another day. So far so good for Freddy. Continuing on with his rock, Freddy encounters an angry warthog on the trail. Still believing the rock to be light as a feather, and believing (falsely) that dancing upon something light deters warthogs, Freddy proceeds to do a two-step on top of the rock directly in the path of the charging pig. The moral of this fable is plain: there are no effective algorithms connecting false belief to appropriate action, as there are when the input is true beliefs and the rules of inference employed are valid or inductively sound. Intelligent action is hard enough for a brain to manage; burdening it with ever-changing, completely arbitrary principles would make the task impossible. Freddy may survive the adder, but he will not live long. Nor will his genetic heritage. (Fales 1996, 442–43)

Given the prevalence of deductive and inductive inference in the reasoning that guides our behavior, and given that false beliefs fed into this reasoning would generate random resultant beliefs that could be either true or false, and given that these false outputs can be hazardous in so many ways, scenario (5), The False Adaptive Beliefs Scenario, strikes Fales as very unlikely.

For the reasons just discussed, Fales believes that Plantinga's five scenarios are not equiprobable alongside the scenarios in which our cognitive faculties are reliable. Consequently, Fales concludes that Plantinga's case against NNE is weak.

PLANTINGA'S REPLY TO FALES

In a recent book, *Naturalism Defeated?* (2002), Plantinga provides replies to various critics of his epistemological views. In doing so he provides a fairly detailed response to Fales's arguments. In what follows I will provide a brief review of the central points he makes in reply to Fales's defense of NNE.

Plantinga essentially gives no reply to Fales' critique of scenarios (1), (2), and (4). He writes:

Fales rejects [scenarios 1, 2, and 4] on the grounds that "The neural systems by means of which organisms generate and manage their beliefs are biologically expensive". I don't know whether that is a good reason for rejecting them, but let's not quibble: let's concede that these three are all unlikely on N&E, unlikely enough so that we can ignore them for present purposes. (Plantinga 2002, 262)

"N&E" refers to ontological naturalism combined with the view that human beings and their cognitive faculties are the products of evolution by natural selection. So Plantinga is willing to concede to Fales that even if ontological naturalism and the evolutionary account of our origins is correct, scenarios (1), (2), and (4) are unlikely.

In contrast Plantinga does criticize Fales's treatment of scenarios (3) and (5), the Syntactic Control and the False Adaptive Beliefs Scenarios. Recall that in reply to the Syntactic Control Scenario Fales argues that many naturalists reasonably believe mental representations get their semantic content by being caused in the right way by items in the environment. Plantinga's reply to this point is akin to the problem I raised earlier in discussing Fales's treatment of this scenario. He says Fales's reply assumes that the following proposition expresses a conceptual necessity and goes on to challenge this assumption:

> Semantic content maps onto neurophysiological properties (syntax) just if the propositions that get somehow associated with neural structures, or perhaps adaptive neural structures, as their content are *true* propositions. (Plantinga 2002, 262)

Plantinga questions this assumption, by arguing that many beliefs—adaptive as well as maladaptive—are false and that consequently it is hard to see how this can be a conceptual truth. He concedes that semantic content maps onto neurophysiological (syntactic) properties but he doesn't see why the content that maps onto it must be true. He writes:

> Fales makes still another suggestion: ". . . if a mental representation is caused in the right way by heat, then it's a representation of heat; and if it is not so caused, then it's not a representation of heat." Now of course we are thinking about *beliefs*, so if this remark is apposite, Fales must be thinking of beliefs as among the representations. Perhaps there are representations of various kinds, but among them are beliefs. Well, suppose what he says is so: a mental representation is a representation of *x* just if it is caused in the right way (whatever that is) by *x*: why think the representation (belief) in question must be a true representation? Suppose a representation (a belief) is caused in me in the right way so that it is a representation of a tree: why suppose it must be a *true* representation of a tree?

Can't I have a false belief about a tree? Maybe the tree is a beech, but I think it's an elm: can't that happen? Why does Fales overlook this question? (Plantinga 2002, 263)

At best Plantinga finds Fales's critique of the Syntactic Control Scenario to lack the requisite support.

Fales responds to the False Adaptive Beliefs Scenario by arguing that it looks like false beliefs could be adaptive if one just considers perceptual, noninferential beliefs. But he says that when you consider how false beliefs used in inductive and deductive reasoning can lead to all kinds of maladaptive false conclusions, it is terribly unlikely that a being with unreliable cognitive faculties could be well adapted.

Plantinga looks at this point at a challenge for him to explain further how the possesion of unreliable faculties could be adaptive. To meet this challenge he presents us with the following scenario:

> Suppose naturalism is true and in fact there is no such person as God. Now several naturalists (E.O. Wilson and Michael Ruse, for example) have argued that belief in God, while false, is nonetheless adaptive. So suppose a tribe of cognitively gifted creatures believe that everything (except God Himself) has been created by God; they therefore think everything is a *creature*, i.e., something created by God. Suppose further that their only way of referring to the various things in their environment is by way of such definite descriptions as 'the tree creature before me' or 'the tiger creature approaching me.' Suppose still further that all their beliefs are properly expressed by singular sentences whose subjects are definite descriptions expressing properties that entail the property of creaturehood—such sentences as 'The tiger creature approaching me is dangerous' or 'The tree creature before me is full of apple creatures'. Suppose, finally, that their definite descriptions work the way Bertrand Russell thought definite descriptions work: 'The tallest man in Boston is wise', for example, abbreviates "There is exactly one tallest man in Boston, and it is wise'. Then from the naturalist perspective all their beliefs are false. Yet these can still be adaptive: all they have to do is ascribe the right properties to the right 'creatures'. (Plantinga 2002, 260)

In this way Plantinga thinks he has described a way in which our cognitive faculties could be unreliable but very adaptive. Thus, he thinks he has answered Fales's challenge.

With regard to the view that naturalism implies the unreliability of our cognitive faculties Plantinga thinks that even if he were wrong about scenarios (1), (2), and (4), the case made by the Syntactic Controls and False Adaptive Beliefs Scenarios is strong enough to support this thesis. As we have seen, he defends these against Fales's criticisms, so he thinks his case against naturalism or NNE is still strong.

<h2 style="text-align:center">REFLECTIONS ON PLANTINGA'S DEFENSE</h2>

The False Adaptive Beliefs Scenario tells us that if we are not God's creatures and are simply products of natural selection then it could well be that we have unreliable cognitive faculties leading us to all manner of false beliefs which are nonetheless adaptive. Fales argues that there is no way having many false beliefs could be adaptive and challenges Plantinga to explain how this could be so. Plantinga accepts this challenge and has us suppose that there is no God and that there is a culture which thinks there is and the people of which always refer to the things of this world as creations of God. These people would have tons of false beliefs which are nonetheless adaptive.

One possible way of responding to this might employ the concept of partial truth. Consider the situation where God does not exist and the statement "That tiger creature is dangerous". When uttered by a woman who sees a tiger giving her a fierce and hungry look this statement is partly true. It is true that it's a tiger; it's true that it's dangerous; but it's false that it's a creation of God. In addition the true aspects of this belief are adaptive. Fales objects to the idea that beliefs that are "wildly wrong" can be adaptive. It is the case in which the woman believes such a tiger is a friendly, playful puppy that troubles Fales. How can *this* be adaptive? It cannot, and this is why he objects to The False Adaptive Beliefs Scenario as any kind of evidence for the naturalistic unreliability thesis.

In Fales's defense it could be argued that the religious people Plantinga describes formulate all kinds of partial truths that are quite adaptive and thus they do not consistently form "wildly wrong" beliefs. Thus, one could easily view their case as consistent with the view that from the evolutionary naturalistic perspective reliable cognitive faculties are likely to exist in human beings because of their adaptive value.

In the end, however, it seems that this strategy which appeals to partial truth will not suffice. On Plantinga's behalf, it could be argued that it is not good enough to argue that "wildly mistaken" beliefs cannot be adaptive. His point is that if we are not products of God's intelligent design but are simply the products of the blind forces of natural selection then it is unlikely that our cognitive capacities are reliable, because according to the theory of natural selection it is adaptive beliefs that count, not true beliefs. The examples Plantinga presents in which, for instance, there is no God but people look at all things as being creatures of God show how we can have cognitive faculties with many false beliefs and yet these faculties would still function adaptively. He could concede that the cognitive faculties considered in these examples would produce many partial truths. But the problem is that with all these partial truths come a hell of a lot of false beliefs, and the number of false beliefs produced would clearly be sufficient for concluding that the cognitive faculties considered in these cases are unreliable. Thus, he could still reasonably maintain that according to the theory of natural selection it is unlikely that we have reliable cognitive faculties, so that NNE does give way to skepticism.

In reply it could be argued, contra Plantinga, that there is enough reliability preserved among these partial truths for NNE to avoid skepticism. But I do not see how this approach could work. So what are we to make of Plantinga's argument at this point? I think he shows quite convincingly that we could get on quite well in the world with many false beliefs. At the same time, though, we have to get many things right to make our way in the world. Lacking the capacity to distinguish reliably between dangerous situations and safe ones, for instance, cannot be adaptive. Clearly, reliability of our faculties in at least some contexts is needed. The problem here is clarifying just what these contexts are and figuring out what significance reliability in these contexts might have for the reliability of our cognitive faculties in general.

Reliability will be important in the contexts of recognizing danger, finding food, finding mates, meeting the needs of children, as well as other related sorts of things. Additionally, the reliability of one's capacities in discerning these things will have important implications for the reliability of our cognitive capacities in general. When you look at things from the evolutionary biological perspective, it is quite reasonable to think that early humans or our proto-human ancestors were primarily concerned with the kinds of fundamental issues referred to above—avoiding danger, finding food and water, and so forth. These issues would have been the central focus of their thought. Consequently, very early on in the evolutionary history of humans or our proto-human ancestors, having reliable cognitive capacities was important, because the pressing issues of the day arose in those contexts where accuracy counts. Additionally, it seems doubtful that such humans or proto-humans would have any beliefs at all about whether things were creatures of God. Beliefs were probably more along the lines of "That's dangerous," "That's food," or "That's a possible mate." Getting these things right is important and referring to things as "this" and "that" does not commit one to any position on whether they are creatures of God. The identification of something as a creature of God requires a mode of thought that is too sophisticated to be reasonably attributed to the primitive sorts of ancestors to which I am referring here. For these reasons I think it reasonable to conclude that in our proto-human and early human ancestors having reliable cognitive capacities was very adaptive and lacking them was maladaptive. Thus, from the evolutionary biological perspective it is reasonable to conclude that we have inherited these reliable cognitive capacities.

In reply to this Plantinga might argue that even though reliable cognitive capacities were needed by our evolutionary ancestors, these reliable capacities were designed to serve them well for survival and reproductive success in their own environments. The point could be made that we live in rather different environments today, where, for instance, food production, presentation, and delivery, has changed radically. It might be argued that the processes which were reliable in the environment of our ancestors are not reliable today given our changed environment.

However, this kind of reply is answerable. While it is true that our environment has changed and, for instance, we have to be able to distinguish between a package of candy and a package of pills or poison in order to survive, whereas our ancestors didn't, it is also true that like our ancestors we must be able to reliably distinguish between food and not-food, mate and not-mate, and so on. Some learning will be needed to do this well in our environment, just as some learning was probably needed for this by our ancestors in their environments, but it also seems very likely from an evolutionary biological point of view that the more fundamental conceptual capacities that enable this kind of learning, resulting in the development of reliable capacities for drawing these distinctions, have been inherited from our evolutionary ancestors. Thus, despite the change in the evolutionary conditions faced by our distant human or proto-human ancestors, it is likely that they would have had some of the same basic conceptual capacities that we have and which enabled them and enable us to reliably distinguish between food and not-food or mate and not-mate.

A related but different objection could be made concerning the fact that today we have theoretical knowledge in such diverse fields as the natural sciences, mathematics, and history. Plantinga might argue that while we do have knowledge in these subjects, they involve thinking about things for which our cognitive capacities were not originally adapted. Thus, even if I am right that at some point in early human or proto-human history reliable cognitive capacities were required, enabling the detection of food and mates and the avoidance of danger, there is no reason to think that the reliable capacities needed for advanced mathematical or scientific understanding were produced through the processes of natural selection. For there is much scientific, mathematical, and historical knowledge that has little value for survival or reproductive success.

This kind of reply won't work either, for it is more reasonable to look at the cognitive labor employed in science and math as an extension of reliable cognitive capacities into new domains than the ones in which they were originally put to use. The most fundamental inductive and deductive reasoning principles that helped our ancestors acquire vital true beliefs in our distant evolutionary past are used today in science and math but have been refined and extended into more elaborate systems of thought. These are logical extensions upon basic principles of rationality that were already present in our ancestors, enabling them to accurately represent and infer the nature of reality so as to survive and reproduce. Since the methods of contemporary science and math are logical extensions of what we have good reason to believe were originally basic principles of reason employed by the reliable cognitive systems of our ancestors, it is reasonable for the evolutionary naturalist to regard our cognitive capacities as reliable producers of true beliefs even in the context of contemporary science and math.[5]

Perhaps, at this point Plantinga would concede that there is some good reason to think evolution alone, without the guidance of God's direction, could explain the existence of our cognitive faculties, and perhaps he would even concede that a certain degree of reliability might be required of these faculties to enable reproductive success. But he might also contend that due to what I shall call "the problem of false positives" we can never really be warranted in claims about the reliability of our faculties. Thus, he might say that NNE still results in skepticism.

The problem of false positives might be expressed in terms of the following example: imagine a species of bird the individual members of which believe danger is present whenever they hear noises other than bird songs. As a consequence of this they fly away from where they are whenever they hear noises other than bird songs. Now not all noises indicate danger. So, these birds will form many false beliefs and act on them, flying away from what they perceive as danger. But these birds can get on quite well with all of these false beliefs as long as they still get enough moments of quiet to eat and mate. Also, since they will flee when there *is* danger, the belief that noise indicates danger will serve adaptive purposes.

This example is intended to show how cognitive faculties which frequently produce such false positives and are, consequently, unreliable, may persist within a species and even serve adaptive ends. Thus, Plantinga might argue that if one accepts NNE then one could have no ground for believing in the reliability of one's faculties and no ground for thinking one knows anything.

---

[5] For an excellent summary of the view that the reasoning used in contemporary science and mathematics is an inherited adaptation from our protohuman ancestors, see Ruse 1998. See also Quine's essay, "Natural Kinds," in *Ontological Relativity and Other Essays* (1969), 114–138. The relevant empirical research concerning cross-cultural similarities in systems of logic and mathematics can be found in Staal 1967 and Bochenski 1961. For relevant empirical findings concerning the innate mathematical and reasoning abilities of children, see Gelman 1980; Gelman and Gallistel 1978; Marks 1969; and Seligman 1972. And for empirical data on the mathematical and reasoning abilities of chimpanzees, see King and Fobes 1982; Premack 1976; Gillan, Premack, and Woodruff 1981; and Gillan 1981.

But in reply I would contend that we do know things and we have grounds for thinking we do. Thus, if we are the products of the blind forces of natural selection then there must be some plausible Darwinian explanation for why we have cognitive capacities which are sufficiently reliable for the possession of knowledge. Is there one? Of course, there is! Thus, I am inclined to think the problem of false positives poses no serious threat to my case.

While it is true that the members of some species may get on quite well while forming many false beliefs and acting on them, as the birds mentioned above do, this does not mean that a human being would do well if he functioned like this. Since we have knowledge, our cognitive capacities must be reliable producers of true belief. Plantinga and I agree about this. But, unlike Plantinga, I do not view the acceptance of NNE as a defeater for my claim to knowledge, because as noted above there are perfectly plausible Darwinian explanations for the reliability of such capacities. I have already suggested how such an explanation might proceed. For a more developed account one should see Michael Ruse's *Taking Darwin Seriously*.

If it is demanded that the problem of false positives be answered, then I would respond as follows: since we know things now, our cognitive capacities must be reliable. Cognitive capacities which produce many false positives, as the birds' in our example do, would not be reliable. So, we must not have those kinds of cognitive capacities. That is, our cognitive capacities should not produce false positives in this way. What is the Darwinian explanation for this? Well, suppose that at some point in human or proto-human history our ancestors acted as the birds do, believing danger was present whenever there was noise and running away. Such individuals could get on quite well like this as long as they found enough quiet time for eating and mating. But now let's suppose that random mutation produces some human beings or proto-humans, that have a more reliable method for discerning danger, a method that does not produce so many false positives. Certainly, this is likely to provide them with adaptive advantages. While their competitors are running away in terror due to mistaken beliefs about the dangers of a situation, these humans or proto-humans will carry on getting more food, better shelter, and perhaps more or better mates—all of which would favor them in reproductive success. Thus, given that the elimination of such false positives would serve adaptive ends and given that random mutations do occur, there *is* a plausible Darwinian explanation for the reliability of our cognitive capacities. For all of these reasons, then, I contend that the problem of false positives poses no threat to my argument.

The points I have just made in discussing the False Adaptive Beliefs Scenario should be carried over into a discussion of the Syntactic Control Scenario. I have just argued that the kinds of issues our distant human or protohuman ancestors faced were the kinds that required true beliefs. Thus, those of our ancestors with unreliable cognitive capacities would not have done well at surviving and reproducing. So, in all likelihood we are the ancestors of beings who had reliable cognitive capacities, so that we have probably inherited such capacities ourselves.

In the Syntactic Control Scenario Plantinga argues that even though beliefs play a role in causing human behavior they may do so only through their syntax, not their semantics. "Syntax" here is taken to refer to the neurological processes that give rise to the semantic content, the representations of what one is actually thinking about. If syntax alone is the only part of our beliefs involved in causing behavior, then, according to Plantinga, the truth of our beliefs would be adaptively irrelevant, meaning that from the naturalistic perspective there would be no reason to think our cognitive faculties are reliable.

But, as I have just argued, the contexts in which our human or proto-human ancestors found themselves were the kinds of contexts in which having true beliefs was fundamentally important. Those proto-humans who for example mistakenly believed poisonous snakes were cuddly, friendly pets were killed off! Fales says that when mental representations are caused in "the right way" by the environment they will generally be true. While his comments are somewhat vague here (and Plantinga picks up on this), I think "the right way" here is intended to mean the adaptive way. Adaptive beliefs are the ones that foster survival and reproductive success. Those among our early human and proto-human ancestors who were better adapted to their environments survived and reproduced more successfully. But if so, those creatures most likely *formed beliefs* in "the right way," that is, adaptively, and given the nature of the belief systems they were probably operating with— "This is food", "That is a mate", "This is dangerous"—it is extraordinarily difficult to see how anything but true semantic content could have been correlated with their adaptively successful syntactical structures. How could thinking "Trees are mates" or "Rattlesnakes are safe" translate into behaviors that are consistently reproductively successful? It seems terribly unlikely, and so, for these reasons, it is reasonable to conclude that our early human or proto-human ancestors did possess reliable cognitive capacities, and because of this it is reasonable to think that our cognitive capacities are reliable too.

In reply Plantinga might say, "Of course it's hard to see how 'Rattlesnakes are dangerous' could be false. That is because it is associated with adaptive behaviors. But if it's the syntactic component of this belief which governs the behavior and the semantic content is uninvolved, then there really is no reason for us to think it is true even though it is adaptive." In response I want to say, "But look around you and you will see how common it is for people with false beliefs to be hurt by these beliefs! Doesn't this give us grounds for thinking that, whatever the syntactic components of adaptive beliefs and maladaptive beliefs, the former are generally true and the latter are generally false?"

Plantinga might respond that I am supposing that whatever has been syntactically coded for successful behavior will be true and whatever is coded for unsuccessful behavior will be false, and this begs the question against his argument. According to Plantinga, as strange as it may seem, if naturalism is true and if syntax alone might control our behavior, there is then no reason to think our cognitive faculties are reliable. All the beliefs we typically accept as being true and which help us navigate our way through life are such that we cannot ever really know them to be true. Hence, Plantinga would conclude that NNE leads to skepticism.

At this point it looks as though Plantinga has the defenders of naturalism over a fence. But in the end I think that after a re-examination of what his position and theirs amount to and a consideration of the explanatory weakness of his and the strength of theirs, we will see that there really is more reason to accept the naturalistic perspective. Plantinga's position is that if naturalism is true then, when I perceive a rattlesnake before me and I believe there is one before me, I have no more reason to think my belief is true than to think it is false. In contrast, I have contended that our ancestors must have had cognitive faculties that were reliable pro-

ducers of true beliefs in order for them to have survived and reproduced, giving rise to us. Thus, on my view and other things being
equal, we have good reason to think our faculties are reliable and
good reason to think the belief formed in this scenario is true.

The question, then, becomes which of these views is more reasonable. I think the latter is more reasonable because it is simply
too difficult to see how unreliable capacities could be beneficial.
Plantinga says unreliable faculties could be beneficial if they produced false beliefs that had adaptive syntactical structures. But this
is too sketchy. How exactly would this work? In contrast, it is fairly
easy to make sense of how true beliefs are for the most part adaptive. And, yes, any explanation of how true beliefs are for the most
part adaptive is likely to assume that semantic content plays a role
in our behavior, *but given the explanatory power we gain by assuming this*, doing so is justified.

As a consequence of the preceding considerations, we have reason to reject Plantinga's scenario (3), the Syntactic Control
Scenario, as giving us any reason to doubt the reliability of our
cognitive faculties. I have also argued that Fales's attack on scenario (5), the False Adaptive Beliefs Scenario, can be given an adequate defense, and, as noted earlier, Plantinga himself does not
challenge Fales's attacks on scenarios (1), (2), and (4). Thus, all
things considered, Plantinga's critique of NNE fails.

Conclusion

In this chapter I have tried to do two things. First, I wanted to
explore further the possible religious implications of evolutionary
biology. Second, I wanted to look at some of the possible epistemological implications of evolutionary biology. Alvin Plantinga
uses evolutionary biology to argue that if there is no intelligent,
benevolent designer of the universe and we are simply the products of the blind forces of natural selection, then we could not
really know anything. In this way he uses evolutionary biology
against a naturalistic ontology and in support of theism. The kind
of argument he makes here opens the door to a consideration of
the epistemological implications of evolutionary biology, and
through a consideration of Plantinga's work as well as that of
some of his critics we were able to explore some of these epistemological issues.

Besides having provided a clear and accurate account of the views of Plantinga, Ruse, and Fales, I hope to have established several points in this chapter. First, I hope to have shown that Ruse's internal realist reply to Plantinga is problematic in various respects. Second, by defending the critical reply of Fales to Plantinga I hope to have shown that there are good replies to the latter's argument that can be made from the perspective of realism. It is my strong sense that evolutionary biology has no significant implications for the rationality of faith. In this and the previous chapter I have given critical consideration to the strongest arguments that it does have significant implications for this and in each case I have argued that these arguments fail in significant respects. Thus, the arguments of these two chapters to some extent support my views on evolution and religion.

7

Psychological Egoism and Evolutionary Biology

In this chapter and the next I want to explore some of the ways in which evolutionary biology has been used to approach some questions about the human condition which have traditionally been dealt with by philosophers. The two issues that I will address are psychological egoism and freedom of the will. In this chapter I will take up the topic of psychological egoism. In the next I will discuss freedom of the will.

Psychological egoism is the view that we are all fundamentally selfish, that our ultimate motive in whatever we do is to promote our own self-interest. In this chapter I will explore the question of whether this theory is true by examining the works of various contemporary philosophers who are critical of traditional philosophical attempts at refuting this theory and who think that evolutionary biology can play a significant role in refuting it. The discussion will focus primarily upon the truth of psychological hedonism, since this is regarded as the version of psychological egoism that is the most difficult to refute.

Psychological hedonism is the view that avoiding our own pain and increasing our own pleasure are the only ultimate motives people have. According to this view, every act a person performs is motivated by one or both of these self-interested goals. This view denies the existence of genuine altruism, doing things for others out of an ultimate desire for their welfare or happiness. The truth of psychological hedonism has been debated by philosophers for ages.

In their recent, widely read, and critically acclaimed book, *Unto Others: The Evolution and Psychology of Unselfish Behavior*, Elliott

Sober and David Sloan Wilson argue that traditional philosophical arguments against this view do not work and then go on to give their own evolutionary biological argument against the view. Most of the reviews and discussions of their book have not examined in any detail their argument against psychological hedonism. Instead, most published reactions to the book have focused on their defense of the group selection theory, an issue which is primarily of concern to biological theorists.

In what follows I will explain and critically examine Sober and Wilson's evolutionary biological argument, concluding that in its current form their argument is too weak to support the conclusion that psychological hedonism is most likely false. Then I will go on to argue that this should give us no reason to think that psychological hedonism is true, because, despite recent criticisms of it, Robert Nozick's experience machine argument (1974) is still a good philosophical argument against psychological hedonism. In the second half of the chapter I will explain Nozick's argument and defend it against the criticisms of Sober and Wilson as well as the more recent criticisms of Matthew Silverstein.

Sober and Wilson's Argument

Sober and Wilson define psychological hedonism as the view that "attaining pleasure and avoiding pain are the only ultimate concerns that people have" (Sober and Wilson 1998, 296). They say that this view is a variety of psychological egoism and that according to psychological hedonism we are all motivational hedonists. Motivational hedonism (MH) says that the ultimate motive for any act, X, is the belief that X will minimize the agent's pain and maximize his pleasure. In distinguishing psychological hedonism from psychological egoism they write:

> Psychological egoism . . . is more liberal than hedonism. Hedonists are egoists, but not all egoists are hedonists. Egoists may care ultimately about attaining pleasure and avoiding pain, but they also may have ultimate desires that embrace the world outside their own minds. Egoists, for example, may have their own survival as an end in itself; they also may have the irreducible desire to accumulate wealth or scale Mount Everest. (Sober and Wilson 1998, 296)

Sober and Wilson also discuss motivational pluralism (MP), which holds that "the ultimate desires that people have include both egoistic and altruistic motives. People may want to avoid pain as an end in itself, and they also may have their own survival as an ultimate goal, but, in addition, they sometimes care irreducibly about the welfare of others" (Sober and Wilson 1998, 296–97). According to MP, there are some acts that we perform simply because we believe they will do the best job of improving the welfare of someone else and not because they will make us feel better. MP says that some of our ultimate motives are altruistic. Thus it is incompatible with motivational hedonism (MH) and psychological egoism.

Sober and Wilson argue that psychological hedonism is probably false. In doing so they also take themselves to be refuting psychological egoism, since they regard psychological hedonism as the version of egoism that is hardest to refute. In making their case they provide an evolutionary biological argument for this conclusion. The main frame of this argument can be represented as follows:

1. Both MP and MH can generate parental care behavior.

2. If two motivational mechanisms are both capable of generating a certain type of behavior, it remains possible that one of them is more likely to have evolved than the other.

3. MP is more likely to have evolved than MH.

So, 4. it is more likely that we are motivational pluralists than that we are motivational hedonists.

If MP is true then we are sometimes moved to help others, such as our children, out of an irreducible concern for their own well being. Thus if MP is true then psychological hedonism/egoism is false. Consequently, if it were sound, the above argument would show that psychological hedonism/egoism is probably false.

Propositions 1–4 above only express the main frame of their argument. To fully understand the argument we will have to consider the support Sober and Wilson provide for the premises. The bulk of their argument involves developing the case for the third premise. In a moment I will turn to their case for it, but first I will make just a few very brief remarks about the first and second premises.

The second premise is fairly straightforward and requires neither justification nor defense. The first premise is true for the following reasons. Parental care behavior is behavior that aims at helping one's own children. Since a parent can provide this help because it makes the parent happier to do so, it can be generated by MH. Since such parental care can also be provided simply because it is believed by the agent that the care will help the child, MP can generate the behavior as well. So, the first premise certainly seems to be true as well.

So what of the third premise? Why is it true? Sober and Wilson regard MP and MH as mechanisms that trigger behavior. They also contend that the way to determine which of two competing mechanisms is more likely to have evolved requires an appeal to the criteria of *reliability*, *availability*, and *efficiency*. They think that by appealing to these criteria there is good reason to think that MP is more likely to have evolved in humans than MH.

In making their case they focus on parental care behavior, which is highly adaptive, meaning that it greatly increases the chances that one's genes will be passed on to future generations. They believe that when mechanisms which trigger an adaptive behavior, such as parental care behavior, are equally available to and energy efficient for an organism, the mechanism (MP or MH) which more reliably produces the adaptive behavior is more likely to have evolved. They contend that MP and MH are roughly equivalent with respect to availability and energy efficiency, but they also say that MP is significantly more reliable at producing parental care behavior. Thus they conclude that MP is more likely to have evolved than MH. And this in turn would mean that psychological hedonism/egoism is probably false.

Now to understand further their argument we need to: 1) look at why they think MP more reliably produces parental care behavior and 2) look at why they think MP and MH are roughly equivalent with respect to their availability and efficiency. MP more reliably produces parental care behavior because someone who only helps his children when it furthers his own interests, as would the MH, is liable to face situations where helping his children is not in his interest. In contrast the MP who is motivated to help his children out of a basic interest in their welfare, an interest not grounded on the thought that helping his children helps himself, may still be led to help his children even when he thinks it is not in his interest to do so. In this way MP is the more reliable mechanism for producing parental care behavior.

Concerning the equal availability of MP and MH, Sober and Wilson state:

> [W]e think it is implausible to reject the hypothesis of motivational pluralism as an explanation of parental care by claiming that pluralism was not available ancestrally. There is every reason to think that pluralism *was* available; it requires the same basic equipment that hedonism demands. A hedonist must formulate beliefs about whether its children are doing well. It must form the ultimate desire to attain pleasure and avoid pain. And the organism must construct the instrumental desire that its children do well. If this is what it takes for a hedonistic organism to provide parental care, what does it take for a pluralistic organism to produce the same behavior? A pluralistic parent also must form beliefs about whether its children are doing well. In addition, the pluralist must form the ultimate desire that its children do well. We suggest that constructing this *ultimate desire* involves no great innovation, if the organism is already capable of *believing* that its children are doing well or ill. If the propositions available as objects of belief also are available as objects of desire . . . then pluralism will be possible for an organism who is capable of forming beliefs about the welfare of her children. Whereas hedonism requires the organism to form the *instrumental* desire that her children do well, pluralism simply has the organism register this same desire as an end in itself. We conclude that pluralism was probably available ancestrally, if hedonism was. (Sober and Wilson 1998, 321–22)

What Sober and Wilson are getting at here is that according to MH the following three processes must occur for parents to help their children: 1) the parent must form a belief about the well-being of his child; 2) the parent must form the ultimate desire to attain pleasure and avoid pain; and 3) the parent must form the instrumental desire that his child do well. In contrast they contend that according to MP only two steps are needed to trigger a parent into helping his child: 1) the parent must form a belief about the well-being of his child; and 2) the parent must form the ultimate desire that his child do well. They also contend that with respect to the motivational pluralist account of helping behavior, forming the ultimate desire that his child do well "involves no great innovation", since the organism is already capable of believing that its children are doing well or ill. This last point about how forming the ultimate desire to help "involves no great innovation" is significant. In making this point they refer the reader back to points they make in an earlier part of the book. I will return to this point later, but for now let us turn to their case for equal efficiency.

Sober and Wilson contend that MP is just as energy efficient for an organism as is MH. For MP "does not require the organism to build and maintain any new device. Mechanisms for representing beliefs and desires are required by both hypotheses, both require that the organism be able to experience pleasure and pain, and both require the organism to have both ultimate and instrumental desires" (322). They acknowledge that the motivational pluralist will need to form the ultimate desire that its children do well as well as the desire that he himself do well, but they say that it is hard to see why forming this extra ultimate desire should "engender any massive energetic burden. We doubt that people who have more *beliefs* need more calories than people who are less opinionated; the same point applies to *ultimate desires*" (322).

Before concluding their case for equal efficiency they go on to consider a possible objection. They note that MP allows for situations of conflict between ultimate desires. Sometimes my ultimate desire for my own happiness might conflict with my ultimate desire for my child's happiness. In these situations I need some way of adjudicating between these desires. MH would not need an adjudicating mechanism, since it presents us with but one ultimate desire, our own happiness. In this way it could be argued that MH really is more energy efficient, since it does not require the construction of any adjudicating mechanism.

In reply to this they argue that there are different types of pleasures and pains and that an organism can gain one pleasure at the cost of experiencing a very different type of pain. For instance, an organism might be hungry at the same time that its child is hungry, and there might be only enough food for one of them. If the organism feeds its child it will endure the pain of hunger. If the organism feeds itself it will endure the pain of watching its child go hungry. In situations like this even the MH will need some adjudicating mechanism for deciding which of these two different pains to endure. Since, then, an adjudicating mechanism will be needed for either MH or MP, it follows that MP is not less efficient than MH (323).

To sum up, then, Sober and Wilson argue that MP is more likely to have evolved in us than MH, because MP more reliably produces parental care behavior, while being equally available and equally efficient. And since MP would spur us sometimes to help our children for their own sakes and not simply as a means to our own pleasure, this means that psychological hedonism/egoism is probably false.

More on the Case for Equal Availability

As noted above, Sober and Wilson argue that forming the ultimate desire to help one's child "involves no great innovation," since the organism is already capable of believing that its children are doing well or ill. They also note that earlier parts of the book support this contention. In what follows I want to discuss these earlier parts of the book, but first I should note that this is a key element in their argument against psychological hedonism/egoism.

Presumably we are all motivated to act out of our self-interest on many occasions. MH says that we always act out of self-interest. In contrast MP says that on at least some occasions we act altruistically. From the evolutionary biological perspective we are likely to have such an ultimate desire and to act on it only if the capacity to form this desire is available to us and only if forming and acting on such an ultimate desire is roughly equivalent in efficiency to forming and acting on self-interested desires. Sober and Wilson argue that the capacity to form the ultimate desire to help our children is available to us because we are capable of believing that our children are doing well or ill.

Now an important question here is why the capacity to formulate such beliefs entails a capacity to form such ultimate desires. To see why they think this one must refer back to certain points they make in their Chapter 6. There they state:

> There is a set of concepts that an organism uses to formulate its beliefs; there also is a set of concepts that an organism exploits in formulating its desires. We might view these sets of concepts as comprising a language out of which various representations that express propositions can be constructed. There is a vital reason why these two

sets of concepts should be the same. A common language should be accessible to the organism in formulating both its beliefs and its desires so that the organism can engage in means-end deliberation. Aristotle discusses the example of a man who wants a covering and believes that a cloak would make a good covering. This desire and belief together lead him to form the intention of obtaining a cloak. In this example, the concepts out of which the desire is constructed and the concepts that figure in the belief overlap. If desires and beliefs were built out of disjoint vocabularies, it is hard to see how they could work together in deliberation. If Jill wants X, but none of her beliefs tell her how to get X, how is she to figure out what she should do?

Psychologists in different sub fields have defended modularity theses (Fodor 1983; Barkow et al. 1992). Rather than postulate an all-purpose mechanism that governs all mental activity, many theorists have defended the idea that there are separate modules for language acquisition, for face recognition, and for other tasks. What we are now suggesting, however, is that belief and desire formation are not rigidly segregated from each other; a common vocabulary must provide the same (or roughly the same) conceptual resources to both the devices that construct beliefs and the devices that form desires. Although believing and desiring are separate activities, they do not exist in thoroughly isolated modules. (Sober and Wilson 1998, 210–11)

In this passage they argue that in order for our means-end deliberations to work the concepts used in the formation of beliefs and desires must be the same. But, as noted in the second part of the passage above, if the concepts used in forming beliefs and desires are the same then "believing and desiring do not exist in thoroughly isolated modules." They argue that since the modules responsible for belief formation and desire formation are not "thoroughly isolated" and since we can obviously form beliefs about the welfare of our children, it would involve "no great innovation" to form the ultimate desire to help our children. Thus, they conclude that "pluralism was probably available ancestrally, if hedonism was" (322).

Thoughts on Their Case for Equal Availability: Some Modularity Issues

The conclusion that Sober and Wilson draw in their case for equal availability does not follow logically from the premises. While it may well be that the concepts employed in belief and desire formation must be roughly the same in order for means-end reasoning to work, and while this means there cannot be "thorough isolation" between belief forming and desire forming modules in the sense that they must be able to share information, this does not imply anything about the probable ancestral availability of pluralism. It could well be that one module of the brain is needed for forming self-interested ultimate desires and another module is needed for forming altruistic ultimate desires. If our ancestors did not possess the module for forming altruistic ultimate desires, then, despite the fact that the concepts of belief and desire formation need to be similar and that, consequently, belief and desire forming modules cannot be thoroughly isolated, *it could still have been very unlikely that pluralism was available ancestrally.* To make their case for the equal availability of the pluralistic mechanism, they need to show that it is unlikely that a separate module is needed for forming altruistic ultimate desires.

They continue to overlook this point in making their case for equal efficiency. They write:

> [P]luralism does not require the organism to build and maintain any new device. Mechanisms for representing beliefs and desires are required by both hypotheses, both require the organism to have both ultimate and instrumental desires. What pluralism requires is that the device for representing the organism's ultimate desires encode an extra representation—namely, the desire that its children do well. Since hedonistic organisms already represent this propositional content as a belief and also as an instrumental desire, it is hard to see why placing that proposition in an organism's "ultimate desire box" should engender any massive energetic burden. We doubt that people who have more beliefs need more calories than people who are less opinionated; the same point applies to ultimate desires. (Sober and Wilson 1998, 322)

Clearly they are again assuming that the module that produces ultimate self-interested desires can also produce ultimate altruistic desires. But this really needs proof and should not be assumed.

As Sober and Wilson note, Jerry Fodor has provided an extensive defense of the modularity view. It might be that to strengthen their case they would have to provide some more extensive reply to the views of Fodor. Indeed I might be able to strengthen my critique by developing some of Fodor's points. But my objective here is simply to suggest, as stated above, that since it could well be that one module of the brain is needed for forming self-interested ultimate desires and another module is needed for forming altruistic ultimate desires, it could still have been very unlikely that pluralism was available ancestrally. See Fodor 1983.

Thoughts on Their Case for Equal Efficiency

Besides these problems concerning issues of modularity, there is reason to think Sober and Wilson's case for equal efficiency is weak. In arguing for the equal efficiency thesis they try to defend two points. First, MP "does not require the organism to build and maintain any new device" (322). Thus they argue that no extra energy is needed in building the kind of mind that acts as a motivational pluralist as opposed to a motivational hedonist. Second, they argue that the day to day lives of motivational pluralists requires no more energy than the day to day lives of motivational hedonists. They argue that the motivational pluralists will need to form ultimate desires that others do well as well as ultimate desires that they themselves do well. But, according to Sober and Wilson, forming extra desires does not require more calories. In additional support of the second point they also argue that since an adjudicating mechanism for solving conflicts of desire will be needed for both the motivational hedonist and the motivational pluralist, no extra energy will be needed to live as a motivational pluralist.

My comments in the previous section suggest that their defense of the first point is weak. They need to do more to show that building a motivational pluralist's mind is just as energy efficient, since this may involve creating a separate module for the construction of altruistic desires. Their second point about energy efficiency is problematic as well. If one keeps in mind that the majority of what we do is aimed at promoting our own well-being, then it is no longer so clear that MP is just as energy efficient as MH. Making decisions on pluralistic grounds will require a shift in procedure that is bound to raise questions and complications that a motivational hedonist is not likely to face. Thus if the motivational hedonist is sufficiently well-adapted, or meeting with sufficient reproductive success, it is hard to see why such a shift in thinking to a pluralistic mode should occur.

Additionally, children are motivated primarily by self-interest, and the work of Lawrence Kohlberg (1981) suggests that humans do not develop concern for the health and well-being of others until later in life. Consequently, looking at things from a developmental point of view, it is likely that if we are motivational pluralists this is the result of a transformation in our thought processes that occurs at some stage of normal human development. The significance of this is that the transformation to such other-regarding modes of thought may well involve a loss of some energy efficiency in the short-run, and there may be no definite efficiency gains in the long-run. These are possibilities that could use further examination by Sober and Wilson.

In the preceding comments I suggest that the shift from self-interested thinking to altruistic thinking may involve some loss of energy and/or present complications that would not arise if we always acted out of self-interest. But here the reader will want to know why this is so. After all, Sober and Wilson contend that acting exclusively out of self-interest presents its own complications, i.e. conflicts between types of pleasures and pains, which require an adjudicating mechanism. What problems would arise for the motivational pluralist that requires more energy to deal with than is needed by the motivational hedonist? Sober and Wilson argue that problems of conflict between the interests of others and oneself will need an adjudicating mechanism, but since we would need such an adjudicating mechanism even if we were motivational hedonists, there is no reason to think self vs. other conflicts present any threat to the equal efficiency thesis.

We all must have an adjudicating mechanism to help us sort through conflicts between different types of pleasures and pains we might experience. And, indeed, if we are motivational pluralists we will need a mechanism to adjudicate between conflicts of self-interest and the interests of others as well as between distinct others (such as daughter and son or cousin and daughter or neighbor and son). But there are two problems here. First, it is not at all clear that the same mechanism that allows us to adjudicate conflicts between our own pleasures and pains can also handle conflicts between self and others or conflicts between multiple others. Thus if there is such a separate adjudicating mechanism, it is likely some energy will have to be employed in the construction and maintenance of it. So before accepting the equal efficiency thesis we need some evidence that either the same mechanism can handle both types of conflict or no more energy will be needed to create, maintain, and use a separate adjudicating mechanism.

Second, even if it requires no more energy to have a mechanism that adjudicates conflicts between self and others as well as between different others, it is still not clear that the use of such a mechanism would be as efficient as handling all decision problems through one motivationally hedonistic mechanism in which all decisions are made in terms of self-interest. Several problems come to mind here.

First, if I am a motivational pluralist and, consequently, can be moved to act from an ultimate desire for the welfare of others, then this will raise questions about what will best serve their welfare. And presumably it will take some amount of energy to answer such questions. In reply it might be contended that this problem arises even for the motivational hedonist, since it is also not obvious what one's own welfare consists in. However, while my own welfare may not be obvious to me all the time, it still seems correct to say that more often than not it is more obvious to me than is the welfare of others.

Second, suppose that there is only one skateboard in my neighborhood and that my son, my daughter, my neighbor's kid, and I all want to play with it right now. If I am a motivational pluralist I will be faced not only by conflicts between the welfare of others and myself (Should I play with the skateboard or should my son?) but I will also have to be concerned with arbitrating between the competing concerns of different others (Should my son, my daughter, or my neighbor's kid get to play with the skateboard?). Sober and Wilson talk about how there would need to be a mechanism to adjudicate conflicts between self and others if we are motivational pluralists. They regard this as no problem with respect to efficiency, since you would need to adjudicate between conflicting pleasures and pains for yourself anyway. But if we keep in mind that there will be 'other versus other' conflicts that we must be concerned with as motivational pluralists, then the frequency of conflicts needing adjudication is likely to increase along with the complexity of the adjudication procedures.

Third, MP tells us that we can be motivated by altruistic ultimate desires as well as egoistic ultimate desires. MH tells us that we can only be motivated by egoistic ultimate desires. Most of the dilemmas that we face in life can be assessed through either an altruistic or an egoistic lens. Let's go back to the skateboard example. Suppose the kids are young and weak and I am older and stronger and have little conscience as well as a strong desire to use the skateboard. From the egoistic perspective I will have good reason to use the skateboard even though some of the children would enjoy it more. From the altruistic perspective I might have good reason to forgo my own pleasure to let a child use it who would enjoy it more than I. My point here is that motivationally hedonistic decision making can lead to different conclusions from altruistic decision making. Thus if we are motivational pluralists capable of acting either altruistically or egoistically we will occasionally need an additional meta-level adjudicating mechanism to help us decide between which of two lower level adjudicating mechanisms (altruistic or egoistic) to use. Such meta-level adjudicating mechanisms would not be needed if we were all motivational hedonists. The construction, maintenance, and use of such meta-level adjudicating mechanisms would make life as a motivational pluralist less energy efficient than life as a motivational hedonist.

For all of these reasons we have good grounds for doubting the strength of Sober and Wilson's case for the equal efficiency thesis. In the previous section I argued that we also have reason to doubt the strength of their case for the equal availability thesis. Thus, on the whole it is reasonable to conclude that their evolutionary biological argument against MH is weak.

Not to Despair: Nozick's Argument Reconsidered

So far I have argued that in its current form Sober and Wilson's evolutionary biological argument against psychological hedonism is not sufficiently strong to refute the view. Moreover, I disagree with their views about the merits of the traditional philosophical arguments against this view. I think the experience machine argument that Robert Nozick provides in his *Anarchy, State, and Utopia* gives us good reason to reject psychological hedonism. In what follows I will briefly explain Nozick's argument and then go on to defend it against Sober and Wilson's criticism, as well as the more recent criticism by Matthew Silverstein.

In Nozick's experience machine argument he has us imagine that there is a machine that we could plug into, have our brains connected to, that would be able to simulate any pleasurable experiences we want to have. In their book Sober and Wilson develop the idea quite well in the following way:

> Suppose you were offered the chance to plug into the experience machine for the rest of your life. The machine would be programmed to make you instantly forget that you had chosen to plug in and then would give you whatever sequence of experiences you would find maximally pleasurable and minimally painful. If your wishes involve the experiences associated with being the world leader who finally eradicates world hunger, that can be arranged. If you would like to have the experience of being the greatest athlete who ever lived, that too would be no problem. And if the happiness that comes from deep and sustained relationships of love and friendship is what you crave, the machine can provide that as well. The only catch, of course, is that your beliefs will be illusory. You will *think* you are a politician, a great athlete, or involved in a loving relationship, but your belief will be *false*. If you choose to plug into the experience machine, you will live your life strapped to a laboratory table with tubes and electrodes sticking into your body. You'll never *do* anything; however, the level of pleasure you'll experience, thanks to the machine, will be extraordinary. (Sober and Wilson 1998, 282)

The idea of the experience machine can be used to develop an argument against psychological hedonism. The argument goes like this:

1. Suppose there is an experience machine.

2. If everyone were offered a chance to plug into it, some people would choose not to.

3. Those who choose not to plug into the machine must have something besides their own pleasure as an ultimate motive, so that their own pleasure cannot be their only ultimate motive. For if their own pleasure were their only ultimate motive, they would have no reason to forgo a life plugged into the experience machine.

4. So, psychological hedonism is false.

Sober and Wilson's Objection Considered

After considering what they regard as some flawed hedonistic replies to this argument, Sober and Wilson go on to present what they think is the real problem with this argument. They write:

> Quite apart from the amount of pleasure and pain that accrues to subjects *after* they decide [whether to plug in or not], there is the level of pleasure and pain arising in the deliberation process itself. The hedonist can maintain that *deciding* to plug into the machine is so aversive that people almost always make the other choice. When people deliberate about the alternatives, they feel bad when they think of the life they'll lead if they plug into the machine; they feel much better when they consider the life they'll lead in the real world if they decline to plug in. The *idea* of life attached to the machine is painful even though such a life would be quite pleasurable; the *idea* of real life is pleasurable, even though real life often includes pain. (Sober and Wilson 1998, 285)

They go on to explain further why some people who consider plugging in will refuse to plug in. In describing such people they write:

> They realize that plugging in will mean abandoning the projects and attachments they hold dear; plugging into the machine resembles suicide in terms of the utter separation it effects with the real world. The difference is that suicide means an end to consciousness, whereas the experience machine delivers (literally) escapist pleasures. Hedonism is not betraying its own principles when it claims that many people would feel great contempt for the idea of plugging in and would regard the temptation to do so as loathsome. People who decline the chance to plug in are repelled by the idea of narcissistic escape and find pleasure in the idea of choosing a real life. (Sober and Wilson 1998, 285)

Now, contra Sober and Wilson, I believe hedonism is betraying its own principles when it claims many people would feel great contempt for the idea of plugging in. We need to consider why people are "repelled by the idea of narcissistic escape" and why they "find pleasure in the idea of choosing a real life." Why is this the case? It is only because people are moved by considerations other than their own pleasure. It is only because our own pleasure is not our ultimate motive that we can make sense of people's repulsion at the narcissistic escape offered by the experience machine. I agree with Sober and Wilson that people will not choose to plug in because they find the idea of giving up a real life unpleasant. But this explanation of their refusal is incomplete. To complete it one needs to consider why people find this unpleasant. And the best explanation refers to the fact that they value something other than their own pleasure, such as "real life." This non-hedonistic value serves as the ultimate motive for their refusal to plug in. Thus, I contend that Sober and Wilson have not shown why Nozick's experience machine argument is flawed

In defense of Sober and Wilson it could be argued here that my defense of Nozick rests upon reasoning very similar to that of Joseph Butler. Butler is one of the most famous critics of psychological hedonism, and Sober and Wilson criticize Butler's argument in an earlier section of their book. According to Sober and Wilson, Butler's argument, "Butler's stone," can be outlined as follows:

1. People sometimes experience pleasure.

2. When people experience pleasure, this is because they had a desire for some external thing, and that desire was satisfied.

---

3. So, hedonism is false. (Sober and Wilson 1998, 278)

The conclusion that hedonism is false rests upon the assumption that according to hedonism the only thing we desire is our own pleasure. Sober and Wilson respond to this argument by denying the latter assumption. They do not think that hedonism is committed to the view that we only desire our own pleasure. Rather, they think hedonism allows that we desire other things, but when we do it is only because we desire pleasure and view other things as things that will give us pleasure. For instance, they would say a hedonist can acknowledge that we desire things other than pleasure, such as food, but when we do it is only because we desire pleasure and we think food will provide it (278).

It could be argued that my insistence that people who refuse to plug into the experience machine are not hedonistically motivated rests upon the assumption that a hedonist could not allow that people desire other things such as a real life. Here Sober and Wilson would contend that the hedonist could allow such a desire as long as it is grounded in the refusers' beliefs that real life will bring them pleasure. In this way Sober and Wilson could argue that my defense of Nozick falls into the same trap that Butler's argument falls into.

However, in reply to this I would argue that Nozick's experience machine example actually provides us with the means for showing why Butler's original insight was the correct one. For in the case of the experience machine one cannot reasonably opt for real life on the grounds that real life is pleasant. If that is the basis of one's decision then one's decision is plainly irrational, because the illusions offered by the experience machine are guaranteed to be more pleasurable than anything one could experience in real life.

In defense of Sober and Wilson it could be argued that anyone who refuses to plug into the experience machine acts irrationally. But Sober and Wilson reject this move in their own discussion of Nozick's experience machine argument. They write:

> When people say they are unwilling to plug into the experience machine, this isn't because they don't understand the problem posed or reason incorrectly in thinking it through. (Sober and Wilson 1998, 283)

For all of the above reasons I think we have good reason to conclude that Sober and Wilson's critique of Nozick's experience machine argument fails.[1]

Silverstein's Objection Considered

Besides Sober and Wilson's critical reply to Nozick's argument, Matthew Silverstein has published one of the very few other critical responses to Nozick's argument. As he notes early on in his article, the vast majority of philosophers acquainted with Nozick's argument believe that it is sound, and he goes on to argue that it is unsound. The basic structure of Silverstein's argument can be expressed as follows:

---

[1] I develop this reply to Sober and Wilson's critique of the experience machine argument in more detail in Lemos 2002.

1. If the experience machine argument refutes hedonism, then we must have an irreducible desire to "track reality," to remain connected to the the real world.

2. We only desire this because tracking reality generally leads to happiness.

So, 3. the desire to track reality is not irreducible.

So, 4. the experience machine argument does not refute hedonism.

To say that a desire is irreducible is to say that it cannot be explained with reference to any other desire. Thus, Silverstein's point is that since tracking reality generally leads to happiness and since we desire to be happy, we can, then, explain the desire to track reality with reference to the desire to be happy, so that such a desire is not irreducible. "Tracking reality" is to be understood as having true beliefs.

The crucial premise in this argument is premise 2, and Silverstein takes pains to make the case in support of it. He writes:

> The experience machine thought experiment appeals to our intuitions as evidence against hedonism. Our intuitions tend to reflect our desires and preferences. In particular, our experience machine intuitions reflect our desire to remain connected to the real world, to track reality. But . . . the desire to track reality owes its hold upon us to the role it has played in the creation of happiness. We acquire our powerful attachment to reality after finding again and again that deception almost always ends in suffering. We develop a desire to track reality because, in almost all cases, the connection to reality is conducive to happiness. Our intuitive views about what is prudentially good, the views upon which the experience machine argument relies, owe their existence to happiness.
>
> We miss the mark, then, if we take our intuitions about the experience machine as evidence against hedonism . . . Our desire to track reality—like all of our intrinsic desires—is related to happiness in an important way: it owes its existence to happiness. Even though it leads us away from happiness in the case of the experience machine, our desire to track reality points indirectly to happiness . . . Any inclination to seek happiness directly is thus overwhelmed by our desire to

track reality. Happiness itself, therefore, is what fundamentally effects our intuitive fear of the experience machine, and we must not be misled by that fear. The mere existence of our intuitions against the experience machine should not lead us to reject hedonism. Contrary to appearances, those intuitions point albeit circuitously—to happiness. And as a result, they no longer seem to contradict the claim that happiness is the only thing of intrinsic prudential value. Our experience machine intuitions do not disappear, but they now fit comfortably into a hedonistic theory of well-being. (Silverstein 2000, 296)

Silverstein believes that whatever we desire, even those things we desire intrinsically, i.e. for their own sake, we desire because they tend to lead to happiness. Thus on his view no desire is irreducible except the desire for happiness. He says that the experience machine argument makes us think we have an irreducible desire to track reality. But, he thinks, in reality we only desire to track reality for its own sake because we have been conditioned to desire it due to the positive reinforcement tracking reality brings. Thus, even though the experience machine argument makes us aware that we desire to track reality for its own sake, this desire is not irreducible, since its existence is ultimately explicable with reference to our desire for happiness.

> Happiness stands at the center of our motivational system; it is the ultimate source of our desires. Thus, all of the evidence to which the experience machine argument appeals—all of our desires, including our desire to avoid the machine itself—ultimately points towards happiness as the source of prudential value. But that is precisely the doctrine of hedonism. (Silverstein 2000, 297)

At this stage of the argument Silverstein has, for the most part, simply explained how we can view all our desires, including our intrinsic desire to track reality, as existing to satisfy a more fundamental desire for our own happiness. Next he goes on to argue that this hedonistic understanding of the nature of our desires is justified on the ground that it solves a mystery that would otherwise be unsolvable.

> Hedonism explains what would otherwise be a mysterious coincidence, namely, the fact that all of our desires point towards happiness. No non-hedonistic theory of well-being can account for this fact. In

other words, without hedonism we cannot explain why all of our desires are related to happiness in this way. The most plausible explanation is a hedonistic one: the reason all of our desires point towards happiness is that happiness is the only thing that is intrinsically prudentially valuable. So the psychological account of happiness and desires does more than account for the experience machine intuitions. It actually suggests that hedonism is true. (Silverstein 2000, 297)

In responding to Silverstein I would note that the second premise of his main argument, "We only desire to track reality because doing so generally leads to happiness," is false. Many people are quite aware that illusions and deceptions, self-deceptions in particular, can be quite beneficial, can help us lead happier lives. For instance I might really feel better believing that when I was younger I was a good athlete and that women were attracted to me. Living with these illusions about my past might really make me feel better, if, for some reason, it is important for me to think that I had these qualities. Similarly, a colleague who is denied tenure might feel better about the whole thing if he continues to live under the illusion that the members of his department were jealous of his publication record rather than facing up to the fact that he was not a very good teacher. In our lives many illusions are maintained with relative ease and often lead us to be happier than we otherwise would be.

Someone who is cognizant of this fairly obvious fact of life is likely to see that the life of total illusion presented by Nozick's experience machine would provide happiness. I might be aware of the pleasures that I or others have derived from engaging in self-deception and, keeping this in mind, I might find the idea of life plugged into the experience machine to be quite attractive in certain respects. However, I still might refuse to plug in. Why? Not because I think tracking reality generally leads to happiness. For I am all too aware of the pleasures illusion and self-deception can bring. But rather, because, despite my tendency to enjoy illusions about my past, I might still want to *be* a certain sort of person in the future, such as a good husband and father and teacher. And these are not things that I can *be* if I am plugged into the experience machine.

It is because we have fundamental desires to *be* certain sorts of people that many of us are led to deceive ourselves about what we are or were. It is because being a good athlete is or was so important to me that I now tell myself that I was one even though I wasn't.

My point here is that tracking reality does not *generally* lead to happiness. Rather, sometimes it does and sometimes it doesn't. And someone quite familiar with the pleasures of illusion can still refuse to plug in to the experience machine. Such a person cannot plausibly be understood as refusing because of the positive reinforcement brought on by tracking reality. Thus, his refusal more likely than not stems from the fact that he values being a certain sort of person more than pleasure or happiness.

I will consider two possible replies Silverstein might make. First, he might argue that even if a person refuses to plug in out of a desire to be a certain sort of person, such as a good husband and father, we can still understand such a desire hedonistically. He might argue that these desires themselves exist only because being these things would make one happy. Thus, Silverstein might contend that my reply is inadequate. Second, he might also have us reconsider his argument that all desires must exist for the sake of a more fundamental desire for happiness, for otherwise it would be a mystery as to why all desires point towards happiness. If this argument is sound, then our desires not to plug in must also be motivated by a more fundamental desire for happiness.

Neither of these possible replies works. The first one won't work, because if I know I can be happier living in the illusion of the experience machine, which I can know because I am familiar with happy illusions, then I could not reasonably refuse to plug in unless I valued being a good husband and father for reasons independent of their effect on my own happiness. The second reply won't work either, because, contra Silverstein, there is no mystery for the hedonistic theory of desire to solve. The reason why all our desires point towards happiness is no mystery, because happiness involves the satisfaction of desire. Desires point towards happiness because we are made happy by their satisfaction. Accepting hedonism is not necessary to see this point.

Conclusion

I hope to have demonstrated the truth of two main points. First, I hope to have shown that in its current form Sober and Wilson's recent evolutionary biological argument against psychological hedonism is too weak to support its conclusion. And, second, I hope to have shown that we need not worry that psychological hedonism is true, however, because, despite recent criticisms, Nozick's experience machine argument gives us good philosophical reasons to think it is false. Before closing I want to note briefly the importance of the fact that I say the evolutionary biological argument does not work *in its current form*. Insofar as Nozick's philosophical argument is a good one, we should expect that eventually there will be good evolutionary biological reasons for thinking psychological hedonism is false. The fact that Sober and Wilson's argument fails does not mean that no evolutionary biological argument, nor even some new and improved version of their own argument, would work. It might be worthwhile for evoutionary theorists or philosophers to continue pursuing this line of argument.

8

Evolution and Free Will: Darwinian Non-Naturalism Defended

With respect to the philosophical issues of freedom, determinism, and moral responsibility, philosophers tend to adopt one of three positions—libertarianism, compatibilism, or hard determinism—and it is generally thought that these are the only viable positions with respect to such issues. However, in his recent publications Bruce Waller has made an interesting, vigorous defense of a fourth position, which he calls "natural autonomy." According to this view, humans possess a kind of autonomy that involves our having the capacity to choose among alternative courses of action, but since our choices are ultimately under the control of genetic and environmental factors this view also states that we are not morally responsible. In defending this view Waller offers criticisms of the three traditional positions and tries to show how his own position overcomes their defects. He also argues that his position fits better with Darwin's theory of natural selection than do the other more traditional views. Waller's writings have led me to re-examine my views on freedom, determinism, and responsibility, and this chapter is a consequence of that re-examination. Since a study of his views demands such a re-examination of the traditional views, Waller is to be commended for engaging the issues in fresh, clear, and insightful ways.

In what follows I begin by explaining some of the central ideas in and arguments for his theory of natural autonomy. An important aspect of his position which separates it from that of hard determinists is his defense of the ethical principle of non-interference. Waller believes that his theory of natural autonomy allows a defense of this ethical principle, whereas the hard determinist view cannot

173

offer any comparable defense of such a principle. I go on to argue that Waller needs to appeal to a theory like either libertarianism or compatibilism to make his defense of non-interference work, and in the later stages of the chapter I argue that the libertarian position is a live option for Darwinians because, contrary to what Waller tells us, it is both compatible with the theory of natural selection and internally coherent. In making my case I appeal to certain insights from Roderick Chisholm's defense of the libertarian position.

Waller's Theory of Natural Autonomy

In Waller's book, *The Natural Selection of Autonomy*, he begins by outlining three traditional positions on autonomy and moral responsibility. The three traditional views considered by Waller are:

1. Libertarianism: We are uncaused causers of our actions.

As such we are autonomous and morally responsible. He notes that this view has been defended by C.A. Campbell and Roderick Chisholm among others.

2. Hard determinism: All of our choices are causally determined by genetic and environmental factors beyond our control.

Thus, we are not autonomous and we are not morally responsible. He notes that this view has been defended by B.F. Skinner and John Hospers.

3. Compatibilism: Even though all of our choices are causally determined by genetic and environmental factors beyond our control, we are still autonomous and morally responsible.

He says that Daniel Dennett and Harry Frankurt hold this view.

Waller's own position is that we are autonomous but not morally responsible. He argues that the sort of autonomy we have, natural autonomy that is shared with non-human animals, is not the sort of autonomy that is compatible with moral responsibility.

Natural autonomy is the ability to explore alternative courses of action. This ability is enjoyed by other animals, while in humans it is enhanced by higher human intelligence. In developing the concept of natural autonomy Waller talks about the behavior of feral white-footed mice. He cites the following passage from J. Lee Kavanau in which he is discussing investigators' reactions to the behavior of white-footed mice in maze running experiments:

> Investigators sometimes are puzzled by the fact that once an animal has learned a discrimination well, it nonetheless still makes some "incorrect" responses. Actually, these responses are incorrect only from the point of view of the investigator's rigidly prescribed program, not from that of the animal. The basis for these responses is that the animal has a certain degree of variability built into many of its behavior patterns. This variability is adaptive to conditions in the wild, where there are many relationships that are not strictly prescribed. (Waller 1998, 7)

In reflecting on Kavanau's comments Waller writes:

> Thus if the white-footed mouse never strayed from the one true path, she would miss the opportunities that might subsequently appear along other routes and would be ill-equipped to respond rapidly should her most beneficial route be closed off or run dry. By occasionally taking alternative paths, the white-footed mouse keeps her options open. (Waller 1998, 7)

Waller refers to this capacity of the white-footed mouse to pursue alternative paths as "natural autonomy" and "autonomy-as-alternatives." And, as noted above, he believes that in humans it is enhanced by our higher intelligence.

> Human intelligence generates important differences between the autonomy of white-footed mice and the autonomy of humans, but the differences are best understood by examining their common roots in the exploration of alternative paths. The white-footed mouse explores alternative paths with keen scent and sharp eyes and swift feet. Our reflective analytic intelligence is our best exploratory device, and without it we are as ill-equipped for examining a variety of paths and behavioral patterns as would be a white-footed mouse deprived of scent and sight. So reason is essential to full autonomy: reason opens a wide range of possibilities and options and facilitates careful assessment of those options. (Waller 1998, 8)

Waller goes on to contend that this natural autonomy which we and other animals possess is adaptive.

> The natural world is exactly the place for an autonomy of alternative
> possibilities. Our "survival strategy" has shaped us, like our mam-
> malian relative the white-footed mouse, to keep our options open. We
> might have evolved like the insects, with rigidly programmed behav-
> ioral patterns. Our evolutionary process took a different tack: we are
> "programmed" to favor a variety of paths and to maintain such possi-
> bilities even when one path is the most immediately beneficial. (Waller
> 1998, 9–10)

The idea here is that natural autonomy is adaptive because in a
changing environment the ability to pursue alternative paths aids
one in the struggle to survive and reproduce. If I am programmed
to pursue only one survival strategy that works in certain environmental conditions, whereas other humans have the capacity to pursue a vast array of survival strategies, then when environmental
conditions change I am going to be disadvantaged. Thus from a
Darwinian perspective it should be no surprise to find that humans
and other animals possess natural autonomy.

Now, as noted earlier, Waller thinks that this natural autonomy
is not compatible with moral responsibility. While we have the
capacity to choose between a variety of different courses of action,
he believes that the ways we do choose are controlled by genetic
and environmental factors beyond our control. Thus, praise and
blame and the attendant notion of moral responsibility are all misguided. So, even though we are autonomous in the sense outlined
above we are not morally responsible. While I see that there are
different courses of action that I might follow and while I can
choose to follow one course rather than another, it is Waller's view
that my choice is controlled by psychological states which were in
turn causally determined by genetic and environmental factors
beyond my control.

Despite his claim that we lack moral responsibility, Waller
goes on to contend that his position leaves room for the making
of moral judgments. He makes two points in defense of the
rationality of moral judgments in a world without moral responsibility. First, he says that when people do not act as we think
they should then disapproval of their behavior and telling them
they ought not to do X but ought to do Y may encourage them
to change their ways. Second, he says that even if someone is not
responsible for being a lying, murdering sort we may still rea-

sonably express our disapproval of him by saying that he is a "moral scum" without thereby blaming him or punishing him (Waller 1998, 59–60).

Waller's Position Contrasted with Hard Determinism

Waller and hard determinists reject moral responsibility, but he believes we are autonomous whereas hard determinists deny this. However, upon closer inspection one might wonder whether the autonomy that Waller says we have is something that hard determinists could be willing to accept. Thus, one might wonder whether he really offers us a position that is different from that of hard determinists.

Waller contends that there is something about his position that makes it significantly different from that of hard determinists. He contends that his notion of autonomy-as-alternatives makes sense of the concept of "take-charge-responsibility (TCR)" and the consequent value that we place upon the ethical principle of non-interference. Thus, he argues that there is a relevant difference between his position and that of hard determinists because his position allows us to make sense of certain concepts and principles that are fundamental to our moral experience and that hard determinists cannot make sense of these.

TCR is accepting one's role or job and the obligations that come with having that role or job. In accepting a job as a professor I take responsibility for meeting my classes regularly and on time and grading papers. TCR can be distinguished from "just-deserts-responsibility (JDR)," which Waller identifies with moral responsibility. If I am JDR then I can rightly be praised or blamed for my successes and failures. According to Waller, TCR does not imply JDR. Just because I take responsibility for the decisions I make as a professor does not mean that I should be praised for my successes and blamed for my failures, because whether I do well or poorly is beyond my control. Genetic and environmental factors govern how well I will do in this role.

Waller goes on to discuss TCR for self. This is accepting the responsibilities of being a self or person, which is to accept the obligations which come along with being a decision-maker. He writes:

> TCR for one's own self is supremely important, but it is not moral (just-deserts) responsibility. Certainly it is my responsibility to consider the values I hold and the sort of person I am and wish to be. I may seek advice and consider criticisms, but I have responsibility for myself and I—not my parents, my party, nor my therapist—will make the decisions. If I am denied that responsibility (if someone else has take-charge-responsibility for me), then I suffer important and demeaning and even depersonifying loss. (Waller 1998, 44)

According to Waller, acknowledging natural autonomy and that we consequently have choices between different alternative paths is what allows us to make sense of TCR. For it is only through the recognition that I make the decision among alternative possibilities that I can reasonably take responsibility for making those decisions and prepare myself to do well in making them.

He also believes that it is the concept of TCR which explains and supports the ethical principle of non-interference.

> Denial of moral responsibility is often treated as equivalent to the denial of all individual rights and responsibilities, and thus is thought to open the door to the most brutal and repressive methods of shaping character and controlling behavior. When it is recognized that what is denied is moral responsibility (JDR) and not role-responsibility-for-self (TCR), it is clear that denial of moral responsibility is not a threat to individual rights. We want the right to follow our own paths, to engage in our own self-making; and that right is fully protected by respect for take-charge-responsibility-for-self. So denial of spurious JDR does not threaten the genuinely valuable TCR, nor the individual rights (such as rights to noninterference) it supports. To the contrary, clear focus on TCR skills (without the fog of moral responsibility) offers new opportunities to nurture and enhance autonomous self-making capacities. (Waller 1998, 47)

His view is that his own conception of autonomy as being able to choose among alternatives makes sense of TCR. And our capacity for TCR makes sense of our desire not to be interfered with. Hard determinists who deny the existence of any autonomy will not be able to explain and/or justify our concern with the protection of individual rights. When the hard determinist denies the existence of any kind of autonomy the ascription of neither TCR nor JDR (moral responsibility) makes any sense. But as Sidney Hook says in noting the implications of this hard determinist view:

one feels lessened as a human being if one's actions are always excused or explained away on the ground that despite appearances one is really not responsible for them. It means being treated like an object, an infant, or someone out of his mind. (Hook 1958, 189)

Do Waller's Accounts of TCR for Self and the Principle of Non-interference Fit with His Conception of Autonomy?

As we think about Waller's views on autonomy and responsibility a couple of questions come to mind immediately. First, I wonder whether we can really divorce TCR from JDR in the way that Waller says we can. In other words, is it true that TCR does not (at least typically) imply JDR? It certainly seems that if someone takes on the responsibilities of a job and if he can be expected to know (1) what the job demands and (2) whether he is competent, then if he screws up on the job, we can reasonably blame him for his failure and hold him accountable. And since conditions (1) and (2) are usually met in situations where people take on the responsibilities of a job, it would seem that in most cases of TCR there is also JDR (or moral responsibility) as well.

While I think this first criticism is worth developing, in this section I want to develop briefly another criticism which drives us to reconsider the libertarian and compatibilist views on freedom. As noted earlier, Waller talks about TCR for self, which is our ability to take on the responsibilities of being decision-makers. But one might wonder whether this really makes sense. It would seem that I am inevitably a decision-maker. Thus, it is not clear how I can "take on" this responsibility. For I have it whether I want it or not.

In response Waller would most likely agree that we all do inevitably have the responsibilities of being decision-makers. But not all of us own up to this aspect of our lives. Those of us who don't own up to it act irresponsibly, not getting information and considering it before making decisions. Such people do not take on the responsibilities of being a decision-maker. This is what TCR for self is all about. And the recognition of our natural autonomy, autonomy-as-alternatives, helps to remind us that it is up to us which course we will follow in life. Failure to recognize such autonomy might encourage one to shirk such responsibilities in the belief that there are no alternatives to the course one follows.

In reply I would note that recognition of my natural autonomy does not really give me reason to think that my future decisions are up to me. For ultimately on Waller's view the decisions I make are under the control of genetic and environmental factors beyond my control. Whether I do well or poorly in my decision making or whether I am even able to accept the responsibilities of being a decision-maker is beyond my control. And since my decision making is not under my control my valuing of non-interference is not really justified. For I value this only insofar as I want to have control over my own life. Since Waller's view does not make sense of my having this control, it can provide no adequate explanation nor justification for my valuing non-interference. In the end the justification for non-interference must rest upon a conception of the self that does not view it as simply a machine receiving input from genes and environment and then cranking out decisions from such determining factors. Something like either the libertarian or compatibilist positions must be held in order to make sense of the value of non-interference.

The Libertarian Position Revisited

In *The Natural Selection of Autonomy* (1998) Waller gives reasons for rejecting both the libertarian and the compatibilist positions on autonomy. As I have just argued, he needs to accept one of these positions in order to make his defense of the value of non-interference work. While I find his treatment of the compatibilist position interesting and worthy of some discussion, in what follows I want to focus my attention on his treatment of the libertarian position. Contra Waller, I will argue that the libertarian position is a live option for Darwinians.

Waller rejects the libertarian view on the ground that it is shrouded in "mystery and miracles." According to the libertarian view, autonomous action is caused not by antecedent events but by human agency. Each of us is an unmoved mover, capable of being the original uncaused source of actions. In *The Natural Selection of Autonomy* he offers two main arguments against the libertarian position. One of his main arguments is an attempt to show that the libertarian position is incompatible with Darwinism. The other is an attempt to show that the libertarian position cannot make sense of one's choices being one's own.

Is the Libertarian Position Incompatible with Darwinism?

Waller's first argument runs as follows:

> libertarian alternative choices—choices exercised independently of the environment—corrupt the natural value of alternative possibilities. As products of our natural environment, we want alternatives shaped by their long-term or short-term usefulness in the environment in which we live, alternatives available for selection in response to our changing environment. The sterile insulated libertarian alternatives required by moral responsibility are not shaped by the environmental forces to which we must respond effectively. To the contrary, libertarian choices must be isolated from environmental influences: libertarian choices must be something for which I am "responsible without qualification" and thus "not affected by heredity or environment." But natural autonomy-as-alternatives (practiced by humans as well as white-footed mice) is tightly linked to environmental shaping. (Waller 1998, 11)

According to Waller, if we are Darwinian naturalists then we must look upon the capacity for autonomous decision making as adaptive. And if so, then the alternatives that we have as a result of such an adaptive capacity must aid us in the struggle to survive and reproduce, and such alternatives should then be shaped by our genetic and environmental conditions. However, he also contends that the libertarian position requires that our decisions should not be shaped by heredity or environment if they are to be autonomous.

This argument is problematic. It is not true that libertarian choice need be understood as so insulated from genetic and environmental factors. Contra what Waller states, the libertarian can concede that genetic and environmental factors play a role in shaping the alternative courses of action that one might consider before making a choice. The libertarian can even concede that genetic and environmental factors will incline a person to act one way or the other in the face of such alternatives. But what the libertarian will not concede is that all human decisions among such alternatives are ultimately controlled entirely by genetic and environmental factors. While our genetics and environment might *incline* us to act a certain way, they cannot be *completely determinative* of our actions when we are acting autonomously.

Roderick Chisholm (1991) discusses how our desires may incline us to act a certain way without necessitating us to act that way. Since desires may well have genetic and environmental causes, Chisholm's account of desires inclining us to act a certain way without necessitating us to do so could also be extended to talk of genetic and environmental conditions inclining without necessitating us. Additionally, C.A. Campbell, another libertarian, maintains that much of the evidence we have for the truth of the libertarian position appeals to our own subjective awareness of moral struggles against inclinations that we have acquired due to genetic and environmental factors. Campbell believes that our awareness of our own internal struggles against these forces informs us of our ability to act as uncaused causers of action. But while our struggle against genetically or environmentally produced inclinations is a sign of our libertarian autonomy, Campbell admits that much of the time we act in accordance with the dictates of heredity and environment. Yet, when we do act in accordance with the dictates of heredity and environment it does not necessarily follow that we lack autonomy and moral responsibility for what we are doing, since as beings with the capacity to fight against these drives it is up to us whether we will obey their directives or not.

To maintain that humans possess libertarian autonomy and moral responsibility, whereas other animals do not, does not violate any Darwinian principles. While from the Darwinian point of view this might at some level be "surprising" or "unexpected," it is not surprising when we take into account other features of our biology, such as our large brains, and other aspects of our lives that really do seem to mark us human beings off as unique and different in kind from the other animals. In responding to the biological determinism of the sociobiologist E.O. Wilson, Stephen Gould writes,

> [Markedly increased brain size in human evolution] added enough neural connections to convert an inflexible and rather rigidly programmed device into a labile organ, endowed with sufficient logic and memory to substitute non-programmed learning for direct specification as the ground of social behavior. (Gould 1977, 257)

While Gould does not necessarily intend to defend libertarian autonomy here, his point should be of interest to us. Interestingly, while the difference in the size of the human brain as compared to that of other primates is a difference in degree, this is a difference in degree which has enormous implications for the types or *kinds* of things that humans are capable of doing in contrast to other animals. Thus, there is a biological basis for believing that humans may possess a capacity for libertarian autonomy that no other animals possess. Additionally, when one considers the fact that humans alone write novels, compose symphonies, or work in nuclear physics, it should come as no surprise to find that we possess another capacity, libertarian autonomy, that makes us different from the other animals. (For more on the unique capacities of humans suggesting a difference in kind between us and other animals, see Dennett's *Darwin's Dangerous Idea*, especially Part III. Dennett is a Darwinian and a philosopher, who is very well informed about biology. While he is not a libertarian, but rather a compatibilist, he believes that the linguistic capacities of human beings give them other abilities that make them different in kind from the other animals.)

Waller might object to my contention that genetics and environment can incline us to act in certain ways without necessitating us. This claim plays a central role in my argument to the effect that libertarian autonomous choice need not be thought of as being insulated from genetic and environmental factors. Waller might want to know what inclining without necessitating amounts to and whether this is a distinction that makes any sense.

In developing a response to this consideration I would have us consider the views of Chisholm. He has us suppose that a person has a desire for some event, A, to occur. He states that this person's desire *necessitates* him to act if he cannot resist the temptation to do something to make A happen and that this person's desire *inclines* him to act if he cannot resist the temptation to allow A to happen. So, for instance, suppose Fred desires to have sex with Barney's wife, Betty. This desire would necessitate Fred if he cannot resist the temptation to do something, such as seducing or propositioning Betty, to bring about his having sex with her. This desire inclines Fred if he cannot resist the temptation to allow sexual relations between him and Betty to occur. Suppose that Betty is attracted to Fred and sneaks into his bed and commences to engage in certain sex acts with him. Fred's desire to have sex with Betty would incline him to do so if he cannot resist the temptation to allow Betty to have her way with him. Since Fred might be able to resist the temptation to bring about sexual relations but not be able to resist the temptation to allow them to occur, it is clear that on this analysis it makes sense to say that a desire can incline without necessitating. It is not uncommon for desires to incline without necessitating. There are many things that people desire to have happen that they cannot bring themselves to do or cause, but which they might allow to happen. This is one of the ways in which many of us discover the limits of our virtue.

What Chisholm says about desires inclining without necessitating can be extended in such a way as to make sense of genetic and environmental conditions inclining without necessitating, since such desires can plausibly be viewed as the products of genetic and environmental factors. It therefore makes sense to talk of desires or genetic and environmental factors inclining us to act in certain ways without necessitating us to do so. Thus, we need not view libertarian autonomous choice as being completely insulated from genetic and environmental factors. Instead, our libertarian autonomous decision making is shaped by desires or genetic and environmental factors that incline without necessitating. This can and frequently does occur even when we are both (1) acting in a manner consistent with our desires and (2) not simply allowing something to occur.

Suppose that Fred, instead of contemplating having sex with his friend's wife, Betty, is contemplating having sex tonight with Wilma, his own wife. He might be moved to consider this because of his desire to have sex with Wilma. Now let us also suppose that he initiates such sexual relations with her this evening. The fact that he ends up having sex with his wife does not mean that he was necessitated by this desire. The mere fact that he follows the dictates of this desire does not mean that he was necessitated by the desire. For acting on the desire is compatible with having the capacity to resist the temptation to do something to bring about the satisfaction of the desire. It could be that the desire inclined him without necessitating him and that this inclining but non-necessitating desire was part of the data considered in the forming of a reflective, all things considered judgment that sex with his wife tonight would be a good thing. Having come to such a considered judgment which is shaped by desires or genetic and environmental factors, Fred might have been moved to initiate sexual relations with his wife. But this would be an action shaped by desires or genetic and environmental factors, which incline but do not necessitate. Many of our libertarian autonomous decisions are shaped by non-necessitating desires or genetic and environmental factors in this way.

Can the Libertarian View Not Make Sense of My Choices as Mine?

Waller also argues that while the libertarian position is intended to preserve the concept of moral responsibility, it does so in a way that makes it impossible to see how a person's actions can reasonably be thought of as his own. In referring to libertarian choice he writes:

> But for the naturalist, frustration rapidly boils over into impolite questions: where does this choice come from, if not from my formed character? If the choice transcends my history and my character and my desires and my intellect, then how can it be my choice at all? Such miraculous autonomous choices seem completely detached from me and my choosing and my deliberative processes, all of which have been shaped by my cumulative genetic and learning and social histories. The miraculous saving of moral responsibility seems to be at the expense of a coherent account of autonomous choice. (Waller 1998, 36)

This argument assumes that libertarian choices "transcend" one's history, character, desires, and intellect. But it is not clear what is meant by this. Certainly the libertarian does *not* think that in free-willed action character or desires necessitate action. But he does think they can incline one to act a certain way. And we very often give in to such inclinations. Hence, our ability to predict what people will do when we have knowledge of their character or desires. But still these do not necessitate action, and that is part of the reason why we frequently witness ourselves and others engaging in acts that are out of character or contrary to desires.

So if by "transcend" Waller means "not necessitated by" then it is true that libertarian autonomy transcends character or desires. But so what? This leaves room for their shaping our decisions or inclining us in certain ways without necessitating those acts. This is no more a role than we should expect them to have, given the prevalence of actions performed that are out of character or contrary to desire. Do we really want to say of anyone who acts out of character on some occasion that he was not responsible for so acting because only actions proceeding from one's character are one's own? Should we say the person who is typically brave but who today acted cowardly should not be blamed because his cowardly acts today were not his? It is all too common for people of a certain character to act out of character. Consequently to suggest that an act belongs to an agent only when it flows from his character will imply that many actions we typically ascribe to people and hold them accountable for will no longer reasonably be regarded in this way. Indeed, if we assume (1) I am a just person and (2) I am known in my community to be such and (3) Waller's view is true, then this would license me to go on a rampage of injustice tomorrow, for on Waller's view none of those acts could really be mine.

In responding to this line of argument Waller might contend that he is not necessarily committed to the view that when an act is out of character it is not an act *of* the agent. For he could always say that this is just a sign that we did not know the character of the agent after all. What seems like an act done out of character is not really an act done out of character; rather we were just ignorant of the person's true character. Consequently, he might contend that my reference to the phenomenon of people acting out of character as support for the claim that character does not causally necessitate us to act as we do is ineffective. However, this sort of response does not ring true. It is all too common for people who really are generally disposed to do the right thing, people of good character, to act wrongly on some occasions. We could know that someone is a just person, someone who almost always does what justice requires, and see them engage in an unjust act on some occasion. Perhaps on this occasion they are tempted to do an injustice by one of the very few things that could get them to engage in injustice.

The only way to get the reply under consideration to work would be to maintain that having a certain character trait, such as justice or courage, would require that one *always* do the just thing. Thus, whenever anyone who seems to be just or courageous given their record of past actions ends up doing something unjust or cowardly, we have reason to believe that we really did not know their character. But this raises the standards for having a certain character trait too high. No one reasonably expects the just person always to do what justice requires or the courageous person always to act in a courageous fashion.

Another possible reply to my argument might involve noting that there is an overemphasis on character in my critique. Even if one is just one can engage in an unjust deed and have the action belong to him, as long as there is some other aspect of the agent's psyche that explains why the action occurred. So, for instance, if my desire for fame leads me to engage in injustice despite the fact that I am a just person, then since the desire which causes the act is mine the act is mine also even though it is out of character. So, contra my argument, it could be contended that Waller's view does not require that character cause an act for it to belong to an agent; rather it simply requires that some aspect of the agent's psyche, such as character or desire cause the act.

Consider someone who is just but who also really wants fame. One day, seeing that he can get fame quickly and easily through one act of injustice, he succumbs to the desire and does the unjust deed. Typically, the just person in such circumstances will deliberate, perhaps agonize, over the situation. Presumably a just person will be concerned with doing what justice requires and so, when faced with a strong desire to act unjustly, he will deliberate before acting. This deliberative process is suggestive of the possibility that one could act in either of at least two ways. But if so then the desire, which I would agree *explains* the action, does not necessitate it. Rather it gives the agent a certain inclination or a certain reason to do a certain thing, but it is an inclination which in the process of deliberation is weighed against alternatives. Things like our character, desires, values, shape what is considered in the deliberative process. But it is the agent himself who deliberates, decides, and acts. And as such the agent is something over and above his character and desires. As such the agent is free in the sense implied by the libertarian position.

Furthermore, to say that the agent is something over and above his character and desires is not to imply that we cannot make sense of his actions as his. For whenever there are non-necessitating reasons (inclinations) for his actions that are internal to the agent, reasons that can be given consideration in a deliberative process which is indicative of libertarian choice, then the action belongs to the agent. If I have a non-necessitating desire to hit my friend in the head and I am capable of deliberating about whether I should do this, and if I go ahead and hit him, then, whether I deliberated about it or not on this occasion, the action is mine though not causally necessitated by any desires of mine. The having of a reason or inclination that I could have included in a deliberative process suggests this reason is non-necessitating. And even though the reason (inclination) does not necessitate, it is *my* reason (inclination) and so it makes the act mine.

Conclusion

In this chapter I hope to have accomplished several things. First, I have tried to present a clear and accurate account of the central ideas in Waller's theory of natural autonomy. Second, I have argued that in order for Waller to make his argument for the ethical principle of non-interference work he needs to adopt either a libertarian or a compatibilist position. And, third, contra Waller I have tried to show that the libertarian position is a live option for Darwinians. In support of this last point I defended two main points. First, while the libertarian view does indicate that humans have a unique capacity for libertarian autonomous choice that is not shared by other animals, this is not incompatible with Darwinism nor even all that surprising given (1) other aspects of our biology (our large brains) and (2) the vast array of other human actions that make us special, such as our engagement in the arts and sciences. Second, I argued that the libertarian position can make coherent sense of how an agent's freely willed acts belong to the agent.

In closing I would like briefly to discuss the concept of naturalism. Earlier in this chapter I noted that Waller takes naturalism to include a belief in a deterministic universe. If one believes in a deterministic universe then every event is to be understood as having been causally necessitated by earlier events. Waller is not alone in thinking of naturalism as entailing a deterministic universe. In a recent book in which Owen Flanagan defends a compatibilist view of moral responsibility, he characterizes himself as a naturalist and defines naturalism as follows:

> By naturalism I simply mean the view that all phenomena are natural and subject to causal principles. Mind, consciousness, human volition are like other phenomena in that they are made of natural stuff, have

natural histories, and are explicable in terms of natural law. (Flanagan 1996, 56–57)

It is in large measure because of his acceptance of this naturalistic standpoint in which all phenomena are "explicable in terms of natural (deterministic) law" that Flanagan is attracted to the compatibilist position.

The libertarian position I have been defending is incompatible with such a deterministic view of the universe and therefore is incompatible with any kind of naturalism that entails such a deterministic view of the universe. But I believe that a consideration of the data—our intuitive sense that we could act and decide in ways other than the ways in which we do act and decide, the frequency of people acting out of character and contrary to their inclinations, the nature of the deliberative processes that we sometimes engage in, the fact that there is already so much that separates us from the other animals—gives us good reason to reject such a deterministic view of things. But, as I have argued, this does not mean that one must give up one's Darwinism. Thus, I have in a sense taken some strides in developing and defending a view that could be described as "Darwinian Non-Naturalism."

9

Recent Developments in the Philosophy of Evolution

This book draws upon essays that were written over a period of several years. Since the time that these essays were originally produced and brought together along with some new material to produce this book, there has been continued research and publication in the field. The study of the philosophical implications of evolutionary biology has been an especially hot topic in recent years.

In this chapter I want to address some of this more recent research, putting it into context with my own conclusions. In places I will note where the research of others supports my findings; in other places I will express points of disagreement. In places I will try to give further support for some of the central theses of this book by critically responding to some of this recent research. This chapter comprises eight sections, corresponding to each of the eight preceding chapters of this book.

1. Defending a Sociobiological Account of Morality

In Chapter 1, I gave a defense of Michael Ruse's sociobiological account of morality, in which he argues that human beings have an innate predisposition to accept certain fundamental principles of morality and that with the help of culture they build systems of morality from these fundamental principles. Ruse argues that there are adaptive reasons for why human beings are inclined to accept these fundamental principles. Thus, our acceptance of them is most likely a product of natural selection.

In recent years there has been a good bit of work which gives additional support for the Rusean theory. Richard Joyce's *The Evolution of Morality* is a very clear and readable book which provides an extensive defense of the sociobiological account of morality. Ruse has argued that there are evolutionary biological reasons for why we intuitively accept certain very basic moral principles. In contrast, Joyce argues that the moral sense is a product of evolution. Thus, he gives an evolutionary biological account of the human tendency to think of things in moral terms. In the last two chapters, Joyce moves on to elaborate on the metaethical implications of this account, arguing, like Ruse, that such a sociobiological account of morality undermines the objectivity of morality. Also, see works by Frans de Waal, such as his *Good Natured: The Origins of Right and Wrong in Primates and Other Animals* and his *Primates and Philosophers: How Morality Evolved*. The latter book includes responses to de Waal from various authors, such as Christine Korsgaard, Peter Singer, and Philip Kitcher. I also recommend among other works, Marc Hauser's *Moral Minds: How Nature Designed Our Universal Sense of Right and Wrong*, and various works by Marc Bekoff, such as his 2004 piece in *Biology and Philosophy*. Bekoff has done a lot of research on the behavior of wild dogs, and he argues that in supporting the case for the evolution of morality it is important that we look for evidence of moral or proto-moral behaviors in creatures besides primates and human beings.

Not all of the recent work has been so supportive of the sociobiological account of the origins of morality. One especially intriguing argument has been forwarded by David Lahti, who focuses his critical attention on Ruse's sociobiological account. He views morality as a set of universal, prescriptive, objective guidelines, articulating how we ought or ought not behave. According to Lahti, it is a mistake to think that morality understood in this way is a product of evolution by natural selection. In support of this he makes several interesting points. He notes that if morality is a product of evolution, then it should exist as an adaptation aiding individual human beings in the struggle to survive and reproduce. Presumably, morality would do this by encouraging human beings to engage in adaptive cooperative behaviors, such as those favored by principles of kin selection and reciprocal altruism. However, he argues that it is very unlikely that there is any genetic or biological basis for the existence of morality.

In support of this he notes that prior to the formation of moral systems human beings were, like many other animals, moved to engage in adaptive cooperative behavior by innate desires to help others, by having a genetically evolved tendency to have sympathy for others. Lahti contends that early humans living in hunter-gatherer communities probably relied solely upon such emotional mechanisms to spur cooperative behavior, having no systems of morality. For Lahti, the pre-existence of this emotionally driven impulse for adaptive cooperative behavior is significant. He argues that this means morality becomes unnecessary as a spur to such behavior; it is redundant and so it is unreasonable to think of it as a product of evolution by natural selection. He also argues that morality, which is characterized by a great deal of reflection and deliberation in the making of moral decisions, is a very inefficient means of encouraging adaptive cooperative behavior. Since emotional spurs to cooperative behavior, such as feelings of sympathy, are more efficient, it is, again, unlikely that morality is a product of evolution.

In the conclusion of his essay on the subject, Lahti contends that, more likely than not, morality came into existence not as a product of biological evolution but as "a cultural surrogate for genetic adaptation" (2003, 650). He writes that

> the moral law, in Ruse's sense of a set of universal, prescriptive, and nonsubjective guidelines, is likely a recent phenomenon, postdating the hunter-gatherer period. This concept of a moral law may function to update our behavior to the present social environment from that of our paleolithic ancestors. (2003, 649)

And,

> [Moral guidelines] are hypothesized to be the product of the period since the agricultural revolution, when our culture began to change too quickly to be effectively tracked by organic evolution. (2003, 650)

Before responding to Lahti, I would note that his attack on Ruse's sociobiological account of morality is part of his attempt to show that Ruse's claim that morality is an illusion is ill-founded. That is, Ruse believes objective morality presupposes the existence of moral facts when, according to Ruse, they don't really exist. Lahti thinks this thesis is ill-founded because it rests on what he regards as a problematic sociobiological account of morality.

I would remind the reader that I too believe Ruse's critique of moral realism—the view that there are objective moral facts—is ill-founded. My case for this was made in Chapter 2. However, my disagreement with Ruse is not the same as Lahti's. I actually find Ruse's sociobiological account of morality quite plausible. In what follows, I will clarify my points of disagreement with Lahti.

In general I don't think Lahti is sufficiently sensitive to the resources Ruse has at his disposal in defending his position. For one thing Ruse concedes that culture plays a very large role in shaping the nature of our moral systems. Ruse writes:

> The claim is that human moral thought has constraints, as manifested through the epigenetic rules, and the application of these leads to moral codes, soaring from biology into culture. The question is not whether every last act of Western Man or woman is governed by kin selection or reciprocal altruism or some such thing. I am quite sure it is not. (Ruse 1998, 230)

Ruse's sociobiological account of morality states that there is an evolutionary biological basis for why we accept certain fundamental principles of morality, such as "Love they neighbor as thyself" or "Treat human beings as ends in themselves", and that there are evolutionary biological constraints on what we can accept as moral norms. He allows that culture, not biology, plays a large role in shaping the development of moral systems, which is to say that it plays a large role in shaping the more specific moral principles that are derived from fundamental, basic principles that we are biologically predisposed to accept.

Lahti's contention that morality is "a product of the agricultural revolution, when our culture began to change too quickly to be effectively tracked by organic evolution" is perfectly consistent with Ruse's sociobiological account of morality. For Ruse can plausibly maintain that the fundamental, basic moral principles upon which moral systems are built first need our intuitive acceptance, and were it not for the fact that we evolved certain sympathies for others when living as hunter-gatherers for thousands of years, we wouldn't have found these basic foundational moral principles intuitively attractive.

This problem with Lahti's argument suggests another problem. He maintains that moral systems were developed during the agricultural revolution to help modern human beings cope better in the novel social environments they had created for themselves. The agricultural revolution gave rise to human communities much larger than the kin groups that were predominant in hunter-gatherer societies. But if Ruse and I are right that the development of sympathy for others was necessary to our intuitive acceptance of the basic moral principles of moral systems—the moral systems needed for cooperation in these newer social environments—then, contra Lahti, evolution plays a significant role in the development of these moral systems, meaning moral systems are not redundant since they are needed for us to cope in these newer, larger communities we find ourselves in.

While I find Lahti's argument quite intriguing, I believe it fails for all of the above stated reasons.

2. Nonobjectivist Evolutionary Ethics

In Chapter 2 I explained and criticized Ruse's argument that his sociobiological account of morality implies there are no objective moral truths. This contention of his is highly controversial. The third chapter of my book would suggest this since it surveys the work of various contemporary thinkers who believe, *contra* Ruse, that the sociobiological account of morality actually contributes to the case for objective morality. While I take issue with the arguments of the latter thinkers, I agree with them that Darwinism poses no threat to the objectivity of morality. In Chapter 4 I outline a way in which objective moral values can be defended on Aristotelian grounds, and I even suggest a way in which evolutionary biology can be used to support such an Aristotelian ethics. Since the time I wrote those essays there have been publications supporting Ruse's contention. In what follows I would like to address a couple of these.

SOMMERS AND ROSENBERG'S ANTI-OBJECTIVISM

In a recent publication, Tammler Sommers and Alex Rosenberg uphold the Rusean line in responding to the brand of ethical naturalism expressed by Daniel Dennett in the later chapters of his book, *Darwin's Dangerous Idea*. They argue that Dennett's acceptance of the existence of objective moral values in the later parts of his book does not fit with the Darwinism that he so ably defends throughout its earlier parts. While I cannot do full justice to Sommers and Rosenberg's argument here, I will say that I remain unconvinced of their nihilistic thesis and I think points I make in Chapters 2–4 of this book provide some reasons in support of my position.

Sommers and Rosenberg maintain:

> Darwinism . . . puts the capstone on a process which since Newton's time has driven teleology to the explanatory sidelines. In short it has made Darwinians into metaphysical Nihilists denying that there is any meaning or purpose to the universe, its contents and its cosmic history. But in making Darwinians into metaphysical nihilists, the solvent algorithm should have made them into ethical nihilists too. For intrinsic values and obligations make sense only against the background of purposes, goals, and ends which are not merely instrumental. (Somers and Rosenberg 2003, 653)

The "solvent algorithm" referred to here is the mechanism of random variation and natural selection which, according to Sommers and Rosenberg, "operates at every level of organization from the macromolecular to the mental, at every time scale from the geological epoch to the nanosecond" (653). Sommers and Rosenberg contend that the all pervasive operation of Darwinian natural selection makes the assertion of meaning or purpose in the universe unwarranted. Hence, they conclude Darwinism entails metaphysical nihilism. I have my doubts about this. To see why consider what I say in response to Rachels in Chapter 5. But I am willing to grant them their metaphysical nihilism.

From here Sommers and Rosenberg go on to contend that Darwinism also implies ethical nihilism, the belief that there are no objective moral values, because such values "only make sense against the background of purposes, goals, and ends which are not merely instrumental." I reject the reasoning behind this argument for Darwinian nihilism. As I argued in Chapter 4, even if species arise from a process of natural selection there will still be characteristic, or defining, features of organisms in virtue of which we can provide objective assessments of value. So, even if human beings are products of natural selection, there will still be some sense of rationality in virtue of which it can be said of humans that they are rational animals. Thus, it will still be true that we can objectively assess the merits of humans in terms of how well they do at reasoning and we can determine the virtues as those traits necessary for doing well at reasoning, the characteristic activity of human beings.

Darwinism undermines Aristotelian biology. For instance, Aristotle believed species were fixed and permanent, and this is clearly mistaken, according to the Darwinian evolutionary theory. But it does not undermine Aristotelian ethics. It is my hope that Chapter 4 of this book takes us some way in understanding why not. I am not alone in holding this view about Aristotelian ethics. For more on this see Arnhart 1998, Casebeer 2003, Foot 2001, Hursthouse 1999, and Thompson 2004. Each of these thinkers and I (see Lemos 2007) believe that an Aristotelian ethics can provide the basis for objective moral norms and they see Darwinism as no threat to this thesis.

JOYCE'S ANTI-OBJECTIVISM

Richard Joyce has also argued that evolutionary biology undermines belief in the objectivity of ethics. Like Ruse, Joyce believes that there is a good evolutionary biological explanation for the human capacity for moral judgment. Also like Ruse, he believes the existence of such an evolutionary biological account of our moral capacities implies there are no objective moral truths.

In Joyce 2006 he considers the possible objection that mathematical beliefs are formed from an adaptive inbuilt faculty for simple arithmetic, but this does not lead us to deny the objectivity of math—the point here being that since we do not deny the objectivity of math despite its adaptive basis, then the adaptive basis of morality should not lead us to deny its objectivity. In reply, Joyce contends that the adaptiveness of mathematical beliefs presupposes their truth. That is, they are adaptive only because they are objectively true. Thus, the evolutionary account of the mathematical faculties does not undermine the objectivity of math. In contrast, he says that the adaptiveness of moral beliefs does not presuppose their truth. He contends that moral beliefs would be adaptive even if they were false. Thus, the evolutionary account of our capacity for moral judgment *does* undermine the objective truth of our moral beliefs (Joyce 2006, 182–84).

Joyce goes on to align himself with Gilbert Harman, whose views I discuss in Chapter 2. Like Harman, Joyce believes that since we can explain the existence of moral beliefs without appeal to moral facts (objective moral truths), there is no good reason to believe in them. He goes on to note that if moral facts could be reduced to the nonmoral facts used in explaining moral beliefs, then Harman's and Joyce's argument could be answered. But Joyce argues that no such naturalistic reduction is workable or defensible, because no such reduction "can accommodate the sense of inescapable practical authority with which moral claims appear to be imbued" (Joyce 2006, 190).

This last point is an important one. It plays a key role in his evolutionary argument against the objectivity of morality, and he appeals to it in critically responding to various evolutionary naturalistic moral objectivist theories, such as those of William Rottschaefer and Robert Richards (Joyce 2000) and William Casebeer (Joyce 2006, 168–174). When Joyce says moral claims have "inescapable practical authority," what he means is that they have an intrinsic action-guidingness. Consequently, if there are any, moral properties must "provide a person with reasons for acting irrespective of that person's ends" (Joyce 2006, 173). As he notes, this is part of the reason why J.L. Mackie was led to say that moral properties are so *queer* that we have reason to believe they don't exist. (See Mackie 1977.)

Joyce believes moral assertions place demands upon us and they have their demand giving structure built into them (Joyce 2006, 174). It is this aspect of the nature of moral assertion which he argues naturalist objectivist reductionism cannot account for, and so he feels vindicated in endorsing Harman's argument against the objectivity of morality.

In response to Joyce, I am inclined to argue along the same lines that Brink has argued in response to Mackie. (See Brink 1998.) Joyce unwarrantedly assumes that moral assertions have intrinsic action-guidingness, that they have a demand giving structure built into them. Rather, whether moral assertions make any demands upon us has to do with whether we are morally decent people. This is why it is so easy for many bad people to know full well what they ought to do and still not do it.

The moral objectivist can reasonably respond that it is not his job to give everyone, including the morally worst sorts, overriding reason to do what is right. Rather, the ethicist's job is to give a clear and accurate account of the nature of morally good person-hood, the virtues requisite to it, and the rights and duties corre-spondent to these virtues. If such an account is not intrinsically action-guiding for all those cognizant of it, this is no failing on the part of the ethical theory. Rather, it may well be a sign of the moral failings of those who don't act in conformity with it.

Here I'm responding to Joyce in a manner akin to Paul Bloomfield. In a review of Joyce 2006, Bloomfield writes:

> The moral naturalist will say that the moral facts, like facts about good parenting, are what they are. What we make of them, how they make us feel, the importance we give them, the practices we adopt for prais-ing and punishing, etc. are all independent of their existence, and it is only establishing their existence that is the concern of the moral nat-uralist. (Bloomfield 2006, 180)

This is a point well-made, and it is in line with what I am arguing here.

As a matter of review, let me just say that Joyce is quite right in feeling the need to respond to naturalist ethical reductionism in defending Harman's anti-objectivist argument. However, in attacking naturalistic ethical reductionism, he unwarrantedly assumes that all moral assertions have an intrinsic action-guiding-ness, thereby placing the standards for a successful naturalistic reduction of ethics at an unjustified and impossible level.

3. Recent Objectivist Approaches to Evolutionary Ethics

A number of contemporary philosophers believe that evolutionary biology provides the basis for an objectivist theory of ethics. Many of them believe that it provides a way to legitimately reason from facts to values or to establish the existence of objective moral facts. As Chapters 2–4 of this book suggest, I certainly agree that there are objective moral truths, but, as I argue in Chapter 3, I believe there are flaws with many of these recent attempts at bridging the is-ought gap with evolutionary biology.

In the years since that chapter was originally published in *The Southern Journal of Philosophy*, there have been other published cri-tiques of some of those objectivist theories. Some of the points I make are repeated in these criticisms. Ferguson (2001) provides a very thorough and, I think, devastating critique of Robert Richards's evolutionary ethics. Richard Joyce (2000; 2006) also provides a critique of Richards's theory. Both Joyce and Ferguson make some of the points I make. In Joyce 2000, Joyce also provides a critique of William Rottschaefer's objectivist evolutionary ethics. The critiques of Rottschaefer and Richards in Joyce 2000 are problematic because they rely too much on the point that such naturalistic justifications cannot makes sense of the "inescapable practical authority" of moral claims. My comments in the previous section relate what I think is wrong with this. Joyce 2006 also provides a critical survey of recent attempts to use evolutionary biology in supporting an objectivist moral theory. Here Joyce engages with Robert Richards and Richmond Campbell, both of whom I discussed in Chapter 3. He also addresses the work of Daniel Dennett and William Casebeer, two figures I have not addressed. Joyce's critique of Dennett is dead-on, but his treatment of Casebeer's Aristotelian evolutionary ethics is highly problematic. I will return to this in the subsequent section, as the points he makes against Casebeer could be seen as a threat to my own Aristotelian approach.

Before moving on I would like to give consideration to one more recent attempt at bridging the is-ought gap with evolutionary biology. I want to give some consideration to William Harms's teleosemantic approach. This is an approach I did not consider in Chapter 3.

Harms has argued, *contra* Ruse and others, that the evolutionary biological account of morality does not imply that there are no objective moral truths. In doing so, he goes on to argue, as others have, that the evolutionary biological account of morality actually supports the objectivity of morality. In Harms 2000, he begins by critically responding to Ruse's case against moral realism, the view that there are objective moral truths. There he makes a point that I very much agree with—namely, that Ruse's argument rests on the mistaken assumption that objective moral standards must be species independent. Like myself, Harms believes objective moral standards can be derived from our evolved and evolving human nature. In Chapter 2 I made this kind of point and in Chapter 4 I sketched an Aristotelian approach to showing how such objective moral norms might be derived from our evolved human nature.

Harms goes on to give his own account of how evolutionary biology provides the basis for objective moral truth. In doing so, he appeals to R.G. Millikan's teleosemantics. According to this theory, "the truth of a signal just is the fact that the signal now stands in the kind of relation to the world which explains the historical contribution to fitness of the signaling system" (Harms 2000, 701). Harms goes on to note that according to teleosemantics there are true and false bee dances, true and false monkey warning cries, and so on. The idea here is that when, for instance, a monkey's warning cry serves the adaptive purpose it has historically served then the warning cry is true.

Harms maintains that morality exists as an adaptation aiding individual human beings in the struggle to survive and reproduce. In accordance with teleosemantics, he is led to maintain that moral claims are true when they serve the adaptive purposes they have historically served. So, for instance, the claim that "Theft is bad" will be true just in case this utterance serves its historically adaptive purpose. The preceding considerations lead him to conclude, "if you believe morality is an adaptation, then you ought to believe that there are objective standards that apply, and that there is a distinctively *moral* kind of truth" (Harms 2000, 701).

While I obviously have sympathy with the notion that morality is an adaptation and with the idea that there are objective moral truths, I find this argument problematic. The kind of critique I would offer has already been expressed in the literature by Richard Joyce (2001). Joyce notes that Millikan's teleosemantics is highly controversial, but for the sake of argument he is willing to grant the truth of the theory in general. (For criticisms of teleosemantics see Fodor 2000 and Botterill and Carruthers 1999, Chapter 7.) Joyce goes on to challenge the supposition that the truth of a moral claim is established by whether it serves its historically adaptive function. In challenging this, he argues by analogy. He has us suppose there is no God and he points out that were this so it still might be adaptive for us to encourage belief in God through using religious language, like "God exists" or "God punishes the wicked." Thus, religious discourse could be false but adaptive; and, *contra* Harms, he concludes the same might hold for moral claims.

Joyce notes how Harms allows that moral realists do not have to contend that there are moral *truths*. Moral realists might say that moral language is not truth-functional, but that there are objective criteria establishing the conditions for correct issuance of moral signals. On this view, "Theft is wrong" wouldn't be true, but when saying this serves the historically adaptive function, then saying it is warranted or fitting. Harms might try to avoid the preceding critique by noting that he wants to support this alternative kind of moral realism.

Joyce notes that this is a problematic construal of the moral realist options, but, again for the sake of argument, he is willing to concede that this is a kind of moral realism. He then goes on to argue that Harms's position would be flawed even in this modified form. Going back to the analogy with religion, he says that, even if there were adaptive functions for non-truthfunctional religious language, like "Repent thy sins!" or "Praise the Lord!", this would not offer support for *theistic* realism. That is, even if there were adaptive functions for "Repent thy sins!" or "Praise the Lord!" this would not mean that the use of such language was ever warranted or fitting. Thus, in keeping with the analogy, Joyce would say the adaptive use of non-truthfunctional moral discourse does nothing to support *moral* realism.

There is more to Joyce's critique than what I've explained here, but I do think I've covered the main points in a way that suggests some real problems with Harms's argument. In correspondence, Harms has told me that, while he has not published a reply to Joyce, he does believe that Joyce has misconstrued his position. After reviewing Harms's piece it is not clear how Joyce misinterprets him. One possibility concerns a section in Harms's essay in which he considers the kind of objection Joyce raises. Harms puts the objection as follows: "Since falsehoods can be adaptive in particular circumstances, then the truth just is not the same as fitness enhancement" (Harms 2000, 707). This seems to be the kind of objection which is the central focus of Joyce's essay. In reply to this, Harms states:

> Again, the proposal is that moral truth derives from the fulfillment of the historical conditions for the satisfaction of a particular signaling system. There is more than one way to exploit a given signaling system for gains in reproductive fitness and not all of these are consistent with *the particular historical function* which sets the truth conditions for moral language. The important point is that semantics are determined by a particular function or range of functions. The fact that

other functions (e.g. deception) can de fulfilled parasitically on the original semantics does not change the semantic rules, since the original function is not modified. There is a large literature that indicates that group adaptations in general have problems with cheating. To say that cheating on a cooperative strategy is adaptive is not to say that it is not recognizable as cheating from a biological point of view. (Harms 2000, 707, my italics)

Harms seems to be suggesting that discourse, whether moral or otherwise, is true when used in its *historically* adaptive ways, but this allows for its being used in different ways that are adaptive in new and/or different circumstances. When this happens you have useful fictions—false but adaptive discourse.

Joyce ignores this passage in his critique and this passage may contain the seeds of a response to Joyce. This is especially troubling when we consider the following passage from Joyce (2001):

The mere fact that we can make *sense* of the idea of a "useful fiction" shows that teleosemantics is not going to automatically secure realism. If what is *ex hypothesi* a fiction can be "useful," then it can, in principle, be favored by natural selection. But something is evidently wrong with the idea that as soon as natural selection gets involved the fiction immediately becomes objectively true. (Joyce 2001, 730)

It would have been nice to see Joyce directly address the passage from Harms that I quote above, because there he seems to be trying to deal with the kind of complaint that Joyce raises. Nonetheless, at this juncture, I am inclined to think that Harms's position is still problematic, because he only seems to allow that useful fictions arise in contexts where a signal is used in adaptive ways that are different from the *historically* adaptive ways. What seems to trouble Joyce, and rightly so, is that a signal could be used in its historically adaptive ways and still be false! In other words, Joyce seems to be suggesting that some signals, quite possibly moral signals, originally came into existence as useful fictions. Joyce seems to be suggesting that Harms's theory cannot make sense of this possibility. Joyce makes a good point here. Consequently, I am inclined to think that Harms's teleosemantic approach to defending an objectivist evolutionary ethics is significantly flawed.

4. Sketch of an Aristotelian Evolutionary Ethics

In Chapter 4 I presented an Aristotelian evolutionary ethical theory, and I argued that it overcomes flaws in the various objectivist theories considered in Chapter 3. I am not alone in seeing a way to connect evolutionary biology with Aristotelian ethics. Larry Arnhart and William Rottschaefer, both of whom I discuss in Chapter 3, have made the connection in their work. William Casebeer (2003) also makes the connection. Other contemporary Aristotelian ethicists see an important role for biological considerations in defending the view, but they don't develop the link with *evolutionary* biology so much. See, for instance, Foot 2001; Hurka 1993; Hursthouse 1999; and MacIntyre 1999.

These various recent defenses of the Aristotelian approach have not escaped critical attention in the literature. Phillip Kitcher (1999) subjects Hurka's Aristotelian theory to thorough and penetrating criticism; Copp and Sobel do the same for Foot's and Hursthouse's theories; and Joyce tackles Casebeer's approach. Each of these critics makes a variety of points, but they share the belief that evolutionary biology makes the Aristotelian approach implausible. These critics believe evolutionary biology is incompatible with the kind of teleology needed for Aristotelian ethics. This is a point that I strongly disagree with. In Chapter 4, I argued that what is essential to the Aristotelian approach is definitive characteristics of human beings, such as their rationality, in virtue of which objective standards of human goodness can be established, and I contend that evolutionary biology helps to explain the emergence of these definitive characteristics. So, *contra* such critics, I see evolutionary biology as an enhancement to the Aristotelian approach and not a threat to it.

In what follows I will develop in detail replies to the points that Joyce has made in criticizing Casebeer's Aristotelian evolutionary ethics. I want to focus on Joyce's argument for two main reasons. First, the points he makes against Casebeer could easily be seen as a threat to my own similar approach to evolutionary ethics. Second, the other critics of the Aristotelian approach, which I mention above, have already been responded to in the literature. Michael Byron provides a thorough and thoughtful response to Kitcher's critique of Aristotelian ethics; and in Lemos 2007 I defend the Aristotelian approach against various criticisms made by Copp and Sobel.

Joyce's critique of Casebeer's Aristotelian evolutionary ethics begins by presenting a general problem for any Aristotelian approach. Joyce notes that it makes sense to say that people with certain social roles, such as carpenter, teacher, or doctor, are good *qua* carpenter, *qua* teacher, or *qua* doctor, when they do those social functions well; and he says it makes sense to say that body parts—hearts, lungs, eyes—are good when they do their function well. But, he says there is no good reason to think humans have a function in the way these other things do and in virtue of which we can say they are good (Joyce 2006, 170). This is a problem for Aristotelian ethics, since Aristotle in the *Nicomachean Ethics* does argue that since these other things have functions in terms of which we can objectively assess their goodness, so too must humans have a function.

Having noted this point, Joyce considers a different kind of Aristotelian approach. He notes that we might consider the goodness of things by reflecting on what it is for a thing to flourish, and he says evolutionary biology might contribute to our understanding of this.

> If as a matter of fact human flourishing requires living harmoniously in a community (say), then, insofar as breaking a promise will upset one's social standing, we could insist on the applicability of the hypothetical imperative "You ought not to break promises." And to the criminal who declares that the community means nothing to him we could say "But existing in harmony with the community is one of your ends [one of your values?], whether or not you recognize or like this fact." Since these natural ends would be in some sense inescapable, then so too would be the associated hypothetical imperatives; the resulting normativity, it might be thought, would have the kind of practical oomph we want from morality. (Joyce 2006, 170–71)

According to this alternative kind of Aristotelian ethics, an accurate and biologically informed conception of flourishing human life would be the basis for identifying a variety of natural ends or goals of human existence in terms of which we could generate a list of binding moral norms, norms with "the kind of practical oomph we want from morality."

Understanding the Aristotelian approach in these terms, Joyce goes on to make four separate arguments against it. I will consider each of these arguments and show why each fails.

(I) CAN THE ARISTOTELIAN APPROACH MAKE SENSE OF TRANSGRESSION?

Joyce writes:

To the extent that we expect a moral system to have room for the idea that a wrongdoer deserves punishment for her crimes, a system of hypothetical imperatives will not serve. The basic problem is that someone who fails to act so as to secure her ends has principally wronged herself, but a value system revolving around self-harm doesn't look much like a moral system. Punishment, in such a system, would amount to a bizarre institution of inflicting further harm upon a person because she has harmed herself. On such a view Jack the Ripper should elicit our deepest sympathy, since what was really wrong about his killing all those women is that he radically undermined his own flourishing. (Joyce 2006, 171)

There are two serious problems with this argument. First, it *can* make sense to punish someone who has harmed himself, because he might not know he has harmed himself and the punishment may motivate him to not continue doing so. Second, the Aristotelian need not view punishment solely as a means to keep people from harming themselves. He may be equally concerned for the flourishing of others. So, the Aristotelian doesn't have to think that Jack the Ripper is bad just because he (unknowingly) harms himself. Rather, he is also bad because he destroys the opportunity for others to flourish, and for this reason he deserves punishment.

(II) CAN THE ARISTOTELIAN APPROACH MAKE SENSE OF PRAISE?

Joyce provides a different kind of argument in the next paragraph. He writes:

Evolutionary biology may license our claiming that a particular heart is good because it pumps blood well, but in saying this we would not really be praising the heart, any more than we would be praising an assassin for his ruthless efficiency if we admitted that he is good at his profession. Thus, if evolutionary biology by the same logic allows us to call a person "good" (in that she is a flourishing example of humankind), this must also be a "praisefree" use of a normative term—hardly a moral usage. (Joyce 2006, 171)

The point about the assassin leads us off track here, but I will return to it later. The crux of the argument is that since we don't praise a heart by saying it's good by flourishing, we don't praise a human being by saying she's good by flourishing. This is a terribly weak argument because it completely overlooks the fact that humans flourish or fail to flourish largely through the decisions or choices they make. Hence, to say a heart is good is not to praise it, because it is *not responsible* for its goodness. In contrast, human beings are largely responsible for their own decisions, and the decisions they make impact their flourishing. Thus, when we say that a human being is good due to his flourishing, this normally does amount to praise, because he is normally responsible for this flourishing.

As noted above, the point about the assassin draws us off track. We don't praise assassins as good human beings because their occupation runs counter to what human flourishing consists in. But we might acknowledge that someone is a good assassin (good *qua* assassin). However, this is not to praise him or her *qua* human being since that which she is good at (being an assassin) is counter to her own human flourishing as well as that of others. And to the extent that she is responsible for being an assassin she deserves blame and not praise. In contrast, consider another example, say, that of a doctor. If the doctor is good *qua* doctor, then to say he is good is normally to bestow praise, because doctors are normally responsible for being good doctors and good doctoring normally contributes to the doctor's flourishing as well as that of his patients.

(III) CAN AN ARISTOTELIAN ETHICS MAKE SENSE OF THE OVERRIDINGNESS OF MORAL NORMS?

Another one of Joyce's arguments runs as follows:

Suppose it is true that evolutionary biology can somehow underwrite the prescription of "Jack ought not to kill people." On what grounds would the "ought" claim override any competing "ought" claims that might arise? Suppose that Jack gets immense pleasure from killing people, and suppose that gaining pleasure is one of Jack's chosen ends; thus there is a competing hypothetical imperative: "Jack ought to kill people." Who is to say that the former overcomes the latter, that the former has for Jack a "to-be-doneness" that the latter lacks? One might answer that the former is based in Jack's biology, or that it is less contingent than the latter, or even (extravagant claim!) that it flows from something that is essential to Jack's status as a human being. But none of these distinguishing characteristics of the former imperative, nor their combination, suffices to provide it with the needed trumping quality. One could, with just as much prima facie warrant, assert that the ends that a person cares about in the most heartfelt way (i.e. the nasty desire, in Jack's case) are the ones from which the overriding imperatives derive. (Joyce 2006, 172)

The point Joyce makes here is closely related to the point he makes in his fourth argument, which I will consider in the next section. This point and the latter are also closely related to his general critique of objectivist, naturalistic ethical reductionism, which I critically addressed in an earlier section of this Afterword. Consequently, what I have to say about this argument will overlap somewhat with points I have already made.

Here, Joyce is arguing that there is a nothing in the Aristotelian approach that can explain why Jack ought not kill people if Jack derives immense pleasure from doing so. Joyce is asking why it is more important to satisfy the end of human flourishing which involves not killing people than to satisfy one's heartfelt desires, which might be satisfied by killing people.

For the Aristotelian, these worries are misplaced. The point of ethics is to give an account of human goodness or human flourishing and then to derive a list of the virtues from that account. Along with the list of virtues, there would be a derivative list of do's and don't's. So, for instance, since justice is a virtue necessary to human flourishing and since killing innocent people is unjust, one ought not to do so. Given that living in community with others is a part of what is involved in human flourishing and since acts of injustice, like killing innocent people, lead to the breakdown of community, the Aristotelian can plausibly maintain that the good or flourishing human being is just and, consequently, one ought not to kill.

Now, if someone, like Jack, comes along and says "What I really want to do in life is kill people, so I ought to kill people," then does this present a problem for the Aristotelian? Not at all. For Jack only has justification for his conclusion ("I ought to kill people") if he can show how that conclusion is derived from a conception of human goodness or flourishing that is equally or more warranted than the Aristotelian conception, and I seriously doubt that he or anyone can show this. Joyce himself does not endeavor to show this, but he does say, "One could, with just as much prima facie warrant, assert that the ends that a person cares about in the most heartfelt way (i.e. the nasty desires in Jack's case) are the ones from which the overriding imperatives derive" (172).

Perhaps, *contra* Aristotelians, Joyce would argue that flourishing involves the satisfaction of one's most heartfelt desires. But are we *really* to think this conception of flourishing can compete with Aristotle's? It is obvious that flourishing involves more than this. Flourishing has to do with the successful performance of activities that are definitive of beings of a kind. That's why the good heart does well at pumping blood, the good stomach does well at digesting, and the good doctor does well at healing. Since there is no essential connection between satisfying one's most heartfelt desires and doing well at the defining activity of human kind, this proposed conception of flourishing is off the mark. Here it might be wondered what the defining activity of humans is. My own position is traditionally Aristotelian—the defining activity is rational activity. I defended this view at some length in Chapter 4, but there are alternative conceptions or accounts of flourishing that are plausible which could also explain why the case of Jack presents no serious threat to the Aristotelian approach. Consider, for instance, the account of flourishing provided by Foot in her *Natural Goodness*.

Perhaps what really bothers Joyce is that the Aristotelian cannot make someone like Jack see that he ought not kill people. The Aristotelian can explain how human flourishing involves living in community with others and how killing is disruptive of killing and so Jack ought not kill; and Jack might say, "Fine, but I really want to kill, so why shouldn't I?" This could certainly happen. In fact, I think it is common for bad people to respond to moral teaching in this way. But this is no shortcoming in the Aristotelian ethics. It is not the job of ethical theory to give every bad person self-interested reason to do what is right. Rather, it is the ethicist's job to give a rationally justified account of the nature of the virtues and of our obligations. The Aristotelian does this by giving a justified account of human flourishing and shows how the virtues and their correspondent obligations flow forth from this conception. If this doesn't convince all listeners to live accordingly, this is by no means a sign of failure by the Aristotelian ethicist. Instead, it may well be a sign of the moral failings of those listeners.

(IV) CAN THE ARISTOTELIAN APPROACH MAKE SENSE OF "THE INTRINSIC ACTION-GUIDINGNESS" OF MORAL PROPERTIES?

According to Joyce, moral properties have "an intrinsic action-guidingness." That is, they provide persons with reasons for acting irrespective of their ends. So, for instance, to say that justice is good is to provide a person with reason to be just whether that person desires to be just or not. Joyce argues that moral realists, such as Aristotelians, must show that there are moral properties with this intrinsic action-guidingness. He also contends that Casebeer's Aristotelian ethics grounded in evolutionary biology cannot yield such moral properties.

> [T]he normativity that may be squeezed from evolutionary biology comes nowhere near to accommodating this desideratum. Just as the fact that the function of the heart is to pump blood doesn't imply that there is a *demand* that it do so, the ascription by the same logic of biological function to humans would not imply any practical demand. Just as the fact that the function of an assassin is to kill people doesn't imply that he has any *reason* to do so (no reason, at least, that should carry weight in his deliberations), the ascription by the same logic of a biological function to humans would not imply any practical reason to fulfill the function. (Joyce 2006, 174)

This argument is similar to one of Joyce's earlier arguments considered here, and it suffers from similar problems. Consider the first premise, "the function of the heart is to pump blood doesn't imply there is a *demand* that it do so." First, it is an odd claim, since there is no point of *demanding* anything of a heart because it has no choice in what it does. It makes sense to say that since the function of the heart is to pump blood it is necessary that a good heart pump blood. To say this might suggest that a good heart is required in some sense to pump blood. Even so, to speak of a heart facing any such requirements is odd, since, again, it has no choice in what it does.

From this point about the heart he goes on to infer by analogy that "the ascription by the same logic of a biological function to humans would not imply any practical demand" (174). As my comments above suggest, the analogy is weak because it makes no sense to demand anything of hearts since they have no choice. In contrast, we can make demands on human beings because they can choose to respond or not.

Having said all of this, the more important question is whether noting the biological function of humans, describing the defining activity (the *ergon*) of humans, places any practical demand on humans. Before going further, let me remind the reader that the issue here is whether noting the biological function of humans has any intrinsic action-guidingness about it. If so, then noting this should give persons reasons to act in certain ways irrespective of their desires. In this sense, noting the human function would imply some kind of practical demand.

Clearly, Joyce thinks that noting the human function implies no such practical demand. But, as I've argued, his support for this by way of the heart analogy is weak. Now I'll add that noting the human function *does* imply certain practical demands of them, because noting this provides the key to giving a correct account of the nature of human goodness and pointing out the nature of human goodness gives humans some reason to pursue human goodness. There is intrinsic action-guidingness in the description of the human function because it leads to an account of the human good, and such an account gives some reason for humans to act so as to attain the human good.

Having said this, let me clarify what I am *not* saying. I am not saying that the clarification of the human function or the human good gives persons *overriding* reasons to act in certain ways. Whether or not reasons are overriding will be relative to the interests of persons. So, for instance, giving a person an account of the human function and/or the human good gives him some reason to pursue the human good, but it does not necessarily give him *overriding* reasons. Whether it does so will depend on how much he cares about being good. Perhaps, he cares more about being pleased and he finds pleasure in things that are incompatible with the attainment of the human good or the attainment of the human function.

Here it might be thought this will not do as a response to Joyce, because what he really means by saying moral properties are intrinsically action-guiding is that they provide *overriding* reasons to act in certain ways. If this is what he intends, then he places too high of a demand on the moral theorist. As I have already argued, it is not the moral theorist's job to convince every person how he ought to act, to give every person overriding reason to do what he ought. It is enough to give an accurate account of the human function and the human good and to show how the virtues are derived from this. If this does not give every person overriding reason to pursue these ends, then so be it. Again, when people do not see a correct account of the human good as overriding reason to act in pursuit of it, this may be more a reflection of their bad character than it is a problem with the account.

5. Evolutionary Biology and the Moral Status of Animals

In Chapter 5, I examined whether evolutionary biology has significant implications for the existence of animal rights. I did so by providing an extensive critical examination of James Rachels's *Created from Animals*, in which he argues at length that evolutionary biology does indeed have such implications.

Rachels defends this view by arguing that evolutionary biology undermines the concept of human dignity. This concept suggests that human beings have a special moral status that no other animals possess which makes them the only animals deserving of moral consideration. He notes that the two main supports for the concept of human dignity are: (1) the image of God thesis and (2) the rationality thesis. The image of God thesis states that of all animals only human beings are made in the image of God. The rationality thesis states that human beings are the only rational animals. Each of these has been used to support the concept of human dignity. But Rachels argues that the facts of evolutionary biology imply that these theses are not rationally defensible. Hence, he concludes that evolutionary biology undermines the concept of human dignity, which in turn implies that nonhuman animals should be granted equal moral consideration alongside of human beings.

My Chapter 5 has two main parts. The first part is a detailed critical analysis of Rachels's thoughts on the image of God thesis.

The second part is a critical analysis of his thoughts on the rationality thesis. The first part was originally published as an article in *The American Catholic Philosophical Quarterly* in 2003. In that same year David Reiter also published an article critically assessing Rachels's views on the image of God thesis. His piece and mine are the only article-length publications dealing with Rachels's views on the subject. There are, of course, some published reviews of Rachels's book. See, for instance, Bradie 1997 and Bekoff 1992.

Rachels argues that evolutionary biology undermines the image of God thesis by taking away the rational support for it; and he says it does this largely by undermining the design argument for God's existence. As noted in Chapter 5, Rachels is not alone in holding the latter view: Richard Dawkins and Daniel Dennett have been saying this sort of thing for years. The work of Dawkins and Dennett has drawn a lot of attention in the literature, and I take note of some of this literature in Chapter 5. (See Sadowsky 1988; Gallagher 1992; 1993; and Harris 1999.) I also note there that Rachels's account of how evolution undermines the design argument is much more detailed than that of Dawkins and Dennett. Dawkins and Dennett mostly present lots and lots of evidence for evolution and how the theory of natural selection can make sense of the complex design of just about all biological phenomena, and then they move rather quickly to the conclusion that the design argument has been debunked. Rachels is more subtle in his approach, confronting at length possible replies. Because of this, I believed it was especially important to give his work extensive consideration. Since the publication of my critique of Rachels's views on evolution and religion, Dawkins and Dennett have gotten busy with more work on the subject. (See Dawkins 2006 and Dennett 2006.)

Some readers familiar with recent controversies surrounding "intelligent design" might find it odd that I've included no discussion of the work of figures like Michael Behe or Phillip Johnson, two leading figures in the intelligent design movement. The main reason for this is that I don't find this approach to defending the rationality of faith very plausible, but more on this shortly.

In what follows I will briefly address three related topics that connect up with issues addressed in Chapter Five; these are: (1) Reiter's discussion of Rachels' views; (2) the more recent work of Dawkins and Dennett; and (3) the "intelligent design" movement.

(1) Reiter's Discussion of Rachels's Views

Reiter begins with an explanation of the general structure of Rachels's argument that evolution undermines the concept of human dignity. He notes that Rachels: (1) employs the problem of evil in attacking theism and (2) criticizes the God as first cause, or cosmological, argument. I consider both of these aspects of Rachels's position in my chapter, but Reiter doesn't say much about them, focusing more on Rachels's critique of the design argument.

In discussing the design argument, Reiter considers what he calls "designer evolution"—the thesis that God creates through the evolutionary process. He argues that, despite his efforts, Rachels does not show that there are any significant problems with the designer evolution view. Thus, like me, Reiter thinks Rachels fails to show that evolution undermines the image of God thesis. At this point in his article, he makes another point which I have stressed and with which I very much agree. He notes that even if evolution undermines Paley-type design arguments, arguments which say that the complex design of biological organisms requires an intelligent designer, this would still not mean that it undermines the concept of intelligent design. Like me, Reiter sees that there are other kinds of design arguments that are indifferent to the truth of the Darwinian theory of evolution. (See Reiter 2003, 413, note 12.) Alvin Plantinga has also touched on this point in criticizing Dawkins and Dennett, who, like Rachels, believe that Darwinism undermines the design argument for God. I cite Swinburne's design argument as an alternative approach to the design argument; Plantinga cites Robin Collins's "Fine-Tuning" design argument as another kind of alternative (Plantinga 1996; 2007; Collins 1999). Finally, before moving on, let me also note that I am not maintaining here nor in Chapter 5 that such alternative design arguments are sound. My point is that the truth of the Darwinian theory of evolution is irrelevant to their soundness. Consequently, it is a mistake to say that evolutionary biology undermines the design argument.

In the second half of his article Reiter moves away from criticizing Rachels's argument. He goes on to argue that if we assume the truth of naturalism, the view that there are no supernatural beings, such as God, then evolution does make it prima facie implausible that human beings have a special dignity or moral worth. He reasons as follows: If we have a special dignity, then, like Rachels, Reiter thinks we would get this by either (a) being created in God's image or (b) by being the only rational animals. Reiter points out that if naturalism is true then (a) is not possible, since God would not exist. And, he says if naturalism and evolution are true then (b) is prima facie implausible. The reasoning behind the latter contention is that evolution involves gradual modification of species over long periods of time. This being the case there should be other species with whom we are ancestrally related that possess some degree of rationality. He goes on to emphasize that naturalism and evolution only make it *prima facie* implausible that human being have a special dignity. He acknowledges that a comparative study of human beings and other animals may provide adequate evidence that there are unique aspects of human beings which give them a special dignity and worth.

Reiter's argument is interesting. At this point I am inclined to think he's right that naturalism combined with evolution does make the uniqueness of human rationality (or the uniqueness of any human qualities) prima facie implausible. But, as my comments in the second half of Chapter Five suggest, I do think the comparative study of human beings with other animals reveals significant differences, giving justification for the belief that human beings do have a special dignity and worth.

(II) THE MORE RECENT WORK OF DAWKINS AND DENNETT

Turning to the newer treatments of the subject by Dawkins and Dennett, we see some of the same old problems as well as some interesting new points. There is not much in Dennett's *Breaking the Spell* that is particularly relevant to our discussion here. This book does not focus much on undermining the rationality of belief in God. Rather, it is more of an attempt to explain the persistence of the grip that religion has on human consciousness and how certain forms of religious belief become widespread. It also focuses on the question of what we, as a society can and should do to prevent the spread of dangerous or harmful religious beliefs. In dealing with these issues Dennett applies the theory of memes, which Dawkins introduced in his classic, *The Selfish Gene* (1976), and which Dennett discusses at some length in his opus, *Darwin's Dangerous Idea* (1995). According to the theory of memes, we can understand the persistence of the existence and use of certain ideas and theories in much the same way that the theory of natural selection understands the origin of species. The theory states that ideas and theories compete with each other for survival in the minds of human beings. Those that are more fit for survival persist over time. Sometimes they are altered favorably giving rise to new ideas or theories, etc.

In contrast, Dawkins's *The God Delusion*, is more relevant. While making some of the same old mistakes in his contention that evolution undermines the case for God's existence, Dawkins goes farther in this book. He argues not simply that there is no longer any good reason to believe that God exists, as he does in *The Blind Watchmaker* (1985), but that God's existence is extremely improbable. The central argument for this occurs in Chapter 3 of his book, "Why There Almost Certainly Is No God." In short, the argument states that since there is tremendous complexity found in nature and since the complex can only be created by something at least as complex, if not more complex, then God, if he exists, must be tremendously complex. Further, according to Dawkins, the more complex a thing is the more improbable its existence is. So, God's existence is tremendously improbable.

Notice that the argument here doesn't employ evolutionary biology to show that God's existence is highly improbable. If biological considerations are relevant, they are so in establishing the complexity found in nature. Nevertheless, Dawkins is clearly engaged in metaphysical considerations here, and, as critics have argued, he is overly simplistic in his approach to these issues. For instance, Plantinga (2007) notes that there is a long tradition within philosophical theology which understands God as a simple being, not a complex one. Consequently, he feels Dawkins must do more to show that God would have to be tremendously complex. He also notes that on Dawkins's own theory of complexity, which states that complexity requires parts, God cannot be complex. Plantinga's point is that God, being purely spiritual in nature, would lack parts.

Plantinga also notes that Dawkins ignores the traditional conception of God as a necessary being, a being whose essence includes his existence.

[I]f God is a necessary being, if he exists in all possible worlds, then the probability that he exists, of course, is 1, and the probability that he does not exist is 0. Far from its being improbable that he exists, his existence is maximally probable. So, if Dawkins proposes that God's existence is improbable, he owes us an argument for the conclusion that there is no necessary being with the attributes of God—an argument that doesn't just start from the premise that materialism is true. Neither he nor anyone else has provided even a decent argument along these lines; Dawkins doesn't even seem to be aware that he needs an argument of that sort. (Plantinga 2007)

I'm inclined to think Plantinga is right about this. Dawkins's foray into metaphysics here and elsewhere, such as his critiques of the design argument, are overly simplistic. He should probably stick with writing about evolutionary biology, something he is extremely good at doing.

(III) THE 'INTELLIGENT DESIGN' MOVEMENT

In Chapter 5 I argued contra Rachels that evolutionary biology does not undermine the rationality of belief in God as a wise, good, and loving creator of the universe. On my view, it may well be the case that the biological kingdom and the diversity of life were created by God through the process of evolution by natural selection. Additionally, I contend that there may even be kinds of design arguments, such as Swinburne's, which are immune to arguments based on evolutionary biology and which provide good reason to believe such a creator God exists.

What I did *not* do in Chapter 5 is argue that there are significant weaknesses in the Darwinian theory of evolution which justify an appeal to an intelligent designer at work in producing living things. This approach to defending the rationality of faith is taken by contemporary intelligent design theorists, such as Phillip Johnson and Michael Behe.

Behe has famously argued that there are irreducibly complex phenomena in the biological world that are incapable of being explained by way of the Darwinian theory of natural selection. Because of this, he thinks we are warranted in concluding that some kind of intelligent designer (though not necessarily the Judeo-Christian God) was at work in the creation of living things. In his writings he gives detailed examples of some of these "irreducibly complex" phenomena and explains why he thinks the Darwinian theory cannot explain their existence.

Phillip Johnson has argued that the Darwinian theory has a dubious scientific status. He complains that it is an unfalsifiable theory and that many of its claims cannot be supported with observational data. Additionally, he contends that belief in the Darwinian theory of the origin of species requires an unwarranted assumption that naturalism is true. Naturalism is a metaphysical belief that there are no supernatural beings, such as God. Thus, he thinks the theory is unscientific on these grounds as well as its being unfalsifiable and lacking important observational data.

Like me, these thinkers would object to Rachels's claim (and Dawkins's and Dennett's claims too, for that matter) that Darwinism undermines the rationality of faith. But I didn't discuss them in Chapter 5 for two main reasons. First, adequate response to Rachels, Dawkins, and Dennett does not require it. And, second, the arguments of Behe and Johnson are highly problematic. For criticism of Behe, see Dorit 1997 and Ruse 1998; 2001. For criticism of Johnson, see Scott 1992. The points by Dorit, Ruse (1998), and Scott are all reprinted in Philip Appleman's *Darwin: A Norton Critical Edition* (third edition, 2001). I wholeheartedly agree with their criticisms of Johnson and Behe.

6. Faith, Reason, and Evolutionary Epistemology

The first half of Chapter 5 addressed issues concerning evolution and the rationality of faith. Chapter 6 continued to explore this theme from a very different angle. In Chapter 6 I critically examined Alvin Plantinga's recent evolutionary argument against naturalism. He argues that if there is no God and we are the products of the blind forces of natural selection, then our cognitive capacities are shaped to be adaptive. He maintains that such adaptive cognitive capacities are not likely to be reliable producers of true beliefs. Consequently, if there is no God and we are the products of Darwinian evolution, then we have good reason to doubt the reliability of our cognitive capacities, meaning we are led into skepticism. In contrast, if naturalism is false and we are instead the products of God's creative activities, then we are made in God's image. On the latter hypothesis, we'd have good reason to believe in the reliability of our cognitive capacities.

In Chapter 6 I considered just two recent replies to Plantinga's argument—those of Michael Ruse and Evan Fales. I argued that Ruse's reply is problematic in several respects and I argue that Fales's reply is successful. In defense of Fales's approach I considered various points Plantinga has made in response to Fales, and I argue that Plantinga's replies are answerable.

Plantinga's argument has drawn a lot of attention in the recent literature. Many philosophers have tried their hand at giving sound replies to his argument. The best source for entering into this literature is James Beilby's *Naturalism Defeated?* This edited volume contains essays by many good philosophers critiquing Plantinga's argument. It also contains Plantinga's replies to these criticisms. I should note that this book includes the essay by Fales and the reply by Plantinga which I considered in Chapter 6. Besides the essays in Beilby 2002 there are other important critiques. Ruse's reply, which is developed in his *Taking Darwin Seriously*, is not included in Beilby 2002. One should also consider Sober and Fitelson 1998.

In Chapter 6, I criticize Ruse's argument and I defend Fales's argument. Ruse maintains that evolutionary considerations should lead us to reject metaphysical realism in favor of internal realism. Metaphysical realism states that there's a way the world is independent of our representations of it and that true beliefs accurately represent this reality. In contrast, internal realism views reality as a product of our representations and employs a coherence theory of truth. I maintain that Ruse's case for rejecting metaphysical realism is highly problematic. In addition, the reply which Fales makes to Plantinga and which I defend is firmly rooted in a realist perspective. Consequently, my work in Chapter 6 can be understood as offering support for the view that evolutionary naturalism is consistent with metaphysical realism and that, contra Plantinga, a world understood in such realist terms can be known even on the assumption of a naturalistic ontology.

In the recent literature, Stephen J. Boulter has published a very interesting essay, which, if sound, gives support for the metaphysical and epistemological views I advanced in Chapter 6. He argues that there are good evolutionary biological and neuroscientific reasons to accept metaphysical realism (MR). What he calls "metaphysical realism (MR)" contains both ontological realism (OR) and epistemological realism (ER). He says that OR is "the thesis that there is an extra-linguistic reality whose nature or structure is independent of our representation of it" (Boulter 2004, 245). He states that ER is "the thesis that human beings in full possession of their properly functioning cognitive faculties are capable of ascertaining the nature (at least in part) of this independent reality in thought and non-projective perception" (Boulter 2004, 245). In support of MR he gives separate arguments for OR and ER.

In support of OR, he contends:

1. Without a pre-structured world there is no visual perception.

2. But visual perceptions are commonplace.

---

3. So, (3) there is a pre-structured world. (Boulter 2004, 250)

A "pre-structured world" is a world that exists independent of our perceptions and representations of it and it is a world that contains (a) distinct objects, such as tables, trees, and dogs, with (b) distinct features, such as tops, leaves, tails, and legs, both of which exist as they are independent of our perceptions and representations of them. The belief in such a pre-structured world is antithetical to the anti-realist conception of things, since the anti-realist views the existence and nature of such objects as somehow dependent upon our perception or representations of them.

Boulter rightly takes the second premise as obviously true and argues in support of the first premise. In its support he explains important experimental findings from cognitive psychology and neurophysiology which show that "if a subject is presented with an illuminated field which is homogeneous in every respect and in all direction (a field known as a "Ganzfeld"), the light cannot be focused and no retinal image can be formed. In such cases subjects report that they see nothing, despite the fact that the eye is stimulated by the incoming light" (Boulter 2004, 250). He goes on to maintain, "The conclusion drawn from these (at the time) unexpected experimental results is that stimulation by light is a necessary but not sufficient condition for vision. Only some type of light, i.e., structured light, permits visual perceptions" (Boulter

2004, 251). He adds that further support for this conclusion can be derived from experiments on subjects whose visual systems have been deprived of exposure to structured light.

The importance of structured light for vision can also be established by experiments carried out on subjects whose visual systems have been deprived of exposure to structured light. Hubel and Weisel found significant and irreparable disruption to cell physiology and histology in young animals whose eyes had been sutured shut before the visual system was fully developed. They were also able to establish that the disruption was not due simply to light deprivation. The results of these experiments show not only that visual systems respond only to structured light, but also that visual systems require structured light if they are to develop properly at the cellular level (Boulter 2004, 251).

Taking himself to have established that structured light is necessary for visual perception, Boulter goes on to consider what the most likely source of this structured light is. He considers the Kantian or antirealist proposal that the visual system of the perceiver is the source of this structure, but he rejects this option arguing that:

> If the perceiver were the source of the structure, we would not expect visual impotence in the Ganzfeld, which is what we find. For if perceivers contained structuring principles within themselves, as the Kantian maintains, unstructured light ought to pose no difficulties for visual perception since the perceiver makes up for this deficiency by providing the structure itself. But the experimental results noted above show that this cannot be done. If the light entering the eye is not already structured, the observer remains effectively blind. (Boulter 2004, 252)

From here he goes on to maintain that the best explanation for the existence of the structured light necessary for visual perception is the existence of "a featured, pre-structured world which is received as featured in perception" (Boulter 2004, 252). This, of course, implies that premise (1) in his case for OR is true.

As noted above, epistemological realism (ER) is the view that we are able to ascertain the nature of such a pre-structured reality in thought and non-projective perception. In defense of ER, Boulter invokes evolutionary considerations, arguing that the best explanation for how creatures survive and reproduce in their environs presupposes that they just see "the external, extra-linguistic, independent world or environment as it is in itself" (Boulter 2004, 254). Additionally, he maintains:

> [F]or vision to aid oriented activity within this pre-structured world (as it manifestly does) the content of visual perceptions must be (roughly) structurally identical to that of the external world. If this rough structural identity is not assumed it becomes very difficult to explain how perception allows an organism to cope with its environment.

And,

> If we assume, as I think we must, that organisms and their perceptual systems, including human perceptual systems, have evolved within a pre-existing and pre-structured environment in roughly the manner described by the synthetic theory of evolution by natural selection, then it is difficult to avoid the belief that our perceptual systems have evolved to their current state because they allow organisms to track the structure of this environment. If organisms were not able to keep in touch with the surrounding environment as it is in itself their biological viability would be seriously compromised. The idea that perceptual systems are "built" with a specific environment in mind also helps to mitigate the challenge of radical skepticism with respect to the reliability of sense experience. If sense perception were not generally reliable, we would not be here (or at least not in this form). (Boulter 2004, 253–54)

In further support of ER he goes on to argue that the Kantian or antirealist theory of perception, which is the chief rival to ER, does not fit well with evolutionary biology.

I cannot do full justice to Boulter's article here, but I would note that the points he makes about the way in which evolutionary biology suggests that our perceptual faculties must be generally reliable guides in leading us to beliefs about a mind-independent, pre-structured reality fits perfectly with (a) the metaphysical realist position I defended in Chapter 6 and (b) the kind of reply I make to Plantinga's anti-naturalist argument. Consequently, if Boulter's arguments are sound they lend credence to the metaphysical and epistemological points I made in Chapter 6.

7. Psychological Egoism and Evolutionary Biology

Since the time Chapter 6 was first published as an article in *Philosophy of the Social Sciences*, other published critiques of Sober and Wilson's argument have appeared. Among these other critiques is that of Stephen Stich. In what follows I want to explicate some key aspects of Stich's critique, noting the difference between his and mine and suggesting a possible defense strategy for Sober and Wilson.

Recall here that *psychological hedonism* is the view that the only motivation for human action is to either increase the pleasure of the agent or to avoid pain. According to this view, we never act out of an ultimate desire to benefit others—whenever we benefit others we do so only with the intent of making ourselves feel better. Sober and Wilson explain that this is a kind of psychological egoism. They regard it as the version of psychological egoism that is the most difficult to refute. Thus, they believe their refutation of it strongly suggests that psychological egoism is false.

Sober and Wilson believe that evolutionary biology gives us good reason to think this view is false. In contrast to psychological hedonism they discuss *motivational pluralism*, which is the view that sometimes we act to help others for their own welfare and at other times we act to benefit ourselves. According to this view, we are sometimes motivated to act out of an ultimate desire for the welfare of others and at other times we act out of an ultimate desire for our own welfare.

They argue that since the neurological machinery that is necessary for living as motivational pluralists is equally available and equally efficient as the neurological machinery needed to live as a psychological hedonist and since motivational pluralism would be a more reliable mechanism for producing adaptive helping behaviors, such as parental assistance of offspring, than would be the hedonistic mechanism, it follows that evolutionary biology entails that psychological hedonism is most likely false. It is more probable that we sometimes act on ultimate desires for the welfare of others.

In my critique of Sober and Wilson I granted them their point that motivational pluralism would be the more reliable mechanism for producing adaptive helping behaviors, and I argued that there were problems with their assumption that the pluralistic and hedonistic mechanism were equally available and equally efficient. In contrast, Stich grants the equal availability and equal efficiency theses, while attacking their claim that motivational pluralism would be the more reliable mechanism.

Stich identifies four different arguments they make for the view that motivational pluralism is more reliable, and he contends that each of them fails. Stich regards their fourth argument as the most compelling, but he goes on to contend that like the others it also fails. In what follows I will focus on his treatment of the fourth argument, since it is the most interesting of the four and Stich devotes most of his attention to it.

In presenting the fourth argument, Stich quotes the following passage from Sober and Wilson:

> Suppose a hedonistic organism believes on a given occasion that providing parental care is the way for it to attain its ultimate goal of maximizing pleasure and minimizing pain. What would happen if the organism provides parental care, but then discovers that this action fails to deliver maximal pleasure and minimal pain? If the organism is able to learn from experiences, it will probably be less inclined to take care of its children on subsequent occasions. Instrumental desires tend to diminish and disappear in the face of negative evidence of this sort. This can make hedonistic motivation a rather poor control device." . . . [The] instrumental desire will remain in place only if the organism . . . is trapped by an unalterable illusion. (Stich 2007, 277. See Sober and Wilson 1998, 314–15.)

Here Sober and Wilson argue that motivational pluralism, which would allow parents to help their children out of an ultimate desire for the children's welfare, is a more reliable mechanism than hedonism at producing such adaptive behavior. According to this fourth argument, this is so because a parent may learn over time that helping his or her children may not bring him or her much, if any, pleasure. In this case, the parent will no longer be reliably disposed to help his or her child, because he or she will no longer believe the help brings pleasure to himself or herself

In reply to this argument, Stich introduces the concept of "subdoxastic states." These are belief-like states which are unlikely to be altered by contradicting experiences. He says that the literature in cognitive science and psychology contains important discussions of these states. (See Carey and Spelke 1996; Spelke 2000; 2003.) He contends that the belief that helping one's children will bring one pleasure may be one of these sub-doxastic states that is immune to revision in the light of contradictory experience. Consequently, it may be that this belief which leads to hedonistically motivated help is relatively permanent, meaning we cannot be led by our experience to think otherwise. Given this possibility, Stich concludes that Sober and Wilson have not given us good reason to think hedonism is less reliable than motivational pluralism.

Stich's article is very interesting and he makes a lot of good points. But I do not think that his point here is especially devastating. For that matter it's not clear that he regards his point as devastating either. What Stich's point does is to clarify the need for Sober and Wilson to show that the beliefs needed to hedonistically motivate helping behavior—beliefs like "Helping my child will bring me pleasure"—are not likely to be these sub-doxastic beliefs which are immune to revision in the light of contradicting data. If this could be shown, it would be reasonable to suppose that psychological hedonism is improbable.

I, for one, do think it unlikely that the relevant beliefs are so impervious to revision. It is not uncommon for self-centered parents to take no pleasure in helping their children and, consequently, to act accordingly, providing no help when it is needed. Stich's hypothesis is that parents who initially think helping their children will bring them pleasure will irrationally go on providing hedonistically motivated help even when doing so brings them no pleasure. While I'm willing to concede that there are places where it is common for rationality to breakdown in human thought and behavior, I don't think it is likely that this is one of them. Nonetheless, my comments here are probably too speculative. To resolve these issues would probably require informed empirical research.

Gilbert Harman has also published criticism of Sober and Wilson's argument. He argues that Sober and Wilson cannot consistently maintain that the psychological and philosophical arguments against psychological hedonism fail while their own evolutionary biological argument succeeds. Sober and Wilson do contend that the various psychological and philosophical arguments against psychological hedonism fail. Because of this they think their own evolutionary argument against the view is especially important. However, Harman contends that to adequately refute the psychological or philosophical arguments they need a general procedure for mapping altruistic accounts of motivation into egoistic hedonistic accounts. That is, they need a general procedure which shows that for any given altruistic explanation of human behavior there is an equally, if not more, plausible egoistic or hedonistic explanation. But, says Harman, once this is provided to adequately refute the psychological or philosophical arguments, such a general procedure will undermine their evolutionary biological argument against psychological hedonism.

In support of the latter contention, Harman states:

> [Sober and Wilson's] argument is in part that 'psychological altruism will be more reliable than psychological hedonism as a device for getting parents to take care of their children' (1998, p. 310). But the existence of a general mapping between the theories suggest that any biological mechanism instantiating psychological altruism can also be interpreted as instantiating psychological hedonism, which would mean that psychological altruism could not be more reliable than psychological hedonism in any way whatsoever! (Harman 2000, 220–21)

Harman makes an interesting point here. In contrast to Harman, I argued in Chapter 7, contra Sober and Wilson, that the philosophical arguments give us good reason to reject psychological hedonism. Harman's critique is neutral on the merits of the philosophical arguments against psychological hedonism.

Sober and Wilson respond to Harman in the same volume in which his critique appears. (See Sober and Wilson 2000.) Contra Harman, they contend that they did not intend to suggest that *no* philosophical or psychological experiments could refute psychological hedonism. Rather, they contend that none have yet refuted it. I take it this point is intended, at least in part, to suggest there's no need for them to provide a general procedure for mapping any altruistic account of motivation into a hedonistic account. Additionally, if they don't need this to make their case against *existing* philosophical and psychological arguments, then their own evolutionary biological argument is not endangered. They also go on to state that they believe if their evolutionary biological argument is correct, then eventually there should be some empirical psychological or neuroscientific experiments which support their findings.

In defense of Harman, it might be argued that given the great variety of psychological and philosophical arguments against psychological egoism or hedonism, a general procedure for mapping any altruistic account into a hedonistic account is still needed to convincingly argue that no philosophical or psychological arguments have yet refuted egoism or hedonism. In agreement with Harman, it might again be contended that once this general theory is presented it will undermine Sober and Wilson's own evolutionary biological argument.

The preceding provides a possible defense of Harman's critique. I am not strongly committed to it at this point. I am just throwing it out there as something for the reader to consider before assuming that Sober and Wilson have adequately refuted Harman.

Sober and Wilson's critique of the experimental psychological arguments against hedonism has not gone unnoticed in the recent literature. As I have noted, they think their evolutionary biological argument is very important because of the failure of both the psychological arguments and the philosophical arguments. In the recent literature there have been some defenses of the relevant psychological arguments. (See Batson 2000 and Rosas 2002. See Sober and Wilson 2000 for a response to Batson.)

8. Evolution and Free Will: Darwinian Non-Naturalism Defended

In Chapter 8, I discussed Bruce Waller's views on evolution and freedom of the will. In his treatment of the subject Waller introduces the concept of natural autonomy. This is the capacity to pursue alternative courses of action in response to stimuli as opposed to always following the same course of action. Waller says that both human and many nonhuman animals possess this capacity, but in humans this capacity is significantly enhanced by our higher intelligence.

He also argues that this capacity is a favorable adaptation, giving a competitive advantage to creatures living in changing environments. Consequently, he thinks this capacity is a product of evolution by natural selection. In the recent literature Dennett also discusses the evolution of autonomy or freedom. Like Waller, he views it as a favorable adaptation, but he has a different conception of the nature of freedom, endorsing a compatibilist view which Waller rejects.

Compatibilism is the view that human freedom and moral responsibility exist and that they are compatible with causal determinism, the belief that all events are causally necessitated by antecedent events. This is the conception of human freedom endorsed by Dennett. In contrast, Waller says we have natural autonomy. According to Waller, natural autonomy does not support moral responsibility because on this view the choices we make are ultimately controlled by genetic and environmental factors beyond our control.

Waller goes on to discuss the moral and political principle of noninterference. This principle states that we should respect the rights of persons to make their own choices and to live in accordance with them. He argues that his conception of natural autonomy supports this important principle. In Chapter 8, I argued that Waller's natural autonomy theory cannot really support the principle of noninterference and that some kind of libertarian or compatibilist position is needed. I went on to argue, contra Waller, that the libertarian theory of free will is a live option for the Darwinian.

The libertarian theory of freedom states that free will exists and that it is incompatible with causal determinism. Waller presents two main lines of argument against this view. First, he argues that unlike natural autonomy libertarian freedom cannot plausibly be seen as a product of evolution. Second, he argues that the libertarian view is incoherent, being unable to make sense of how one's choices are one's own. I argue that neither of these arguments succeeds.

Before going further, let me note that I have a lot of sympathy for the view that human freedom is an evolved capacity of human beings, and I find the accounts that Waller and Dennett give of this to be quite plausible. However I don't believe there are any good Darwinian reasons to think the libertarian view is mistaken nor do I find the libertarian theory to be inherently flawed. In more recent writings I have tried to give further support for the libertarian view by answering a variety of arguments against it and by attacking the compatibilist alternative. (See my 2006; and my 2007b). In criticizing compatibilism in my 2006 article, I gave arguments that have a kinship with van Inwagen's famous "Consequence Argument."

(See van Inwagen 1983; 2002.) Dennett (in Dennett 2003) continues to defend the compatibilist approach, but he has been justly criticized for not doing more to confront the Consequence Argument. (See Fischer 2003; 2005.)

In both Chapter 8 and my 2006, I defended an agent-causal brand of libertarianism. There are important alternative libertarian approaches, such as Kane's indeterministic event-causal view and Ginet's noncausal view. (See Kane 1996; 2002; and Ginet 1990: 2002.) According to Kane, free willed acts are caused by causally indeterminate events occurring in the brains of the agents who perform them. According to Ginet, free willed acts are not caused at all, but they are not random either since they are susceptible of being given noncausal explanations. I think all three of these libertarian approaches to free will are compatible with a Darwinian view of evolution. In some of my most recent research (Lemos 2007b), I have given serious consideration to Kane's views and suggested a way of defending it against a powerful criticism known as "the luck objection." (For examples of the luck objection, see Mele 2006; 1999; and Haji 2005; 1999.)

A couple of other recent discussions of evolution and free will have been published by Janet Radcliffe Richards (2000, Chapter 6) and Tammler Sommers (2007). Janet Radcliffe Richards makes clear that there is no good reason to think that Darwinism or plausible forms of evolutionary psychology are inconsistent with freedom and moral responsibility. She is also critical of the libertarian approach to freedom and responsibility. She argues that the libertarian approach is not problematic because it conflicts with Darwinism but because it is conceptually incoherent. I agree with her that Darwinism poses no threat to freedom and responsibility, but obviously I part company with her on the issue of the coherence of the libertarian view. It is my hope that Chapter 8 as well as some of my more recent writings give adequate reason for my difference of opinion here.

Sommers (2007) presents an error theory of responsibility claims. That is, Tammler Sommers believes there is no human freedom sufficient for moral responsibility. Consequently, he thinks all claims we make which presuppose such freedom or responsibility are false. He gives an evolutionary biological account of why these false claims and beliefs are so commonplace. Sommers's piece is quite interesting, but I am not inclined to accept his conclusion since I believe that human beings do possess a kind of freedom which is sufficient for moral responsibility. Sommers himself does not argue for the nonexistence of this in his article, rather he cites Galen Strawson and Derk Pereboom as having made the case. Sommers's project is giving an evolutionary biological explanation for the prevalence of what he takes to be false beliefs in freedom and responsibility.

Bibliography

Alexander, R. 1977. Evolution, Human Behavior, and Determinism. In F. Suppe and P. Asquith, eds., *PSA 1976* (East Lansing: Philosophy of Science Association), 3–21.

———. 1979. *Darwinism and Human Affairs*. Seattle: University of Washington Press.

———. 1987. *The Biological Basis of Morality*. New York: Aldine de Gruyter.

Anselm, St. 1961. *The Proslogium*, in *St. Anselm: Basic Writings*, trans. S.N. Deane. La Salle: Open Court.

Appleman, P. 2001. *Darwin*. Third edition. New York: Norton.

Aristotle. 1987. *The Nicomachean Ethics*, trans. David Ross. Oxford: Oxford University Press.

Arnhart, L. 1997. *Darwinian Natural Right: The Biological Ethics of Human Nature*. Albany: SUNY Press.

Ball, S. 1988. Evolution, Explanation, and the Fact/Value Distinction. *Biology and Philosophy* 3, 317–348.

Barrett, J. 1991. Really Taking Darwin and the Naturalistic Fallacy Seriously: An Objection to Rottschaefer and Martinsen. *Biology and Philosophy* 6, 433–37.

Batson, C.D. 2000. Unto Others: A Service . . . And a Disservice. *Journal of Consciousness Studies* 7, 207–210.

Becker, L. 1983. The Priority of Human Interests. In *Ethics and Animals*, ed. H. Miller and W. Williams (Clifton: Humana Press).

Behe, M. 1996. *Darwin's Black Box: The Biochemical Challenge to Evolution*. New York: Free Press.

Beilby, J. 2002. *Naturalism Defeated? Essays on Plantinga's Evolutionary Argument Against Naturalism*. Ithaca: Cornell University Press.

Bekoff, M. 1992. Review of *Created from Animals* by James Rachels. *Environmental Values* 1, 83–86.

231

————. 2004. Wild Justice and Fair Play: Cooperation, Forgiveness, and Morality in Animals. *Biology and Philosophy* 19, 489–520.

Benson, J. 1978. Duty and the Beast. *Philosophy* 53, 529–549.

Bloomfield, P. 2006. Review of *The Evolution of Morality. Mind* 116, 176–180.

Bochenski, I. 1961. *History of Formal Logic*, trans. I. Thomas. South Bend: University of Notre Dame Press.

Botterill, G., and P. Carruthers. 1999. *The Philosophy of Psychology.* Cambridge: Cambridge University Press.

Boulter, S. 2004. Metaphysical Realism as a Pre-condition of Visual Perception. *Biology and Philosophy* 19, 243–261.

Bradie, M. 1997. Review of *Created from Animals* by James Rachels. *Biology and Philosophy* 12, 73–88.

Brink, D. 1998. Moral Realism and the Sceptical Argument from Disagreement and Queerness. In *Ethical Theory: Classical and Contemporary Readings,* ed. Louis Pojman (Belmont: Wadsworth). Originally in *Australasian Journal of Philosophy* 62, 111–125.

Byron, M. 2000. Virtue and the Reductivist Challenge. *Contemporary Philosophy* 22, 34–41.

Campbell, C.A. 1957. *On Selfhood and Godhood.* London: Allen and Unwin.

Campbell, R. 1996. Can Biology Make Ethics Objective? *Biology and Philosophy* 11, 21–32.

Carey, S. and E. Spelke. 1996. Science and Core Knowledge. *Philosophy of Science* 63, 515–533.

Casebeer, W. 2003. *Natural Ethical Facts: Evolution, Connectionism, and Moral Cognition.* Cambridge, Massachusetts: MIT Press.

Chisholm, R. 1991. Human Freedom and the Self. The Lindley Lecture, University of Kansas (1964). Reprinted in *Metaphysics: Classic and Contemporary Readings,* ed. Ronald C. Hoy and Nathan Oaklander (Belmont: Wadsworth), 360–66.

Cigman, R. 1981. Death, Misfortune, and Species Inequality. *Philosophy and Public Affairs* 10, 47–63.

Collier, J., and M. Stingl. 1993. Evolutionary Naturalism and the Objectivity of Morality. *Biology and Philosophy* 8, 47–60.

Collins, R. 1999. A Scientific Argument for the Existence of God: The Fine-Tuning Design Argument. In Michael Murray, ed., *Reason for the Hope Within* (Eerdmans).

Copp, D., and D. Sobel. 2004. Morality and Virtue: An Assessment of Some Recent Work in Virtue Ethics. *Ethics* 114, 514–554.

Dancy, J. 1985. *Introduction to Contemporary Epistemology.* Oxford: Blackwell.

Darwin, C. 1859. *On the Origin of Species.* London: John Murray.

————. 1868. *The Variation of Animals and Plants under Domestication*. London: John Murray.

————. 1871. *The Descent of Man*. London: John Murray.

Dawkins, R. 1976. *The Selfish Gene*. Oxford: Oxford University Press.

————. 1985. *The Blind Watchmaker*. London: Norton.

————. 2006. *The God Delusion*. New York: Houghton Mifflin.

Dennett, D. 1995. *Darwin's Dangerous Idea: Evolution and the Meaning of Life*. New York: Simon and Schuster.

————. 2003. *Freedom Evolves*. New York: Viking.

————. 2006. *Breaking the Spell: Religion as a Natural Phenomenon*. New York: Viking.

Descartes, R. 1997. *Meditations on First Philosophy*, trans. Laurence J. Lafleur. Upper Saddle River: Prentice Hall.

Devine, P. 1978. The Moral Basis of Vegetarianism. *Philosophy* 53, 481–505.

De Waal, F. 1982. *Chimpanzee Politics: Power and Sex Among the Apes*. London: Cape.

————. 1996. *Good Natured: The Origins of Right and Wrong in Primates and Other Animals*. Cambridge, Massachusetts: Harvard University Press.

————. 2006. *Primates and Philosophers: How Morality Evolved*. Princeton: Princeton University Press.

Diamond, C. 1978. Eating Meat and Eating People. *Philosophy* 53, 465–479.

Dombrowski, D. 1997. *Babies and Beasts: The Argument from Marginal Cases*. Urbana: University of Illinois Press.

Doore, G. 1980. The Argument from Design: Some Better Reasons for Agreeing With Hume. *Religious Studies* 16, 145–160.

Dorit, R. 1997. Review of *Darwin's Black Box* by Michael Behe. *American Scientist* 85, 474–75.

English, J. 1997. Abortion and the Concept of a Person. In *Contemporary Moral Problems*, ed. James White. Minneapolis: West. Originally published in *The Canadian Journal of Philosophy* 5 (1975).

Fales, E. 1996. Plantinga's Case Against Naturalistic Epistemology. *Philosophy of Science* 63, 432–452.

Ferguson, K.G. 2001. Semantic and Structural Problems in Evolutionary Ethics. *Biology and Philosophy* 16, 69–84.

Flanagan, O. 1981. Is Morality Epiphenomenal? *Philosophical Forum* 2/3, 207–225.

————. 1996. *Self Expressions: Mind, Morals, and the Meaning of Life*. Oxford: Oxford University Press.

Fischer, J. 2003. Review of Dennett's *Freedom Evolves*. *Journal of Philosophy* 100, 632–37.

———. 2005. Dennett on the Basic Argument. *Metaphilosophy* 36, 427–435.

Flew, A. 1994. E.O. Wilson after Twenty Years. *Philosophy of the Social Sciences* 24, 320–335.

Fodor, J. 1983. *Modularity of the Mind: An Essay on Faculty Psychology.* Cambridge, Massachusetts: MIT Press.

———. 2000. *The Mind Doesn't Work that Way.* Cambridge, Massachusetts: MIT Press.

Foot, P. 2001. *Natural Goodness.* Oxford: Oxford University Press.

Forrest, P. 1983. Priest on the Argument from Design. *Australasian Journal of Philosophy* 61, 84–87.

Francis, L.P., and R. Norman. 1978. Some Animals Are More Equal than Others. *Philosophy* 53, 507–527.

Gallagher, K. 1992. Dawkins in Biomorph Land. *International Philosophical Quarterly* 32, 501–513.

———. 1993. Dawkins, Darwin, and Design. *American Catholic Philosophical Quarterly* 67, 233–246.

Gelman, R., and C.R. Gallistel. 1978. *The Child's Understanding of Numbers.* Cambridge, Massachusetts: Harvard University Press.

Gelman, R. 1980. What Young Children Know about Numbers. *Educational Psychologist* 15, 54–68.

Gillan, D.J. 1981. Reasoning in the Chimpanzee, 2. Transitive Inference. *Journal of Experimental Psychology: Animal Behavior Processes* 7, 150–164.

Gillan, D.J., D. Premack, and G. Woodruff. 1981. Reasoning in the Chimpanzee, 1. Analogical Reasoning. *Journal of Experimental Psychology: Animal Behavior Processes* 7, 1–17.

Ginet, C. 1990. *On Action.* Cambridge: Cambridge University Press.

———. 2002. Reasons as Explanations of Action: Causalist versus Noncausalist Accounts. In *The Oxford Handbook of Free Will* R. Kane, ed. (New York: Oxford University Press).

Goodall, J. 1971. *In the Shadow of Man.* London: Collins.

Gould, S.J. 1977. *Ever Since Darwin: Reflections in Natural History.* New York: Norton.

———. 1980. *The Panda's Thumb.* New York: Norton.

Gutting, G. 1987. A Modified Version of the Argument from Religious Experience. In *Philosophy of Religion: An Anthology*, ed. Louis Pojman (Belmont: Wadsworth). Originally published in Gutting, *Religious Belief and Religious Skepticism* (South Bend: University of Notre Dame Press, 1982).

Haji, I. 1999. Indeterminism and Frankfurt-Type Examples. *Philosophical Explorations* 2, 42–58.

———. 2005. Libertarianism, Luck, and Action Explanation. *Journal of Philosophical Research* 30, 321–340.

Harman, G. 1977. *The Nature of Morality.* Oxford: Oxford University Press.

———. 2000. Can Evolutionary Theory Provide Evidence Against Psychological Hedonism? *Journal of Consciousness Studies* 7, 219–221.

Harms, W. 2000. Adaptation and Moral Realism. *Biology and Philosophy* 15, 699–712.

Harris, E. 1999. Darwinism and God. *International Philosophical Quarterly* 39, 277–290.

Hartshorne, C. 1967. *Anselm's Discovery.* La Salle: Open Court.

Hauser, M. 2006. *Moral Minds: How Nature Designed Our Universal Sense of Right and Wrong.* New York: Ecco.

Hook, S. 1958. Necessity, Indeterminism, and Sentimentalism. In *Determinism and Freedom in the Age of Modern Science,* ed. Sidney Hook (New York: NYU Press).

Hrdy, S.B. 1977. *The Langurs of Abu.* Cambridge, Massachusetts: Harvard University Press.

Hull, D. 1982. The Naked Meme. *Learning Development and Culture: Essays in Evolutionary Epistemology,* ed. H.C. Plotkin (Chichester: Wiley), 273–327.

———. 1988a. A Mechanism and Its Metaphysics: An Evolutionary Account of the Social and Conceptual Development of Science. *Biology and Philosophy* 3, 123–155.

———. 1988b. *Science as Progress.* Chicago: University of Chicago Press.

Hurka, T. 1993. *Perfectionism.* New York: Oxford University Press.

Hursthouse, R. 1999. *On Virtue Ethics.* Oxford: Oxford University Press.

Jacquette, D. 1989. Moral Value and the Sociobiological Reduction. In Lee, S. ed., *Inquiries Into Values: The Inaugural Session of the International Society for Value Inquiry* (Lewiston: Mellen, 685–694.

Johnson, P. 1991. *Darwin on Trial.* Washington, DC: Regnery.

Joyce, R. 2000. Darwinian Ethics and Error. *Biology and Philosophy* 15, 713–732.

———. 2001. Moral Realism and Teleosemantics. *Biology and Philosophy* 16, 723–731.

———. 2006. *The Evolution of Morality.* Cambridge, Massachusetts: MIT Press.

Kane, R. 1996. *The Significance of Free Will.* Oxford: Oxford University Press.

———. 2002. Some Neglected Pathways in the Free Will Labyrinth. In *The Oxford Handbook of Free Will,* ed. R. Kane (New York: Oxford University Press).

Kant, I. 1981. *Grounding for the Metaphysics of Morals*, trans. James Ellington. Indianapolis: Hackett.

King, J.E., and J.L. Fobes. 1982. Complex Learning by Primates. In *Primate Behavior*, eds. J.L. Fobes and J.E. King (New York: Academic Press), 327–360.

Kitcher, P. 1985. *Vaulting Ambition: Sociobiology and the Quest for Human Nature*. Cambridge, Massachusetts: MIT Press.

———. 1999. Essence and Perfection. *Ethics* 110, 59–83.

Kohlberg, L. 1981. *Essays on Moral Development*. New York: Harper and Row.

Lahti, D. 2003. Parting with Illusions in Evolutionary Ethics. *Biology and Philosophy* 18, 639–651.

Lemos, J. 1998. Evolution and Ethical Scepticism: Reflections on Ruse's Meta-Ethics. *Journal of Social and Evolutionary Systems* 21, 213–221.

———. 1999. Bridging the Is/Ought Gap with Evolutionary Biology: Is This a Bridge Too Far? *Southern Journal of Philosophy* 37, 559–577.

———. 2000. The Problems of Emotivism: Reflections on Some MacIntyrean Arguments. *Journal of Philosophical Research* 25, 285–309.

———. 2001. A Defense of Darwinian Accounts of Morality. *Philosophy of the Social Sciences* 31, 361–385.

———. 2002a. Evolution and Free Will: A Defense of Darwinian Non-Naturalism. *Metaphilosophy* 33, 468–482.

———. 2002b. Sober and Wilson and Nozick and the Experience Machine. *Philosophia* 29, 401–09.

———. 2002c. Theism, Evolutionary Epistemology, and Two Theories of Truth. *Zygon* 37, 789–801.

———. 2003a. A Defense of Naturalistic Naturalized Epistemology. *Critica* 35, 49–63.

———. 2003b. Rachels on Darwinism and Theism. *American Catholic Philosophical Quarterly* 77, 399–415.

———. 2004. Psychological Hedonism, Evolutionary Biology, and the Experience Machine. *Philosophy of the Social Sciences* 34, 506–526.

———. 2006. Flanagan and Cartesian Free Will: A Defense of Agent Causation. *Disputatio* 2:21, 69–90.

———. 2007a. Foot and Aristotle on Virtues and Flourishing. *Philosophia* 35, 43–62.

———. 2007b. Kanian Freedom and the Problem of Luck. *The Southern Journal of Philosophy*, 45, 515–532.

MacIntyre, A. 1981. *After Virtue*. South Bend: University of Notre Dame Press.

———. 1999. *Dependent Rational Animals*. Chicago: Open Court.

Mackie, J.L. 1977. *Ethics: Inventing Right and Wrong.* New York: Penguin.

———. 1982. *The Miracle of Theism.* Oxford: Oxford University Press.

Marks, I.M. 1969. *Fears and Phobias.* New York: Academic Press.

Mavrodes, G. 1987. 'Creation Science' and Evolution (letter). *Chronicle of Higher Education.* January 7th, 43.

Mele, A. 1999. Kane, Luck, and the Significance of Free Will. *Philosophical Explorations* 2, 96–104.

———. 2006. *Free Will and Luck.* New York: Oxford University Press.

Miles, J. 1998. Unnatural Selection. *Philosophy* 73, 593–608.

Millikan, R.G. 1984. *Language, Thought, and Other Biological Categories: New Foundations for Realism.* Cambridge, Massachusetts: MIT Press.

———. 1993. *White Queen Psychology and Other Essays for Alice.* Cambridge, Massachusetts: MIT Press.

Nagel, T. 1980. Ethics as an Autonomous Theoretical Subject. In G. Stent ed., *Morality As a Biological Phenomenon* (Berkeley: University of California Press), 196–205.

Narveson, J. 1977. Animal Rights. *Canadian Journal of Philosophy* 7.

Nozick, R. 1974. *Anarchy, State, and Utopia.* New York: Basic Books.

———. 1981. *Philosophical Explanations.* Cambridge, Massachusetts: Harvard University Press.

Pereboom, D. 2001. *Living Without Free Will.* Cambridge: Cambridge University Press.

Petrinovich, L. 1995. *Human Evolution, Reproduction, and Morality.* New York: Plenum.

Plantinga, A. 1974. *God, Freedom, and Evil.* New York: Harper and Row.

———. 1993. *Warrant and Proper Function.* Oxford: Oxford University Press.

———. 1996. Darwin, Mind, and Meaning. *Books and Culture* (May–June).

———. 2002. Reply to Beilby's Cohorts. In James Beilby ed., *Naturalism Defeated?* Ithaca: Cornell University Press, 204–275.

———. 2007. The Dawkins Confusion: Naturalism ad Absurdum. *Books and Culture* (March–April).

Premack, D. 1976. *Intelligence in Ape And Man.* Hillsdale: Erlbaum.

Priest, G. 1981. The Argument from Design. *The Australasian Journal of Philosophy* 59, 422–431.

Putnam, H. 1981. *Reason, Truth, and History.* Cambridge: Cambridge University Press.

———. 1982. Why Reason Can't Be Naturalized. *Synthese* 52, 3–23.

Quine, W.V. 1969. *Ontological Relativity and Other Essays.* New York: Columbia University Press.

Rachels, J. 1990. *Created from Animals: The Moral Implications of Darwinism.* Oxford: Oxford University Press.

————. 1999. *The Elements of Moral Philosophy.* New York: McGraw-Hill.

Radcliffe-Richards, J. 2000. *Human Nature after Darwin.* New York: Routledge.

Regan, T. 1983. *The Case for Animal Rights.* Berkeley: University of California Press.

Reiter, D. 2003. Rachels, Naturalism, and the Status of Animals. *Journal of Philosophical Research* 28, 403–414.

Richards, R. 1986a. A Defense of Evolutionary Ethics. *Biology and Philosophy* 1, 265–293.

————. 1986b. Justification through Biological Faith: A Rejoinder. *Biology and Philosophy* 1, 337–354.

————. 1987. *Darwin and the Emergence of Evolutionary Theories of Mind and Behavior.* Chicago: University of Chicago Press.

————. 1989. Dutch Objections to Evolutionary Ethics. *Biology and Philosophy* 4, 331–343.

Robinson, P. 1995. A Reply to Antony Flew's Discussion of "E.O. Wilson after 20 years." *Philosophy of the Social Sciences* 25, 216–218.

Rodd, R. 1990. *Biology, Ethics, and Animals.* Oxford: Oxford Univ. Press.

Rorty, R. 1980. *Philosophy and the Mirror of Nature.* Princeton: Princeton University Press.

Rosas, A. 2002. Psychological and Evolutionary Evidence for Altruism. *Biology and Philosophy* 17, 93–107.

Rottschaefer, W. 1991. Evolutionary Naturalistic Justifications of Morality: A Matter of Faith and Works. *Biology and Philosophy* 6, 341–349.

————. 1998. *The Biology and Psychology of Moral Agency.* Cambridge: Cambridge University Press.

Rottschaefer, W., and D. Martinsen. 1990. Really Taking Darwin Seriously: An Alternative to Michael Ruse's Darwinian Metaethics. *Biology and Philosophy* 5, 149–173.

————. 1991. The Insufficience of Supervenient Explanations of Moral Actions. *Biology and Philosophy* 6, 439–445.

Ruse, M. 1986. Evolutionary Ethics: A Phoenix Arisen. *Zygon* 21, 95–112.

————. 1990. Evolutionary Ethics and the Search for Predecessors: Kant, Hume, and All the Way Back to Aristotle? *Social Philosophy and Public Policy* 8, 59–85.

————. 1993. The New Evolutionary Ethics. In D. Nitecki and M. Nitecki, eds., *Evolutionary Ethics* (Albany: SUNY Press).

————. 1995. *Evolutionary Naturalism*. London: Routledge.

————. 1998. *Taking Darwin Seriously: A Naturalistic Approach to Philosophy*. Amherst: Prometheus.

————. 2001. *Can a Darwinian Be a Christian? The Relationship between Science and Religion*. Cambridge: Cambridge University Press.

Sadowsky, J.A. 1988. Did Darwin Destroy the Design Argument? *International Philosophical Quarterly* 28, 95–104.

Sahlins, M. 1965. On the Sociology of Primitive Exchange. In M. Banton, ed., *The Relevance of Models for Social Anthropology* (London: Tavistock), 139–236.

Schmid, W.T. 1996. The Definition of Racism. *Journal of Applied Philosophy* 13, 31–40.

Scott, E. 1992. Review of *Darwin on Trial* by Phillip Johnson. *Creation/Evolution* 13, 36–47.

Seligman, M.E.P. 1972. Phobias and Preparedness. In M.E.P. Seligman and J.L. Hager, eds., *Biological Boundaries of Learning* (New York: Appleton Crofts), 451–460.

Silverstein, M. 2000. In Defense of Happiness: A Response to the Experience Machine. *Social Theory and Practice* 26, 279–300.

Singer, P. 1975. *Animal Liberation*. New York: Avon.

————. 1981. *The Expanding Circle: Ethics and Sociobiology*. New York: Farrar, Straus, and Giroux.

Smith, Q. 1998. Swinburne's Explanation of the Universe. *Religious Studies* 34, 91–102.

Sober, E. and Fitelson, B. 1998. Plantinga's Probability Argument Against Evolutionary Naturalism. *Pacific Philosophical Quarterly* 79, 115–129.

Sober, E., and D.S. Wilson. 1998. *Unto Others: The Evolution and Psychology of Unselfish Behavior*. Cambridge: Harvard University Press.

————. 2000. Morality and 'Unto Others': Response to Commentary Discussion. *Journal of Consciousness Studies* 7, 257–268.

Sommers, T., and A. Rosenberg. 2003. Darwin's Nihilistic Idea: Evolution and the Meaninglessness of Life. *Biology and Philosophy* 18, 653–668.

————. 2007. The Illusion of Freedom Evolves. In D. Ross, D. Spurrett, H. Kincaid, and G.L. Stephens, eds., *Distributed Cognition and the Will* (Cambridge, Massachusetts: MIT Press).

Spelke, E. 2000. Core Knowledge. *American Psychology* 55, 1233–243.

————. 2003. Core Knowldege. In N. Kanwisher and J. Duncan, eds, *Attention and Performance, Volume 20: Functional Neuroimaging of Visual Cognition* (Oxford: Oxford University Press).

Staal, J.F. 1967. Indian Logic. In P. Edwards, ed., *The Encyclopedia of Philosophy*, Volume 4 (New York: Macmillan), 520–23.

Steinbock, B. 1997. Speciesism and the Idea of Equality. In *Contemporary Moral Problems*, ed. James White (Minneapolis: West). Originally published in *Philosophy* 53 (1978).

Stevenson, C.L. 1941. *Ethics and Language*. New Haven: Yale University Press.

Stich, S. 1990. *The Fragmentation of Reason: Preface to a Pragmatic Theory of Cognitive Evaluation*. Cambridge, Massachusetts: MIT Press.

———. 2007. Evolution, Altruism, and Cognitive Architecture: A Critique of Sober and Wilson's Argument for Psychological Altruism. *Biology and Philosophy* 22, 267–281.

Strawson, G. 1986. *Freedom and Belief*. Oxford: Oxford University Press.

Sturgeon, N. 1998. Moral Explanations. In *Ethical Theory: Classical and Contemporary Readings*, ed. Louis Pojman (Belmont: Wadsworth). Originally in D. Copp and D. Zimmerman, eds., *Morality, Reason, and Truth* (Rowman and Littlefield, 1984).

Swinburne, R. 1991. *The Existence of God*. Oxford: Clarendon.

Thompson, M. 2004. Apprehending Human Form. In A. O'Hear, ed., *Modern Moral Philosophy* (Cambridge: Cambridge University Press).

Unwin, N. 1990. Can Emotivism Sustain a Social Ethics? *Ratio* 1, 64–81.

van Inwagen, P. 1983. *An Essay on Free Will*. Oxford: Clarendon.

———. 2002. Free Will Remains a Mystery. In R. Kane, ed., *The Oxford Handbook of Free Will* (New York: Oxford University Press).

Voorzanger, B. 1987. No Norms and No Nature: The Moral Relevance of Evolutionary Biology. *Biology and Philosophy* 3, 253–270.

Waller, B. 1986. The Virtues of Contemporary Emotivism. *Erkenntnis* 25, 61–75.

———. 1990. *Freedom Without Responsibility*. Philadelphia: Temple University Press.

———. 1996. Moral Commitment Without Objectivity or Illusion: Comments on Ruse and Woolcock. *Biology and Philosophy* 11, 245–254.

———. 1998. *The Natural Selection of Autonomy*. Albany: SUNY Press.

Williams, P. 1990. Evolved Ethics Re-examined: The Theory of Robert J. Richards. *Biology and Philosophy* 5, 451–57.

Woolcock, P. 1993. Ruse's Darwinian Meta-Ethics: A Critique. *Biology and Philosophy* 8, 423–39.

Index